ANTHROPOLOGICAL PAPERS

MUSEUM OF ANTHROPOLOGY, UNIVERSITY OF MICHIGAN
NO. 24

LATE WOODLAND CULTURES OF SOUTHEASTERN MICHIGAN

by
JAMES E. FITTING

ANN ARBOR
THE UNIVERSITY OF MICHIGAN, 1965

ISBN (print): 978-1-949098-21-1
ISBN (ebook): 978-1-951519-44-5

Browse all of our books at
sites.lsa.umich.edu/archaeology-books.

Order our books from the University of Michigan
Press at www.press.umich.edu.

For permissions, questions, or manuscript queries,
contact Museum publications by email at umma-pubs@umich.edu or visit the Museum website at
lsa.umich.edu/ummaa.

PREFACE

The following study is a revised version of a doctoral dissertation submitted to The University of Michigan in the spring of 1964. Recorded herein are the results of a long period of archaeological investigation in southeastern Michigan carried out by myself and others. The bulk of the material examined was from the Riviere au Vase site excavated by Dr. Emerson F. Greenman. Dr. Greenman has influenced this work by both personal conversation and by his numerous publications on Michigan archaeology.

My doctoral committee, under the chairmanship of Dr. James B. Griffin, Director of the Museum of Anthropology, offered many helpful suggestions on both preliminary and final drafts of this study. Dr. Greenman's comments on Great Lakes Archaeology, Dr. Richard O. Keslin's suggestions on ceramic classification, and Dr. F. Clever Bald's background information on Michigan history have been incorporated into the present version. Dr. Arthur J. Jelinek deserves special thanks for keeping me at the task of writing for the past year.

Many other persons have also contributed directly or indirectly to this document. Mr. Henry Wright has read and commented on all of Part II and most of Part I. Mr. Alan McPherron read the section on ceramics in an earlier draft. His suggestions, based on his unpublished Juntunen studies, were extremely helpful. Discussions with Mr. Richard Flanders on the transition from Middle to Late Woodland were beneficial. Mr. Charles Cleland spent many hours on faunal identification and edited the section on the fauna from the Riviere au Vase site.

Dr. Leonard Moss, chairman of the Department of Sociology and Anthropology at Wayne State University aided and encouraged me while I was on the faculty at Wayne during the 1963-64 academic year. Dr. Arnold R. Pilling, Director of the Wayne State University Museum of Anthropology, deserves an additional note of thanks. Pilling's extensive survey work in Macomb County has been invaluable. I am heavily indebted to him for his identification of the historic materials from the Riviere au Vase site. As a friend and colleague he has served as a sounding board for many of my ideas on southeastern Michigan archaeology.

The maps for the Fuller and Verchave sites were drawn and drafted by Mr. Henry Wright. All other drawings were drafted and lettered by Mr. George Stuber. The plates are the work of Mr. Michael Ashworth and Mr. Stuber. Miss Anita Bohn aided me in cataloging, sorting, and classifying archaeological materials.

The first draft of this study was typed by Miss Anita Bohn, Miss Frances Steketee, and myself. The second draft was typed by Mr. Jerry Fields and the final copy by Mrs. Harry Rechkemmer. My wife, Molly, read and proofread all of the above copies with great patience. Final editing was done by Mrs. Clara Johnston of the University of Michigan Publications Office.

Financial support for various parts of the excavation and analysis presented in the following pages has been received from the Horace H. Rackham School of Graduate Studies and from the National Science Foundation.

James E. Fitting

CONTENTS

TABLES

FIGURES

PLATES

(Plates I-XLVIII follow page 165)

CONTENTS

INTRODUCTION

Southeastern Michigan has for centuries, served as a meeting ground—a passage from the lower to the upper Great Lakes. This area was Tieugsachrondio, the place of many beaver dams, to the Iroquois. It was Wawyachtenok or whirlpool to the Algonquian speaking groups in the area. Claimed by warring bands, it was a no man's land at the time of first European contact. This was the situation in 1701 when Detroit was founded.

Today the southeastern counties of Michigan are the most densely populated area of the state. With the growth of this population came the destruction of archaeological monuments. In this part of the state we have recorded archaeological excavations taking place in the early years of the nineteenth century.

More has been written about the archaeology of this area than about any other part of Michigan. In addition to many nineteenth-century works there are more recent compilations. Greenman's Younge, Wolf, and Furton site reports have presented intensive examinations of material from these sites. Many articles on southeastern Michigan have appeared in the *Michigan Archaeologist,* the journal of the Michigan Archaeological Society, and *The Totem Pole,* the journal of the Detroit Aboriginal Research Club. There would appear to be no lack of published material for this area.

There has been, however, a lack of synthesis of the archaeological material from southeastern Michigan. This was particularly true for the Late Woodland period, the period of most intensive occupation in this area. In 1962 the University of Michigan Museum of Anthropology excavated a number of small sites in Macomb County. Most of the material from these sites was Late Woodland. Here is where the problem began; for all of the excavation and publication we could only say that it was Late Woodland, a broad classification covering nearly 1,000 years.

The published syntheses by Greenman (1939*a*) and Quimby (1952, 1960) proved to be of little assistance. It was evident that a re-examination of the southeastern Michigan Late Woodland would have to be undertaken in order to interpret the sites excavated in 1962.

The key to this re-examination was the Riviere au Vase site. This was a very large site in Macomb County which was excavated by the University of Michigan Museum of Anthropology in 1936 and 1937. No detailed site report had ever been written but the quantity and variety of cultural material suggested that a long span of occupation was represented.

The following course of action was suggested by the available data:

1) An examination of the cultural material from the Riviere au Vase site and an interpretation of its occupational history.

2) An examination of the Late Woodland sites excavated in 1962 by the University of Michigan Museum of Anthropology. This material would be analyzed in light of the Riviere au Vase site.

3) A re-interpretation of the published material in this area. This would be based on the new evidence from southeastern Michigan and adjacent areas. This would include, if possible, a chronological ordering of Late Woodland sites. The radiocarbon dates for the northeastern part of North America, which dated material related to that from southeastern Michigan, would also be examined.

This was the pattern used in the analysis presented in the following sections.

PART I

THE RIVIERE AU VASE SITE

I

EXCAVATIONS AT THE RIVIERE AU VASE SITE

The Riviere au Vase site, also known as the Graham site, the Greene School site, and the Mud Creek site, is located in section 28 (T.3N, R.14E) of Chesterfield Township, Macomb County, Michigan (Figure 1). It has been given the designation of 20 MB 3 in the Michigan Archaeological Society site-numbering system. This is the site number on file at the Wayne State University Museum of Anthropology and was confirmed by personal communication from Dr. Emerson F. Greenman to Dr. Arnold R. Pilling in 1959.

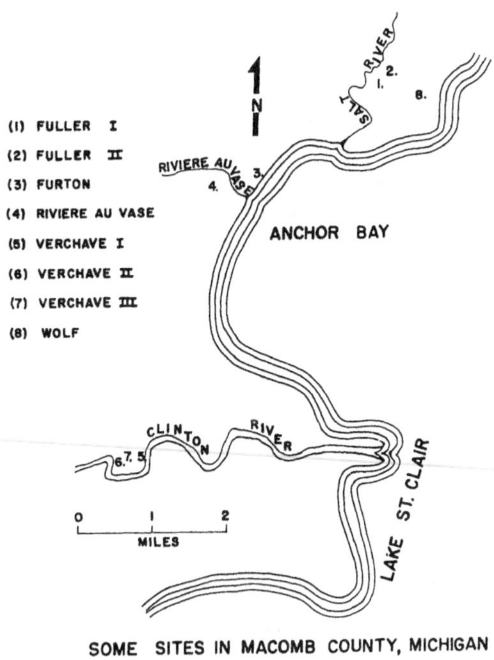

Fig. 1

In the summer of 1936 Greenman and a field party from The University of Michigan started excavations at the Riviere au Vase site. It was possible to spend only a few weeks at the site in 1936 but the number of burials which were encountered and the number of artifacts recovered were impressive enough to warrant returning to the site in 1937.

In the spring of 1937 excavations were undertaken for a period of several weeks and in the summer of that year a full field party returned to the site. The excavation was under the direction of Greenman with Mr. Robert Benton acting as assistant field director in the summers of 1936 and 1937. The excavations undertaken in the spring of 1937 were, apparently, under the direction of Mr. George I. Quimby who also spent some time on the site during the regular season. John Alden, Gretchen Beardsley, H. Holmes Ellis, Virginia Griffin, Alfred Guthe, Norman Humphrey, Helen Stevenson, Gail Wellwood, and Walter Woodward also participated in the excavation of the site. A number of other persons participated in the University of Michigan Museum of Anthropology excavations for short periods of time.

The site is located on a sand ridge running approximately east-west between Sugarbush Road and Lake St. Clair (Figure 2).

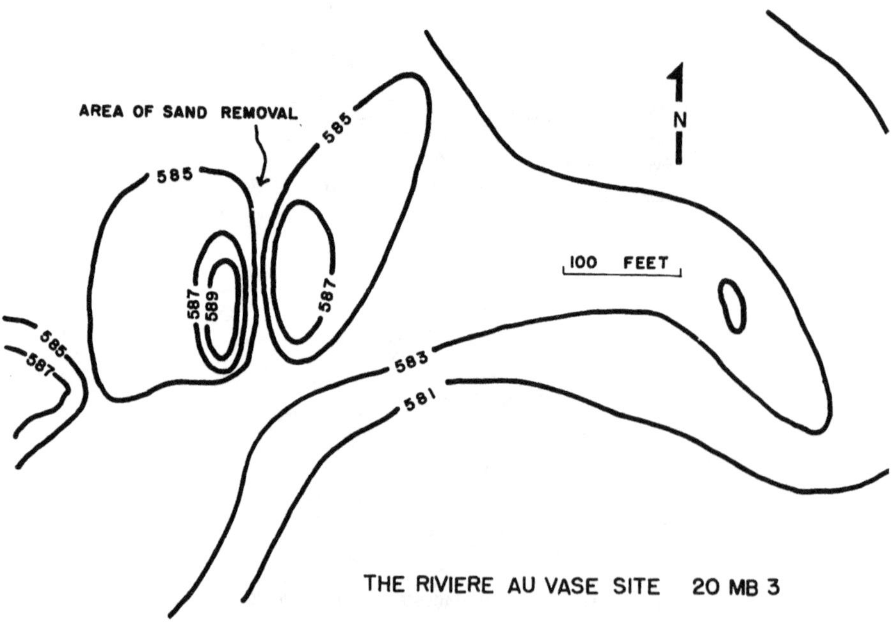

Fig. 2

The elevation of this ridge varies from 581 feet above sea level at the bottom of its slope to 589 feet above sea level at its highest point in the central area of the site. The Riviere au Vase, or Mud Creek, flows toward Lake St. Clair on the northern and eastern sides of the site.

The most distinctive beach formation in this area is the sand ridge at 595 feet above sea level which present-day Sugarbush Road follows. This is a roughly north-south ridge and marks the last major lake phase in the Lake St. Clair basin prior to the modern Lake St. Clair stage. The smaller ridge on which the Riviere au Vase site lies is not a part of this beach system. It is set apart from the beach and is at a slightly lower elevation, which, coupled with the observation that it follows the course of the Riviere au Vase, suggests that it was formed in connection with the river.

The University of Michigan Museum of Anthropology excavations in 1936 and 1937 did not take a unit down to the water table. The units which were taken down to a depth of 40 inches, however, showed a profile not unlike that from the Verchave I site. The upper humic zone had probably been plowed although no evidence for plow scars was recorded in the field notes. This zone was about 1 foot thick. Below the humus or plow zone was an area of yellow sand. This varied in depth throughout the site. In the central area it was deep enough to have been exploited commercially before the University of Michigan excavations. Local informants recalled that this sand removal had taken place in 1927 and that a number of burials were uncovered during its removal.

The yellow sand gave way to lighter colors with increased depth and the deepest recorded deposits were of a whitish-yellow sand with ferric stains. No information was recorded on deposits underlying the whitish sand. In this area there are two possibilities: either bedded lacustrine clays, as at the Fuller sites or cross-bedded coarse sand and gravels of river and delta deposits such as were found at the Verchave sites. Since the ridge follows the course of the stream, the latter suggestion seems to be the most likely alternative. The sand ridge would then be a recent formation on an older channel or delta of the Riviere au Vase.

The present-day Riviere au Vase, or Mud Creek, as it is called locally, is about one-half mile to the north of the Riviere au Vase site. Its old channel has been greatly altered by dredging between the site and Lake St. Clair and near the site the river has been reduced to an insignificant trickle.

The site was tested by means of thirteen excavation units. These were large trenches rather than controlled units. An area would be staked out and the excavators would then attempt to clear this area with shovels using trowels and finer tools when subsurface features and burials were encountered. None of the material from the site was screened and very little of the non-artifactual material was saved.

The field records were of three sorts. A running written account of the excavations was kept in a notebook at the time of excavation. Later this narrative was transcribed into three volumes of field notes totaling 195 pages and covering both years of the excavation.

The second type of records were the maps. These were 8.5- by 11-inch sheets of graph paper recording the position of burials and other features within the excavation units. These were fairly useful in analysis, but the reduplication of corner stake letters and pit numbers in many of the units, coupled with the failure of the recorders to designate which of the thirteen units was under discussion, limited the usefulness of much of this material.

The third set of records were the field catalogs and information from these catalogs entered into the University of Michigan Museum of Anthropology Great Lakes Division catalog. The catalog for the 1937 material furnished more information on the location of the various pits excavated in that season than either the maps or the field notes.

The area of excavation at the Riviere au Vase site (Figure 3) was rather extensive. In the summer of 1936 two major excavation units were opened. The first of these units was Trench A, a 15- by 30-foot trench to the east of the area of sand removal. The area of Trench A excavated in 1936 is designated as A_1 in Figure 3. This was done to distinguish it from the southward extension of the trench excavated by Quimby in the spring of 1937, which we have designated as A_2. This was originally called Trench E, but the subsequent excavation of the larger Trench E shown in Figure 3 suggested the need for a new term to avoid confusion.

The area of Trench B, a 30- by 30-foot unit, was staked out and partly excavated during the summer of 1936. At the close of the field season, the stakes were left in the ground and excavation was completed in Trench B during the summer of 1937.

As previously mentioned, in the spring of 1937 Quimby opened an extension of Trench A, designated as A_2 in Figure 3, to the south of the 1936 excavation. This was a 20- by 40-foot trench.

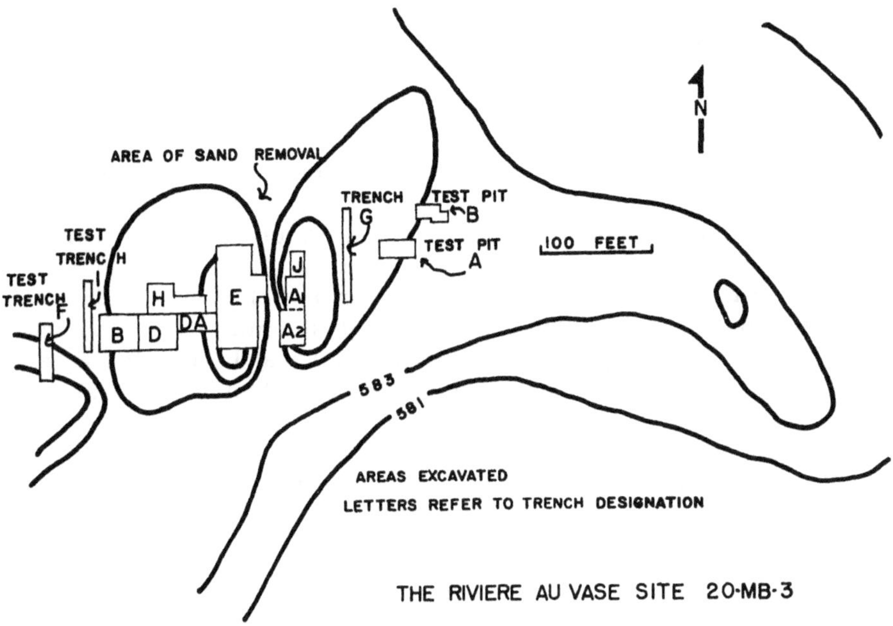

Fig. 3

As in all of the excavation units, the sides were extended to include any burials and other features that might be encountered.

In the summer of 1937, in addition to completing the excavation of Trench B, a second 30- by 30-foot unit was opened to the east of Trench B and contiguous to it. This was called Trench D. The highest remaining area of the knoll, to the west of the area of sand removal, was staked out and opened. This trench, Trench E, was the largest unit opened at the site. It was sectioned off into 5-foot squares. Unfortunately, at least two separate systems were used for designating the squares within Trench E. Not all of the area which was staked out was excavated, and Figure 3 shows the portions which are known to have been excavated. A total area of at least 3,150 square feet was excavated in Trench E.

Trench DA, which was approximately 40 by 15 feet, was opened between Trench D and Trench E. An irregular trench of 20 by 55 feet which had an extension of 10 by 15 feet was excavated to the north of Trenches D and DA. A total area of 1,250 square feet was excavated in this area and designated as Trench H.

A 15- by 25-foot trench was opened to the north of the 1936 Trench A excavations and called Trench J. The above units made up the major parts of The University of Michigan excavations at the Riviere au Vase site.

A number of test pits and test trenches were excavated along the sand ridge in an attempt to define the limits of the site. Test Trench Number 1 was an area 3 feet wide by 69 feet long which was excavated to the west of Trench B. Test Trench Number 2 was a 10- by 20-foot trench 140 feet to the west of Test Trench Number 1. (This trench is not shown in Figure 3.) In between these two test trenches was Trench F, a 10- by 50-foot unit. Trench G was a 5- by 90-foot excavation unit 35 feet to the east of Trenches A and J. The two easternmost units opened on the site were Test Pit A, a 15- by 30-foot unit, and Test Pit B, an irregular unit with approximately 100 square feet of excavated area.

During the excavations of 1936 and 1937 approximately 10,200 square feet were excavated down to the sterile subsoil. The material recovered during these excavations and the surface material from the general site area furnish us with the material to be analyzed in this study.

A number of features were noted during the excavation. These consisted of burials and pits. The term "pit" was used to include both ash lenses and roughly circular, steep-sided refuse pits running from 1 to 2 feet below the plow zone. The problems involved in the analysis of both will follow the description of the artifacts from the site.

At this point we shall only note that there were 145 burial groupings containing the remains of at least 350 individuals. The majority of these burials were located in Trenches A, J, and E. A small number of highly significant burials were recovered from Trench B.

There were numbers for 144 pits but artifacts were recovered from only 101 of these pits. Only sixty-three of these pits were mentioned in the field notes, and many of these were only listed and not described. One important "pit" was Pit 20 in Trench B. This was the site of a historic house. Almost all of the historic material in the University of Michigan Museum of Anthropology collection was from this historic house site.

After the University of Michigan excavations, the site was subject to much indiscriminant collecting. Many burials and features were destroyed and artifacts removed with no record of provenience. Only one other excavation was undertaken in a controlled manner and adequately reported. This was done by Mr. Jerry DeVisscher (1957) of Mount Clemens, and the results of his work will be included in the present analysis of the Riviere au Vase site.

Fragmentary reports and partial interpretations of the material from the site have been published for almost thirty years. A survey of these published references follows:

The first of these references was made in the Younge site report in 1937 (Greenman 1937*a*:96). The Riviere au Vase site was referred to indirectly in the text and directly in a footnote. The presence of perforated crania was noted.

In 1939 Greenman made two references to the Riviere au Vase site. The first of these was in a paper on the cultural relationships of a number of sites in the Great Lakes area (Greenman 1939*a*). No descriptive material was presented in this brief paper, and the focus of the entire work was on fitting the material into the then recently developed McKern classification or midwestern taxonomic method. The similarities between the Younge site and the Riviere au Vase site were reasserted. This paper marks the first use of the term "Owasco" to describe Michigan archaeological material.

The second reference made in 1939 was in the Wolf and Furton site reports (Greenman 1939*b*:26) where the ceramics from the Furton site, two sites in Bruce and Washington townships and from the Riviere au Vase site was referred to as "woodland." In a footnote it was again asserted that the Riviere au Vase site was part of the "Younge focus, Owasco Aspect, Woodland pattern" (Greenman 1939*b*:26).

The first actual description of cultural material from the site appeared in 1945 (Greenman 1945). This was a summary of the material from five burials which appeared to be slightly separated from the main occupation area of the site. It is unfortunate that the term "Hopewellian" appeared in the title of this article. Although Greenman stated, "The only diagnostic Hopewellian trait exhibited by this group of burials was a copper rod with a bone handle, found with burial #1, . . ." (*Ibid.*, p. 458), many people interpreted this article as the identification of a Hopewell component at the Riviere au Vase site.

In 1945 an excellent article on the ceramic technology of the Riviere au Vase site was published by Victoria G. Harper. This was the first of several short descriptive reports on the site. It will be used extensively in the analysis of ceramics presented in this study.

Alfred Guthe (1948:50-60) presented a short description of the cultural material from the Riviere au Vase site. On the basis of Greenman's 1945 paper he divided the material from the site into two components. He lists the cultural material and burials from the site, but there is almost no description and very little discussion of this material.

Greenman published a brief preliminary report in the *Michigan Archaeologist* (1957:9-11) which was very similar to that presented by Guthe in his thesis. It was much shorter, and did not give as complete a list of artifacts and traits as Guthe had done. This study is valuable for its inclusion of information on the historic component.

The 1957 article was used by Greenman as a source for information in 1958 when presenting a survey of the archaeology of the Detroit area (Greenman 1958). Little additional information is offered, and the material from the Riviere au Vase site is again called "Owasco."

Thus, in 1963, when I started my examination of the Riviere au Vase site, I was faced with almost thirty years of analysis, and almost no description of the artifacts. The ensuing study of cultural material and cultural placement of material from the Riviere au Vase site was carried out independently from the earlier studies which were considered only in the final summary. One might even say that a Riviere au Vase site bias was developed, for the Younge site, Wolf site, Furton site, and Gibraltar site collections were examined only after completion of the analysis of artifacts from the Riviere au Vase site, and then in light of that analysis.

As might be expected, since the same material was examined, many of Greenman's conclusions were duplicated. It is also not strange that no two investigators will interpret archaeological data in the same way, and it would be unusual if, after a complete analysis of the artifacts, a second investigator did not produce new information and new interpretations.

II

ARTIFACTS FROM RIVIERE AU VASE

Ceramic Material

Ceramic Technology

A study of the ceramics from the Riviere au Vase site was published in 1945 by Victoria G. Harper. The material in this section is a brief summary of the results of her study which have a bearing on the present ceramic analysis.

Following Greenman (1945) she recognized two components, and separated sherds from these components for her analysis. A series of 1,044 sherds from the more recent component and a smaller number from the earlier component were examined. A microscopic examination revealed that 95.6 per cent of the sherds from the first component had a grit temper. The tempering material was sand and crushed rock. Quartz, orthoclase, acid plagioclase, sericite, kaolinite, biotite, muscovite, magnetite, and hornblende were all present. The occurrence of feldspars was important since this allowed the identification of the rocks crushed for temper. Feldspars occur only in granites and syenits. Granitic material occurred frequently at the site. Some particles of quartz were rounded, suggesting that the clay came from the stream deposits on the banks of the Riviere au Vase.

The particles of temper range from .073 mm to 2.2 mm.

The remaining 4.4 per cent of the sherds from the first component had little or no temper. These may have been sherds from miniature vessels although this was not stated by Harper.

Harper noted that although the temper of the second component appeared to be finer (particles up to 1.46 millimeters, it consisted of the same material, and looked "quite similar under a microscope" (p. 482). The clay from both components appeared to be similar when examined under a microscope.

According to Anna Shepard's texture classification, developed for pottery from the southwestern United States, all of the material from the site falls into the coarse to very coarse categories. Since this is of little help in our present analysis, a more applicable classification was developed for sherds from the Riviere au Vase site.

In the present study we note a fine temper with particles up to 1 mm, a medium temper with particles up to approximately 2 mm and coarse temper with particles over 2 mm. It is to be realized that the coarse-tempered classification includes sherds with finer tempering material as well as the larger particles. The presence of temperless sherds, noted by Harper, is also recognized in this study.

The hardness of sherds from the site was fairly uniform and ranged from 2.5 to 3 on Moh's hardness scale. This is well within the range of most material from the eastern United States.

The color of sherds from the Riviere au Vase site ranges from smokey grey and brown to light buff and cinnamon. Harper established three groups on the basis of color. In the first component she found that 24.5 per cent were well-fired buffs and cinnamons, 52.2 per cent were brown to grey brown and 23.3 per cent of the sample consisted of poorly fired mouse grey to dark grey sherds. The majority of sherds from the second component were within the grey buff and grey categories with a few occurrences of orange to cinnamon sherds.

In her study of clays from the area, Harper found a rather plastic clay with a great deal of shrinkage. She noted that the untempered clay shrunk 6.6 per cent while that which was tempered with crushed rock shrank only 2.1 per cent during firing. This was suggested as the reason for the large amount of temper in the sherds from the site.

By firing a series of clay pellets from the site and refiring sherds it was determined that the pottery had been fired at temperatures between 450 and 550 degrees C. There was apparently little control over the oxidizing and reducing atmosphere as one would expect if the ceramics were fired over an open fire.

In general, Harper's study of the physical properties of the pottery from the Riviere au Vase site showed the material to be remarkably uniform.

A Quantitative Examination of Rim Sherds from the Riviere au Vase Site

The basic tool in this study was the marginal punch card. This was used to facilitate the manipulation of a large amount of data on rim sherds from Riviere au Vase. *KD 585 B* key-sort cards were used, and all attributes were recorded as discrete attributes, that is, they were noted only for their presence or absence. Over 400 rim sherds were used representing 371 distinct vessels. A card was prepared for each vessel represented and the vessel, rather than the individual rim sherd, will serve as the basis for analysis in this study. There were several rim sherds that did not fit into any category and were not coded. These represented unique vessels and will be covered in another section.

In previous studies of ceramics in the northeast (Ritchie and MacNeish 1949; MacNeish 1952) it was found that decoration and technique or method of application were the best criteria for sorting rim sherds into meaningful types. In examining the vessel sample from Riviere au Vase, four principle decorative motifs were noted. The largest group was that of rims with an oblique motif. There were 228 vessels in this group or 62 per cent of the sample. The next most common decoration was a horizontal linear motif. Many of these vessels have an oblique design below the linear design, but in all instances the linear design was superordinant. There were 43 vessels in this group representing 12 per cent of the sample. The two other motifs were minor. The most prevalent was an opposed motif represented by 9 vessels or slightly over 2 per cent of the sample. The smallest category was net or coarse fabric-impressed rims. In this instance, the technique and the resultant motif are identical. There were 3 vessels in this group representing just under 1 per cent of the sample.

There were two residual categories not based upon design elements. One was cord-marked rimmed vessels. These occasionally had lip or interior rim decoration, usually cord-wrapped stick, but the expanse of the exterior rim was decorated with a cord-wrapped paddle. There were 53 cord-marked vessels accounting for 14 per cent of the sample. The remaining category consisted of the rims of 35 miniature vessels (9 per cent of the sample).

The motif division on the sample cards was followed by a series of punches dealing with the technique used in applying the design element. Three techniques were used for applying oblique designs. They were dentate stamping, tool impressions, and impressions made with a cord-wrapped stick or cord-wrapped cord.

Two techniques were used in applying horizontal designs. The most popular of these was a linear cording with either the application of a cord-wrapped stick or cord, or a single cord to the rim of the vessel. An interrupted linear or "stab and drag" technique was also used.

Three methods were used in applying the opposed motif. Three vessels had opposed incising, four had opposed cording and two were opposed dentate stamped.

The net or coarse fabric-marked sherds show evidence of two distinct loosely woven fabrics but the sample size was too small to make a division.

There were three variants of the cord-marked series; a plain cord-marked, a smoothed cord-marked, and a series of cord-marked vessels with small punctates around the rim. The miniature vessels were divided into decorated miniature and undecorated miniature vessels.

The location of the vessel in one, several, or none of the excavation units (i.e., "Surface Collection") was recorded on the card. All of the vessels came from one or more of thirteen separate excavation units or from the general site. If the vessel was associated with either a pit or a burial, this too was noted on the card.

The presence or absence of decoration on the lip or interior of the rim, the presence of bosses, or castellations, and size of temper particles were all recorded. The classification of temper consisted of a coarse category, particles over 2 mm; a medium category, particles up to 2 mm; and fine, particles up to 1 mm. A temperless category was used to include sherds with no apparent temper. All of these attributes were used in this analysis with the exception of the presence of bosses. There were too few sherds with bosses to test for associations with this attribute.

Twelve rim types could be distinguished in profile. These were divided into five series, some with several variants. All collared rims were placed in the "A" group. There were four variants of A rims; A-1 was a collared rim with a rounded lip (Figure 4), A-2 was a rim with a squared lip (Figure 4), A-3 rims looked like an inverted V in profile (Figure 5), and A-4 rims had a thickened lip (Figure 5). Type "B" rims were uncollared and had a thickened lip. There were two variants which were designated B-1 and B-2. The B-1 rims (Figure 6) were marked by a rounded lip while the B-2 rims (Figure 6) had a square lip.

Type "C" rims had a square lip, and were wedge shape in cross section (Figure 7). The lip itself is thicker than the body. No variants could be distinguished in this series.

Type "D" rims were uncollared rims with a square lip. It was possible to distinguish four variants within this group. Rim profile D-1 was a squared rim, but had an inward facing lip (Figure 7); D-2 was a square flat lip variant (Figure 7). Variant D-3 was similar to D-2, but the lip was decorated by incisions or cording running around the circumference of the vessel.

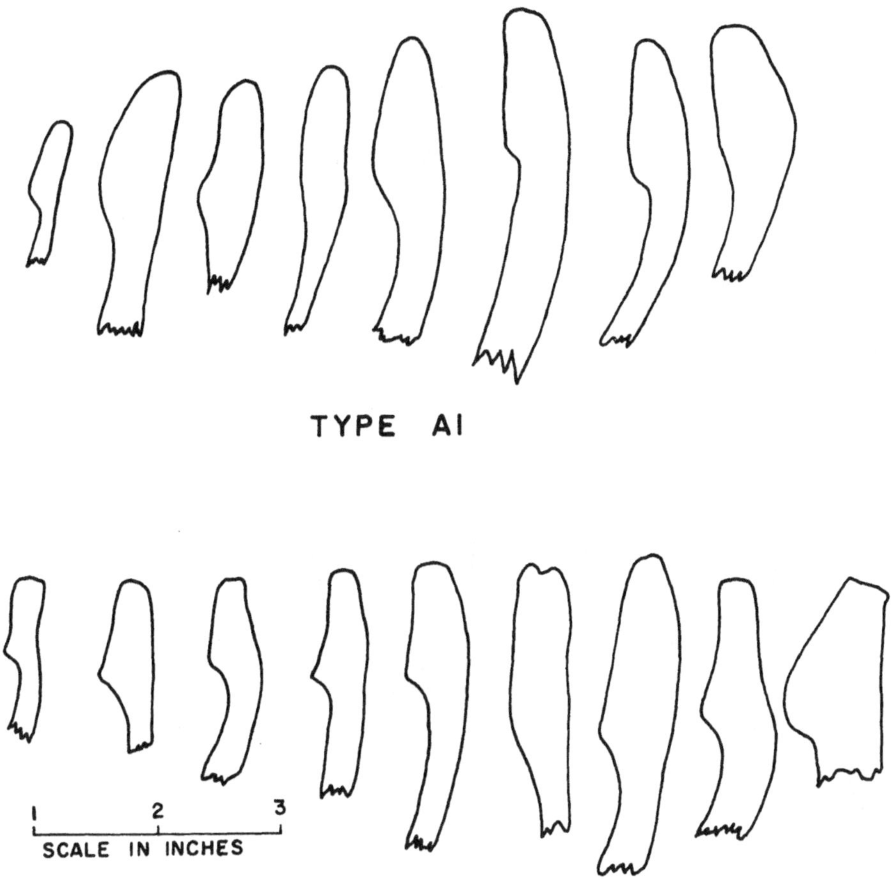

RIM PROFILES ON VESSELS FROM THE RIVIERE AU VASE SITE.

Fig. 4

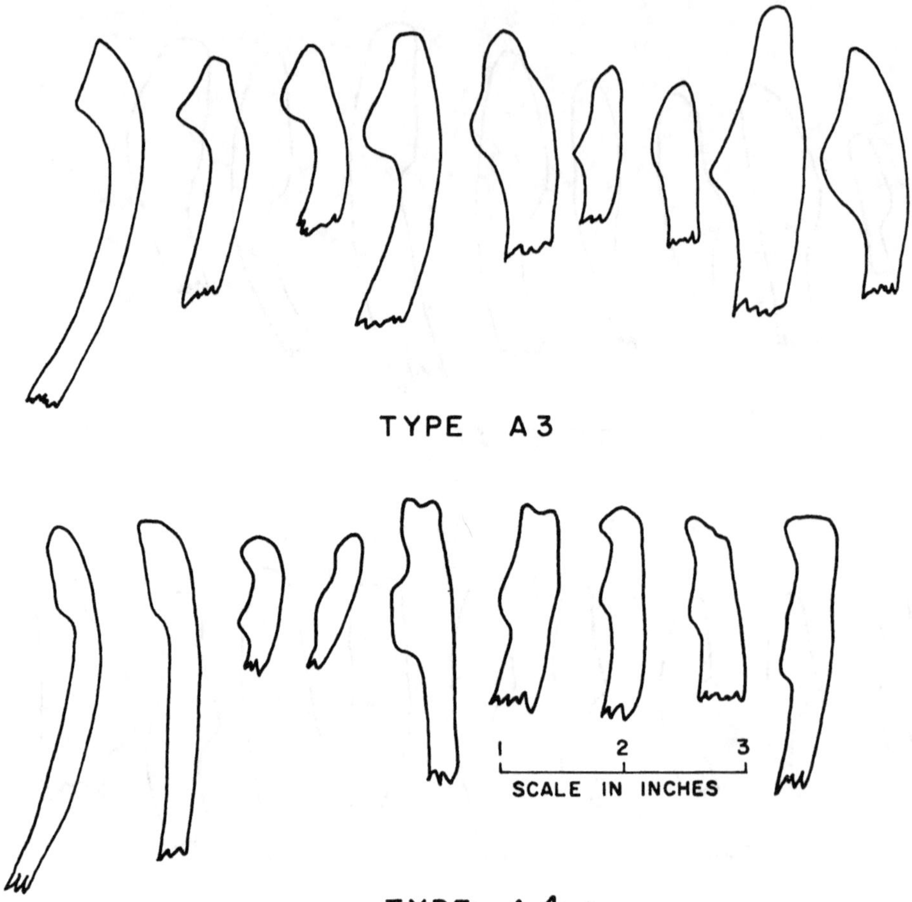

RIM PROFILES ON VESSELS FROM
THE RIVIERE AU VASE SITE.

Fig. 5

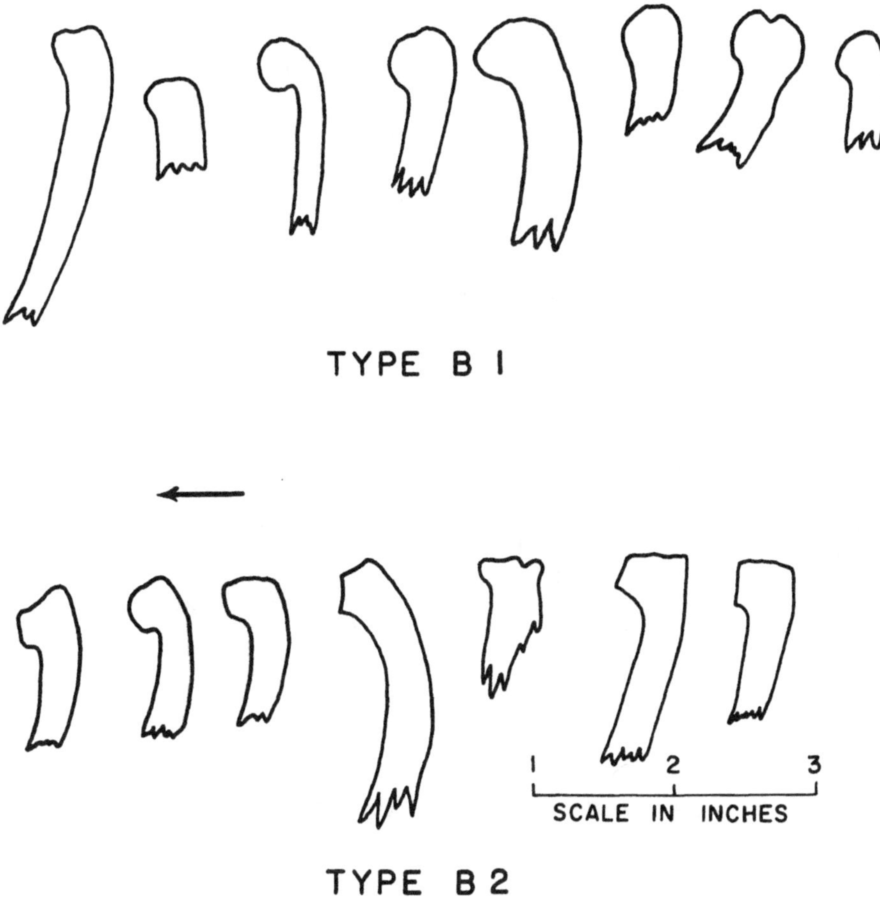

RIM PROFILES ON VESSELS FROM THE RIVIERE AU VASE SITE

Fig. 6

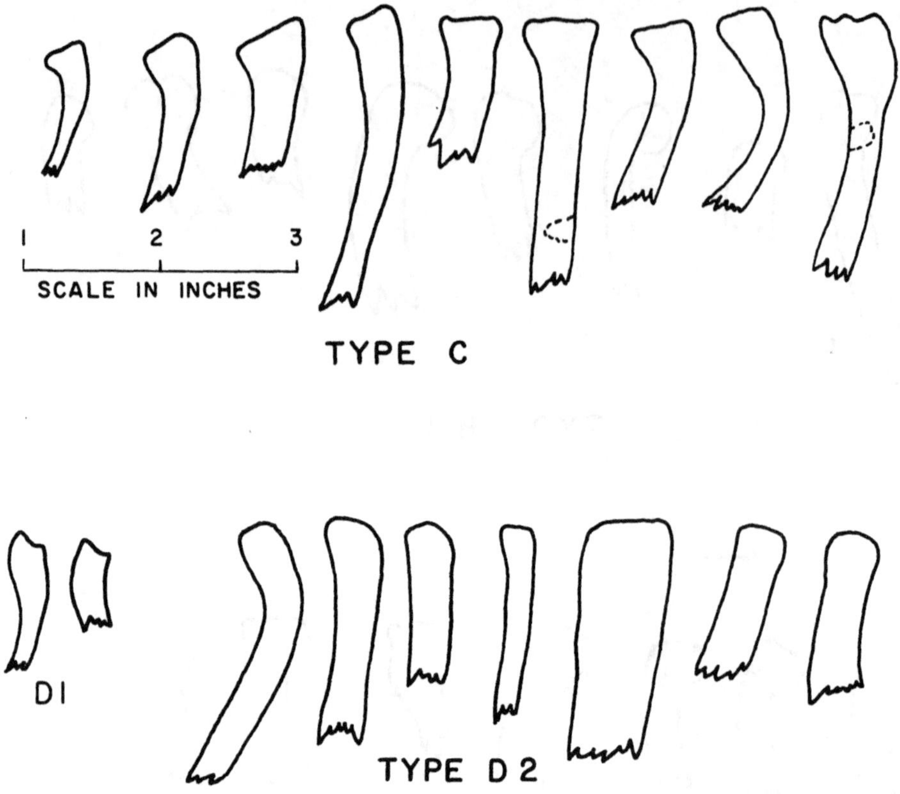

RIM PROFILES ON VESSELS FROM

THE RIVIERE AU VASE SITE.

Fig. 7

Variant D-4 is the counterpart of D-1. It is a square rim but with an outsloping lip.

The final rim type, type E, is a simple rounded rim (Figure 8). There were no distinguishable variants for this type of rim profile.

Since previous investigations by Ritchie, MacNeish, and others had found designs and techniques to be associated with the rim profiles, this was the first thing checked. The statistical technique used was that suggested by Spaulding (1960), for testing attribute associations. Some regrouping of data was

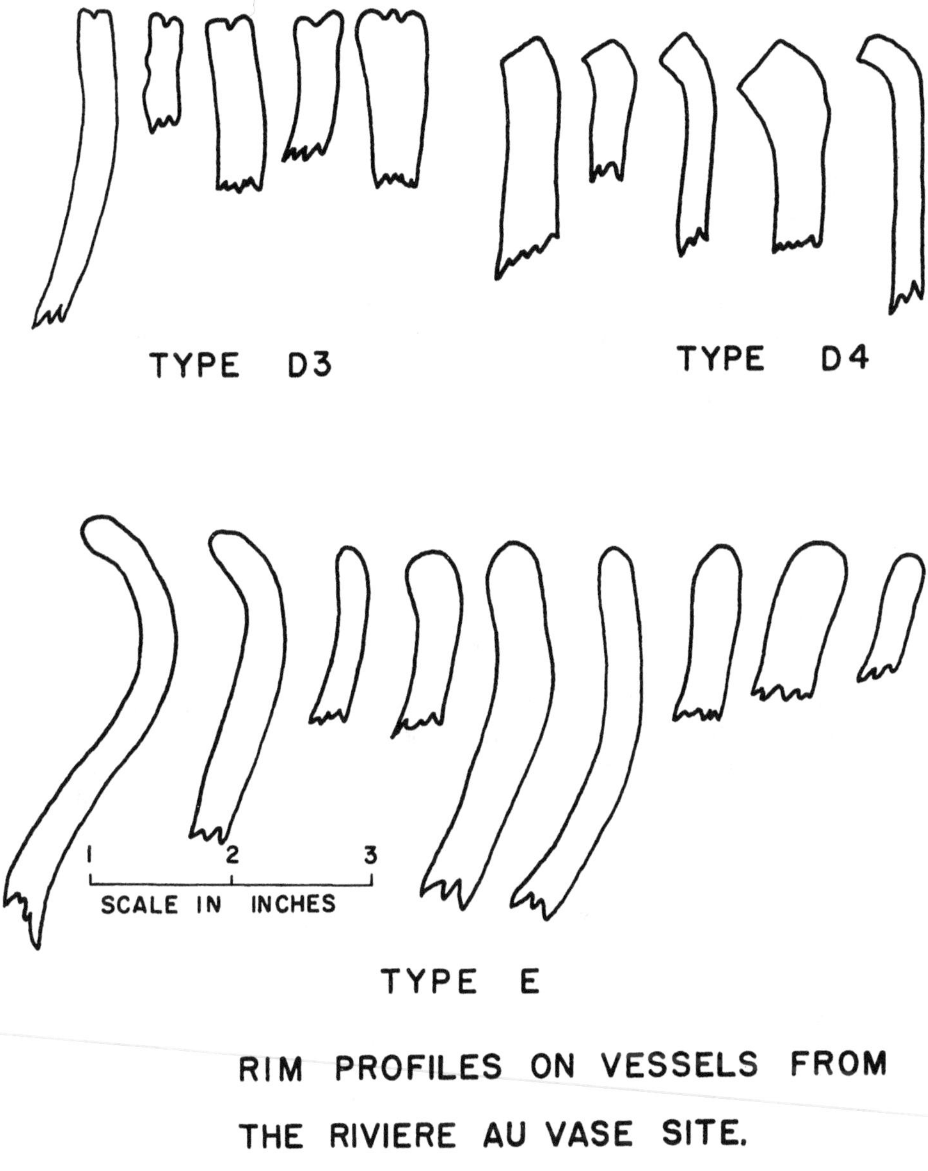

Fig. 8

necessary. The three methods of applying the oblique motif were used as separate categories: dentate-stamped, tool-impressed, and corded. For the horizontal motif the sample was too small to break down. This was also true of the cord-marked ware category. The fabric and opposed categories were too small to include in a quantified examination. Therefore, we had five categories: three composed of techniques for applying oblique designs and two including all of a motif (linear) or lack of it (cord-marked). The subcategories of rims were also too small for quantification so only the five main types could be used.

The first five tables in this section show the clustering of rim types with the categories of design and technique used in this study. Our level of significance is taken from the statisticians (Dixon and Massey 1957:91). In all cases our null hypothesis is that the observed distribution of elements does not differ from the expected random distribution of elements. If, when this is tested by chi square, we find a probability factor of 0.5 or less for the resultant chi square value, we shall reject the hypothesis that there is no difference from the expected random distribution. We can then look for the clustering that is causing so large a discrepancy from chance associations. When we have a probability factor of less than .05, we can speak of a *significant* difference and when it is less than .01, we have a *highly significant* difference.

In Table 1 the test for association of dentate-stamped vessels, as opposed to all other vessels, and rim type is given. Here we have a highly significant difference ($P < .01$) between the observed distribution and the expected distribution, and we must reject our null hypothesis. This is accounted for by the clustering of dentate stamping and type A rims. It is possible

TABLE 1

ASSOCIATION OF DENTATE STAMPING AND RIM FORM

Rim Type	Design and Technique			
	Dentate		All Others	
	Observed	Expected	Observed	Expected
A.	40	29	80	91
B.	9	7	20	22
C.	12	9	23	26
D.	13	21	71	63
E.	5	13	49	41

$\chi^2 = 17.434$; dF = 4; $p < .01$.

to say that there is a significant association between collared rims and dentate stamping.

The same test is used in Tables 2 and 3 for tool impressions and cord-wrapped stick or cord-wrapped cord impressions. In both instances our probability factor is less than .20, but not small enough for the rejection of our null hypothesis. The two techniques of applying oblique designs are distributed fairly evenly among the rim types. We would expect this much variation more than 10 per cent of the time due to chance alone.

We have a probability factor of less than .01 for the test of the association between linear design and rim form (Table 4).

TABLE 2

ASSOCIATION OF TOOL IMPRESSIONS AND RIM FORM

Rim Type	Design and Technique			
	Tool-impressed		All Others	
	Observed	Expected	Observed	Expected
A.	23	25	97	95
B.	4	6	25	23
C.	8	7	27	28
D.	24	18	60	66
E.	8	11	46	43

$\chi^2 = 4.794$; dF = 4; $p < .20$.

TABLE 3

ASSOCIATION OF CORD-WRAPPED STICK IMPRESSIONS AND RIM FORM

Rim Type	Design and Technique			
	Corded		All Others	
	Observed	Expected	Observed	Expected
A.	33	28	87	92
B.	3	7	26	22
C.	7	8	28	27
D.	17	20	67	64
E.	16	13	38	41

$\chi^2 = 5.842$; dF = 4; $p < .20$.

This is highly significant and we must reject the hypothesis that only chance association is operating on this population. It is difficult to explain the clustering which we observe here. There are greater than expected numbers of both collared rims and squared rims. This could suggest either two distinct variants of linear vessels or that much of the square rim category is based on incomplete rims that are actually collared. The sample is too small to check either of these possibilities quantitatively. For now it seems best to suggest that on linear vessels, squared rims are a variant of collar rims.

Table 5 shows the association between cord-marked vessels and rim type. Here our probability factor is less than .001. We

TABLE 4

ASSOCIATION OF LINEAR DESIGNS AND RIM FORM

Rim Type	Design and Technique			
	Linear		All Others	
	Observed	Expected	Observed	Expected
A.	21	15	99	105
B.	1	4	28	25
C.	0	4	35	31
D.	17	11	67	73
E.	2	7	52	47

$\chi^2 = 17.738$; dF = 4; $p < .01$.

TABLE 5

ASSOCIATION OF CORD-MARKED RIMS AND RIM FORM

Rim Type	Design and Technique			
	Cord-marked		All Others	
	Observed	Expected	Observed	Expected
A.	3	22	117	98
B.	12	5	17	24
C.	8	7	27	28
D.	13	15	71	69
E.	23	10	31	44

$\chi^2 = 53.178$; dF = 4; $p < .001$.

would expect this great a disparity from the expected values less than one time in a thousand if chance alone were operative. We reject the hypothesis that the observed distribution is no different from the expected distribution. We have distinct clustering of cord-marked vessels and type B and E rims. These are thickened lip and rounded lip profiles. This test suggests that cord-marked vessels have a strong tendency to have rounded lips which are sometimes thickened.

A second very important characteristic was tested against each design or technique grouping in this study. That was the association of temper with design or technique. The temper classes were judged subjectively after examination of several thousand rim and body sherds from the site. The extremes are obvious and it is felt that since intergradations between categories are random and our level of significance is high, a relatively unbiased test could be made. Since there were only a half dozen temperless sherds in the five categories of design and technique these were placed with the fine-tempered group.

In the oblique group (Tables 6, 7 and 8) no significant deviation from the expected values was found. In all three instances we fail to reject the null hypothesis. There is no demonstrable tendency for a particular temper size to be associated with either dentate stamping, tool impressions, or cord-wrapped stick impressions.

TABLE 6

ASSOCIATION OF DENTATE STAMPING AND TEMPER

Temper	Design and Technique			
	Dentate		All Others	
	Observed	Expected	Observed	Expected
Coarse. . . .	47	43	122	126
Medium . . .	33	30	83	86
Fine*.	3	9	38	32

$\chi^2 = 5.029$; dF = 2; $p < .10$.

*Includes temperless rims.

Table 9 shows the association of temper and linear designs. Here our probability factor is less than .01 so we reject our null hypothesis. The high value of chi square is, in this instance, caused by the association of linear design and coarse temper.

TABLE 7

ASSOCIATION OF TOOL IMPRESSIONS AND TEMPER

Temper	Design and Technique			
	Tool-impressed		All Others	
	Observed	Expected	Observed	Expected
Coarse....	40	35	129	134
Medium ...	21	24	95	92
Fine*.....	6	8	35	33

$\chi^2 = 1.995$; dF = 2; $p < .50$.

*Includes temperless rims.

TABLE 8

ASSOCIATION OF CORD-WRAPPED STICK IMPRESSIONS AND TEMPER

Temper	Design and Technique			
	Corded		All Others	
	Observed	Expected	Observed	Expected
Coarse....	36	42	133	127
Medium ...	34	28	82	88
Fine*.....	10	10	31	31

$\chi^2 = 2.835$; dF = 2; $p < .30$.

*Includes temperless rims.

The highest chi square value in this series was obtained in the test for association of cord-marked vessels and temper. The probability factor was less than .001, and the null hypothesis was rejected. The clustering which caused the high value was between cord-marked vessels and fine tempering.

We have enough information to go beyond the tables at this point. The fact that no significant difference was found between the observed and expected values in the association of temper and the oblique designs has some significance. The oblique designs form 62 per cent of the total sherd count from the site and 70 per cent of the sherd count in this series. They establish the modal values of this test and the modal values are coarse and medium tempering in a definite ratio. The fact that they do not differ from the whole series means that they do not differ among themselves. We seem to have three groups based on tempering: the oblique designs with both coarse and medium temper predominating, a linear group which has coarse temper and a cord-marked group which is fine temper.

TABLE 9

ASSOCIATION OF LINEAR DESIGNS AND TEMPER

Temper	Design and Technique			
	Linear		All Others	
	Observed	Expected	Observed	Expected
Coarse....	33	22	136	147
Medium ...	8	15	108	99
Fine*.....	2	6	39	35

$\chi^2 = 13.208$; dF = 2; $p < .01$.

*Includes temperless rims.

TABLE 10

ASSOCIATION OF CORD-MARKED RIMS AND TEMPER

Temper	Design and Technique			
	Cord-marked		All Others	
	Observed	Expected	Observed	Expected
Coarse....	13	28	156	141
Medium ...	20	19	96	97
Fine*.....	20	6	21	35

$\chi^2 = 47.961$; dF = 2; $p < .001$.

*Includes temperless sherds.

In Table 11 the association between the presence of lip decoration and the design or technique is given. Here the probability factor is less than .001, and we reject our null hypothesis. The high value for chi square is caused by the relative lack of lip decoration on cord-marked vessels. When we exclude cord-marked from the test we obtain a lower value for chi square and the difference is no longer significant (Table 12).

TABLE 11

ASSOCIATION OF LIP DECORATION AND DESIGN OR TECHNIQUE

Design or Technique	Lip Decoration			
	Decorated		Not Decorated	
	Observed	Expected	Observed	Expected
Dentate.	82	76	1	7
Tool-impressed. . .	64	61	3	6
Corded.	72	73	8	7
Linear	38	39	5	3
Cord-marked. .	41	48	12	5

$x^2 = 19.600$; dF = 4; $p < .001$.

TABLE 12

ASSOCIATION OF LIP DECORATION AND DESIGN OR TECHNIQUE AFTER EXCLUDING CORD-MARKED RIMS

Design or Technique	Lip Decoration			
	Decorated		Not Decorated	
	Observed	Expected	Observed	Expected
Dentate.	82	78	1	5
Tool-impressed . .	64	63	3	4
Corded.	72	75	8	5
Linear	38	40	5	3

$x^2 = 7.024$; dF = 3; $p < .10$.

The same thing was found to be true in testing design or technique against interior rim decoration. When we include the cord-marked vessels (Table 13) there is a significant difference from the expected values ($p < .001$). However, when we exclude cord-marked vessels from the test (Table 14) we obtain a non-significant probability factor of less than .30. Here too, the difference between the observed and expected values is caused by lack of decoration on the interior of the rims of cord-marked vessels.

TABLE 13

ASSOCIATION OF INTERIOR RIM DECORATION AND DESIGN OR TECHNIQUE

Design or Technique	Interior Rim Decoration			
	Decorated		Not Decorated	
	Observed	Expected	Observed	Expected
Dentate.	65	57	18	26
Tool-impressed. . .	53	46	14	21
Corded	62	55	18	25
Linear	28	30	15	13
Cord-marked	16	36	37	17

$\chi^2 = 44.916$; dF = 4; $p < .001$.

TABLE 14

ASSOCIATION OF INTERIOR RIM DECORATION AND DESIGN OR TECHNIQUE AFTER EXCLUDING CORD-MARKED RIMS

Design or Technique	Interior Rim Decoration			
	Decorated		Not Decorated	
	Observed	Expected	Observed	Expected
Dentate.	65	63	18	20
Tool-impressed	53	51	14	16
Corded	62	61	18	19
Linear	28	33	15	10

$\chi^2 = 3.918$; dF = 3; $p < .30$.

Table 15 shows the association of castellated vessels and the design or technique. The probability factor of less than .001 shows a highly significant difference. We must reject the hypothesis that there is no difference between observed and expected values. We have larger than expected values for castellated vessels decorated by tool impressions and cord-wrapped sticks and for vessels with linear designs. Castellations are found with the greatest regularity on the corded vessels. Both dentate-stamped vessels and cord-marked vessels are notable for their lack of castellation.

TABLE 15

ASSOCIATION OF CASTELLATION AND DESIGN OR TECHNIQUE

Design or Technique	Castellation			
	Present		Absent	
	Observed	Expected	Observed	Expected
Dentate.	11	25	72	58
Tool-impressed. . .	26	21	41	46
Corded.	35	25	45	55
Linear	18	13	25	30
Cord-marked. .	9	16	44	37

$\chi^2 = 25.913$; dF = 4; $p < .001$.

In testing the association of the various designs and techniques with burials (Table 16) we are handicapped by the fact that only twenty vessels were associated with burials. In testing these associations we obtain a probability factor of .01 which is highly significant. We reject the hypothesis that there is no difference between the observed and expected values. The strongest association is between cord-marked vessels and burials. This is followed by linear vessels which also are associated with burials in greater numbers than we would expect if chance alone were the only factor influencing the distribution. The number of dentate vessels associated with burials could be due to chance alone. Another striking thing about this distribution is the lack of tool-impressed and corded vessels with the burials. We would expect almost half of the vessels associated with burials to fall into these two groups, yet we find only one. This could reflect either a nonmortuary function for the vessels or that the people using these vessels on the site did not bury their dead there or if they did bury them it was without grave goods.

There were a large number of rims in pits throughout the site so we can place more faith in the tests between design or technique and presence in pits than we could the test for presence with burials. The resultant probability factor (Table 17) is less than .05 or barely significant. We reject the hypothesis that there is no difference between the observed and expected frequency. The largest discrepency between observed and expected values is found in the dentate category. Dentate stamping alone accounts for half of the chi square value.

TABLE 16

ASSOCIATION OF VESSELS WITH BURIALS WITH DESIGN OR TECHNIQUE

Design or Technique	Location of Vessels			
	With Burials		Not with Burials	
	Observed	Expected	Observed	Expected
Dentate.	6	5	77	78
Tool-impressed. . .	1	4	66	63
Corded.	0	5	79	74
Linear	5	3	39	41
Cord-marked. .	8	3	45	50

$\chi^2 = 18.041$; dF = 4; $p < .01$.

TABLE 17

ASSOCIATION OF VESSELS IN PITS WITH DESIGN OR TECHNIQUE

Design or Technique	Location of Vessels			
	In Pits		Not in Pits	
	Observed	Expected	Observed	Expected
Dentate.	54	45	29	38
Tool-impressed. . .	31	37	36	30
Corded.	47	43	32	36
Linear	19	24	25	20
Cord-marked. .	27	29	26	24

$\chi^2 = 9.517$; dF = 4; $p < .05$.

One of the most important tests in this study was the test of association of excavation unit and design or technique. Because of the numerous pits and burials the stratigraphy is very confused. In the majority of instances the depth of a find was recorded only when vessels were in pits. The largest body of data on nonpit depths comes from Trench A where there are depths on thirty-eight sherds. This is much too small a sample for a quantified examination. This leaves horizontal distribution throughout the area of the site as the best available method of isolating and ordering cultural complexes.

Table 18 gives the observed and expected values of the several designs and techniques in six excavation units. Only two to ten vessels were represented from each of the remaining seven excavation units so they could not be included in this text. A very large chi square value and a probability factor of .001 was obtained which was highly significant. The null hypothesis is rejected in this instance. In Trench D we have significantly larger amounts of cord-marked vessels than we would expect by chance alone. In Trench B the dominant variants are dentate stamping and cord-wrapped stick impressions. In Trenches E and H we have greater than expected numbers of vessels with a linear design.

A separate category on the same level as design had been established for miniature vessels. The miniature vessels had been separated into decorated and undecorated forms but the division produced groups too small to test. Since almost all miniature vessels were temperless there was no point in testing this attribute. Although it was not tested it did appear that the miniature vessels had an extremely high frequency of castellation. The difficulty here lay in determining what constitutes a castellation on a vessel with a 4 cm rim diameter. It was felt that the most meaningful test would be distributional, in order to find out the designs or techniques with which the miniature vessels were associated. The first such test is given in Table 19. The probability factor is less than .30 which is not significant so we fail to reject the null hypothesis for this test. A cursory glance at Table 18, however, will show that the distribution of miniature vessels is more closely related to the distribution of the oblique designs (dentate, tool-impressed, corded) than to either linear designs or cord-marked vessels. These two categories were eliminated and the material was retested. The results of this second test are given on Table 20. Here our probability factor is less than .90. We, of course, fail to reject our null hypothesis. The thing to note here is that the fit of the distribution of miniature vessels with oblique designs is much better than with vessels from the entire site. This is a good indication that the people making vessels with oblique designs were also responsible for making the miniature vessels.

The above tests point to some very distinct ceramic grouping at Riviere au Vase. The most obvious of these is the cord-marked ware grouping. There are probability factors of less than .001 for the association of the cord-marked ware and rim

TABLE 18

ASSOCIATION OF RIM DESIGN OR TECHNIQUE WITH EXCAVATION UNIT

Design or Technique	Excavation Unit									
	A		B		D		E		H	
	Ob-served	Ex-pected	Ob-served	Ex-pected	Ob-served	Ex-pected	Ob-served	Ex-pected	Ob-served	Ex-pected
Dentate.	14	16	26	21	15	15	10	13	9	8
Tool-impressed. . .	13	11	15	15	9	11	11	10	5	6
Corded.	11	13	25	17	14	12	5	11	5	7
Linear	5	8	4	11	3	8	17	7	7	4
Cord-marked. .	9	10	15	15	15	10	7	9	4	5

$\chi^2 = 39.025$; $dF = 16$; $p < .001$.

TABLE 19

ASSOCIATION OF MINIATURE VESSELS AND EXCAVATION UNITS

Excavation Unit	Size of Vessel			
	Miniature		All Others	
	Observed	Expected	Observed	Expected
A.	5	6	58	57
B.	14	9	79	84
D.	6	6	56	56
E.	2	5	50	53
H.	3	4	30	29

$\chi^2 = 5.496$; dF = 4; $p < .30$.

TABLE 20

ASSOCIATION OF MINIATURE VESSELS WITH EXCAVATION UNITS AFTER EXCLUDING CORD-MARKED AND LINEAR RIMS FROM THE RESIDUAL CATEGORY

Excavation Unit	Size of Vessel			
	Miniature		All Others Except Linear and Cord-marked	
	Observed	Expected	Observed	Expected
A.	5	6	38	37
B.	14	14	92	92
D.	6	6	38	38
E.	2	4	26	24
H.	3	3	19	19

$\chi^2 = 1.347$; dF = 4; $p < .90$.

form, temper, lip decoration, interior rim decoration, and castellation. Cord-marked vessels are more frequently associated with burials than any other form ($p < .01$). The only instance where there are approximately equal values is in the association of pit deposition and vessel decoration or technique. All this leads to a very distinctive picture of cord-marked vessels with rounded or thickened rims and fine temper. There is a significant lack of lip and interior rim decoration as well as a tendency for absence of castellation. These vessels are found primarily in

Trench D and they are found in greater than expected numbers with burials.

The series of vessels with linear designs also forms a distinctive group. Probability factors of less than .01 were obtained in the tests of rim form and temper. There were tendencies toward castellation and lip and rim decoration. A slightly greater than expected number were found with burials although fewer than expected were found in pits. Trench E and, to a lesser extent, Trench H presented greater than expected frequencies of vessels with linear designs. Here is a coarse-tempered ware which has either collared or squared rims, castellations, lip and interior rim decorations, and is found with burials in Trench E and H.

The entire oblique series, as was mentioned before, holds together as far as distribution of temper is concerned. After this there is a separation. Dentate-stamped vessels have a strong tendency ($p < .01$) to be associated with collared rims and a decided lack of castellation ($p < .001$). They are found with burials in about the expected frequencies and are the type most likely to be found in pits. The distribution of dentate-stamped vessels follows that of tool-impressed or corded vessels. No significant rim form seems to be associated with tool impression or cording. Like all the oblique and linear designs there is a strong tendency toward lip and interior rim decoration. Unlike the dentate, however, there is a strong tendency toward castellation. The tool-impressed and corded vessels are almost completely absent in burials. The large numbers of these forms over the whole site makes this very significant.

We can establish three major groupings on the basis of design and temper. The cord-marked vessels and those with linear designs also have distinctive rim forms and a very distinctive distribution on the site. They are found with burials. Within the oblique group the tool-impressed and corded forms are most similar. The dentate vessels are divergent in lack of castellation, tendency toward collared rims, occasional presence with burials and tendency to be found in pits. The miniature vessels from the site are most likely to be associated with the oblique vessels.

The application of quantitative methods to the study of rim sherds from Riviere au Vase has proved very fruitful. A basis for the separation of the sample into wares and types has been obtained and the possibility of a chronological ordering has been suggested.

Analysis of Body Sherds

The analysis of body sherds from the site was carried out in a similar manner to that of rim sherds, but on a smaller scale. The collections were examined, and the sherds were placed in categories on the basis of surface treatment. The catalog numbers were recorded and entered next to the description of the sherds. The provenience was recorded for the sherds and the material was resorted in three separate ways.

First, the different surface treatment categories were totaled for the entire site. The material was then sorted according to major excavation units. Some of the material which was from "the general site" or for which the provenience was vague was deleted from this section. Lastly, the material was sorted as to exact refuse pit or burial with which it occurred. Since the provenience data was usually specific only to the trench designation, the sample size was also cut at this stage. The data on sherds found with burials and pits are given in the sections on burials and pits.

There were a number of extremely small fragments which we called "sherdlets." These were, for the most part, fragments too small to permit accurate identification of surface treatment. An arbitrary cutoff point on maximum size was established in the analysis of sherdlets. All material under the size of a quarter was classed as a sherdlet unless it showed some specific surface treatment, such as dentate stamping, tool impressions, etc. If it was plain and under this size, it was classed as a sherdlet (possibly an interior surface), or if it was cord-marked and under this size, it was classed as a sherdlet (it would be indistinguishable from a fabric-impressed sherd). The sherdlets were weighed and the total and average weights of the sherdlets from the various excavation units are given in Table 21. The productivity of the site, and problem of analyzing the material without resorting to such an expedient, is demonstrated by the occurrence of over 10,600 such sherdlets in the University of Michigan collections from the Riviere au Vase Site.

The body sherds which we are to describe are, therefore, all over the size of a quarter, or distinguished by the same decorative techniques found on the complete rim sherds from the site. There were 1,850 body sherds included in this section of the analysis, which were divided into three groups which were in turn divided into 15 categories.

Because of the admittedly biased method of sorting sherds, we will first consider those that are solely body sherds. This

TABLE 21

DISTRIBUTION OF BODY SHERDS AT THE RIVIERE AU VASE SITE

Trench	A	B	D	DA	E	F	G	H	J	TTA	TTB	TT1	TT2
Cord-marked	72	99	63	2	42	8	10	24	6	2	..	7	11
Smoothed-cord-marked	54	94	76	5	34	11	20	54	2	7	..	10	4
Smoothed	11	31	17	5	42	14	3	20	4	..	..	1	6
Roughened	11	38	16	7	41	2	4	27	1	1	..	1	5
Fabric-impressed	19	18	11	2	12	1	1	3	..	..	..	..	..
Simple-stamped	2	..	..	..	..	1	1	..	..	..	..	..	..
Brushed	..	1	..	..	..	..	..	..	..	..	..	..	..
Incised shoulder	23	87	26	1	44	4	2	17	4	..	..	2	3
Vase Dentate	33	56	35	2	16	4	10	17	4	..	..	..	1
Vase Tool-impressed	13	15	7	..	4	..	1	8	1	..	..	1	2
Vase Corded	19	24	17	..	15	1	3	4	1	..	..	1	..
Macomb Linear-corded	13	24	11	..	6	2	1	6	2	..	..	..	..
Macomb Interrupted Linear	3	8	1	..	..	..	..	1	1	..	..	1	..
Wayne Punctate	..	3	3	..	1	..	..	..	..	..	..	1	..
Miniature vessel	7	20	5	..	5	..	1	3	1	..	..	1	1
Sherdlets	1,514	3,020	2,115	81	1,136	311	206	1,132	86	80	..	81	96
Weight of sherdlets in grams	5,258	7,850	5,934	289	4,085	1,058	785	3,315	172	311	..	316	339
Average weight of sherdlets in grams	3.47	2.60	2.81	3.57	3.60	3.40	3.81	2.93	2.00	3.89	..	3.90	3.53

first group may be opposed to the second group, incised shoulder sherds, and the third group, incomplete rim fragments duplicating the rim sherd patterns. Seven types of surface treatment were noted on sherds in this first group: cord-marked, smoothed-cord-marked, smoothed, roughened, fabric-impressed, simple-stamped, and brushed. About 54 per cent (1,174) of the total body sherd sample fell into this group.

There were 373 cord-marked body sherds, about 32 per cent of the first group, for the site (Plate I, A). This is a very common type of surface treatment, and was apparently caused by the maleation of the unfired and still wet vessel with a cord-wrapped paddle.

Another group of sherds were cord-marked, but there had been an attempt to obliterate the cord-marking. These were referred to as smoothed-cord-marked (Plate I, B). All of these sherds showed evidence of this type of treatment to a greater or lesser degree. There were 413 sherds in this category, or 35 per cent of the first group of body sherds.

The smoothed-cord-marked category graded into the next category, that of smoothed body sherds (Plate I, C). The dividing line between these three categories is fine, although the polar extremes are obvious. From the intergradations evident on some sherds it is very possible that all three types of surface treatment existed on the same vessel (Plate VII is an example of this). There were 151 sherds of this type, or 13 per cent of the first group of body sherds.

The fourth type of surface treatment was a roughened surface (Plate I, D). This type of surface treatment was noted at the Wolf site (Greenman 1939*b*: Plate III, Figure 2, b), and occurs on a vessel found by W. J. Wintemberg at Windsor, Ontario (Lee 1958*b*:18). It is common at a number of smaller sites in Macomb County which the writer has investigated. Greenman has suggested that this type of surface treatment is ". . .apparently the result of washing before firing, with a consequent rough surface formed by extrusion of fine tempering fragments and by angular depressions left by tempering fragments that were detached in the process" (1939*b*:13). There were 146 roughened body sherds from the site constituting a little over 12 per cent of the first group of body sherds.

A number of body sherds in the first group have been impressed with a coarse fabric (Plate I, E). It is probable that the paddle which was usually wrapped with a cord was occasionally covered with a coarse fabric leading to this type of surface treatment. It is often difficult to find a definite evidence of the warp and woof of the very coarse fabric so sherds were only classed as fabric-impressed when plasticene impressions revealed these characteristics. There were eighty-six such body sherds in our sample, or slightly over 7 per cent of the first group.

Four sherds, less than 1 per cent, have been classed as sample-stamped (Plate I, F). It is my impression that this type of surface treatment is very rare in southeastern Michigan. It is common at the Middleport Village site in Ontario (Wintemberg 1948:47, Plate II), and is found at the Boys site in Ontario (Ridley 1958: Plate II, I, J).

A single sherd from the sample appears to have been brushed (Plate I, G). The interior is very irregular. It would have been grouped with the miniature vessel fragments except for its coarse granetic temper (particles over 2 mm in diameter). It is perhaps significant that this sherd was found in Trench B.

The second group of sherds which we are to consider are incised shoulder fragments. A total of 210 sherds were assigned to this group which constituted 11 per cent of the total nonrim sherd sample. This technique of incised chevron shoulder treatment is shown in Plate II. Since most of the incised shoulder fragments from the Riviere au Vase site were small, a fragment of a vessel found near Flat Rock is illustrated.

This type of shoulder incising has been reported in Ontario by Kidd (1954: Figures 7, 8, 9, 10, 12) and Ridley (1958: Plate I, I).

There were 408 sherds, or 22 per cent of the entire body sherd sample, which appeared to be incomplete rim fragments. They had the decorative designs and techniques of the rim sherds, but lacked the complete rim profile. These were distributed as follows: cord-wrapped stick or cord-wrapped cord impressions running obliquely to the rim, or in this case, the base of the collar, 70; tool impressions running obliquely to the base of the collar, 48; dentate stamping, 193; cord-wrapped stick or cord-wrapped cord impressions running parallel to the base of the collar, 66; interrupted linear or "stab and drag" impressions running parallel to the base of the collar, 20; circular punctates on a cord-marked surface, 11.

In addition to these sherds there were over fifty fragments of thin, temperless vessels that fell within the range of miniature vessels. This included both decorated fragments (similar to the rim sherds in Plate XIX) and plain fragments (similar to the rims in Plate XXI and the vessel in Plate XX).

The body sherds which were found in specific excavation units are given in Table 21. The number of sherdlets, the weight of these sherdlets and the average weight of sherdlets in the various excavation units are also given in this table.

There was a large enough sample from Trenches A, B, D, E, and H to plot the observed frequencies of the nine largest categories of body sherds against the expected frequencies. Because of the extremely subjective nature of the cord-marked, smoothed-cord-marked and smoothed-surface categories, no test of chi square was applied to this material. An examination of the observed and expected frequencies did, however, produce some interesting results. Trench A produced considerably larger numbers of cord-marked sherds than would be expected. Trench E, on the other hand, produced larger than expected numbers of smoothed-surface body sherds and roughened body sherds. Trench D was notable for the large occurrence of smoothed cord-marked body sherds. The outstanding thing about Trench B was the high occurrence of incised shoulder fragments. It might also be noted that the largest number of miniature vessel fragments came from Trench B, although this was not true for the sample of miniature vessel rim sherds. This, perhaps is caused by the small sample.

Although the sample is far too small to suggest quantification of such data, it is of interest that two of the four simple-stamped sherds came from Trench A, and that the single-brushed body sherd came from Trench B.

We may also note that the largest numbers of sherdlets were recovered from Trench B, and the second largest amount from adjacent Trench D. The average weight of sherdlets from Trench B was the least of the entire site (excluding Trench J, where only eighty-six sherdlets were recovered, and Test Trench B, where no ceramic material was recovered). The average size of sherdlets from Trench D was intermediate between Trench B, and the rest of the site. By itself this would not be of too great significance, but when coupled with other observations, it suggests a different type of occupation in the western part of the site.

Although not included with the body sherds, we should also note that six fragments of poorly fired clay were found at the site. These are amorphous, but bear the impression of grass or fine sticks. They are temperless. They appear to be fragments of daub used in wattle and daub house construction. Similar fragments were reported from the Wolf site (Greenman 1939*b*:15).

The most common type of surface treatment on body sherds from the Riviere au Vase site was cord marking or smoothed cord marking. Large numbers of both smoothed and roughened body sherds were recovered during the University of Michigan excavations. Smaller numbers of fabric-impressed, simple-stamped and brushed body sherds were in the sample. There was a large group of sherds that appeared to be fragments of incised shoulders of vessels. There were also a number of incomplete rim sherd fragments with decorations and techniques of application similar to those used in the analysis of rim sherds. A number of miniature vessel fragments were included in this group. There were differences in the distribution of body sherds throughout the area excavated by The University of Michigan.

Temporal Placement of Ceramics

In order to describe and manipulate the ceramic material from the Riviere au Vase site, it becomes necessary to describe types and cultural affiliations for these types and to derive a temporal placement for this material. The preceeding sections will furnish a basis for establishment of types.

McPherron (1963) has set the scene for this type of discussion in his paper on Late Woodland ceramics in the Straits of Mackinac. He pointed out that the broad ceramic horizons of the Middle Woodland period diverge into areal traditions around A.D. 700. Similarities in ceramic styles may be found between Virginia and the Northern Plains, until A.D. 1000 or A.D. 1100. After A.D. 1100 we are dealing with local traditions and can trace developmental sequences, in many instances, to historic peoples.

The descriptions given here are not formal type descriptions. The formal type descriptions for the material under discussion are given in the Appendix. What is given here is a brief description and cultural placement for the various ceramic forms from the Riviere au Vase site. Our attempts at dating are based on the theory that similar ceramic forms in closely related areas are of similar age. While these might appear to be the same types, in light of the observations made over several decades on the distinctness of the Younge Focus material, it seems best to establish a new series of types.

As with other investigators (Guthe 1948:10; Kidd 1954:167-68) these types will be left fluid. Other investigators may well feel the need to combine some forms or separate others or to ignore the classification given here altogether. The potential for divisions in some types is included in parts of the present discussion.

Because of the nature of the sample, and the nature of northeastern ceramics in general, our types are sherd types, specifically rim sherd types, rather than whole vessel types. In several instances vessel forms can be associated with rimsherd types but in these cases several vessel shapes may be associated with a particular rim form.

On the basis of Harper's technological examination of the Riviere au Vase sample, and our observations on the association of fine tempering particles and plain rims, it is possible to establish two wares from the site. The first of these is our Wayne ware with ceramic forms similar to those found at the main level of the Fort Wayne Mound and in the primary burial horizon at the Gibraltar site. The second ware is referred to as Riviere ware and constitutes the largest part of the Riviere au Vase sample. Similar forms are found in southeastern Michigan, in intrusive pits at the Fort Wayne Mound and at the Younge site.

Wayne ware is a predominently fine to medium-tempered ware with predominently plain rims. Several restorable vessels were found with burials in Trench B, and are illustrated in Plates III, V, and VI. A number of rim sherds are illustrated in Plate IV.

Only one type with several variants was defined for our analysis of Riviere au Vase material. This is referred to as Wayne Cord-marked. The above mentioned plates are examples of the common form of Wayne Cord-marked. Castellations and collars are rare on the plain forms, but lip decoration is occasionally found, although it is not as plentiful as the lip decoration on Riviere ware.

Two variants were also recognized. One was Wayne Smoothed. This is a basic Wayne Cord-marked form with the cord marking obliterated near the rim. A complete vessel of this type is illustrated in Plate VII and a number of rimsherds are illustrated in Plate VIII.

The second variant was Wayne Punctate. Here the basic cord-marked rim has been altered through either the application of circular or wedge-shaped exterior punctates. This variant was represented by several rim sherds from the Riviere au Vase site (Plate IX).

Wayne ware is related to the "generalized woodland" forms which (Quimby (1941:494, Plate I, A) found associated with Goodall Focus material in western Michigan. It is a type of some persistence for Quimby later noted (1943) that it was found throughout the entire Goodall sequence. From the associations of this material in refuse pits at the Riviere au Vase site it apparently lasted as a minor variant for some time beyond the Middle Woodland period.

It may be contemporaneous with the more elaborately decorated ceramics from the Krieger site in Ontario (Kidd: 1954). The vessel forms are very similar (see Kidd: 1954, Plates VIII, IX), and there is a tendency toward a design on some of the vessels from the Riviere au Vase site (Plate V) (DeVisscher 1957). Dr. William Ritchie (personal communication) suggested that there is a very close resemblence between Wayne Cord-marked and the Krieger types with common attributes ranging from lip treatment to vessel form.

This type may occupy a similar temporal position to Jack's Reef Corded (Ritchie and MacNeish 1949:106). Ritchie and MacNeish suggest that it is a late Point Peninsula type, and that it may intergrade into Levanna Cord-on-Cord, an Owasco type. They suggest wider connections for a "post-Hopewellian Woodland Cord-marked type" which would include Wayne Cord-marked.

Similarities might be noted between the Wayne Punctate sherds from the site and the vessel recovered by W. B. Hinsdale from the West Twin Lake site (1930). Morgan (1952:93) has compared this material to the Intrusive Mound Culture in Ohio which occupies a post-Hopewell position in that area. Quimby (1952:104) has interpreted Gibraltar and West Twin Lake as both being in the transitional period from Middle Woodland to Late Woodland. He also noted the similarity to the Intrusive Mound Culture in Ohio.

Fred Dustin (1932), in his report on Ogemaw County earthworks, illustrated one Wayne Cord-marked sherd (Plate I, C) and several Wayne Smoothed sherds (Plate I, A, B).

Leonard Griffin has reported on a site in Cheboygan County (1953), which was excavated by the Clinton Valley Chapter of the Michigan Archaeological Society, that has ceramics similar to Wayne Cord-marked. The ceramics from this site, the Black Lake site, may eventually furnish the basis for a new type. The Wayne Cord-marked sherds have a modal lip decorative technique of cord-wrapped stick impressions while those from the Black Lake site have oblique and crisscross tool impressions (some made with a reed or cattail stalk). Both forms are, however, present on both sites. In examining material in the University of Michigan collections, it was found that there were very similar occurrences in the earliest dated occupational level at the Juntunen site (McPherron 1963). It is represented by a number of sherds, and has been dated to A.D. 835 ± 75 years (M-1142). McPherron, in turn, related this horizon to the general transitional period between Middle and Late Woodland.

Since this type, while relatively isolated in some of the burials, is found with other later types in burials and refuse pits, it would seem that we could date it to the very end of this transitional period. This would place it somewhere between A.D. 600 and A.D. 900 at the Riviere au Vase site.

Riviere ware is distinguished from Wayne ware on the basis of larger tempering particles, and a tendency for the greater occurrence of collars and, on some forms, castellations. At least four types are present in the University of Michigan sample. These include Vase Dentate, Macomb Linear (with two variants), Vase Corded, and Vase Tool-impressed.

On the basis of association with Wayne Cord-marked, and the lack of late features such as castellations, the type which would seem to be earliest in Vase Dentate. This type had a medium to coarse temper similar to that found in Vase Corded and Vase Tool-impressed sherds. There was a tendency for the rims to be collared and for castellations to be absent. This was the type which was most common in refuse pits. Vase Dentate sherds are illustrated in Plates XI and XII. The dentation was regularly applied with a carved tool.

In addition to the collared type A rims there are also larger then expected numbers of type C or thickened rims. This is also the case for Jack's Reef Dentate Collar, an apparently similar type in the New York Owasco sequence (Ritchie and MacNeish 1949:106). In New York it has been suggested that there might be two types, collared and uncollared. It is a late Point Peninsula type in New York where it is found with Jack's Reef Corded Collar.

At the Krieger site Kidd (1954:168) noted that Krieger Dentate-stamped was a potential type, and a variant of Krieger Stamped. The dentate-stamped rim which he illustrates (Figure 12, 1) has a profile and a general appearance similar to the type C profile dentate-stamped rims from the Riviere au Vase site.

Ridley, at the Frank Bay site, found dentate stamping common in three levels (Ridley 1954). A collarless dentate-stamped form (Figure 18, s, v) was present in the Point Peninsula Strata, and dentate stamping occurred on thickened to collared rims in both the Primary Transitional Strata (Figure 19, a-d, f) and in the Frank Bay Transitional Strata (Figure 20, a). Both of these levels were, in turn, beneath his Barrie-Uren Strata which contained no dentate stamping.

At the Boys site in Ontario (Ridley 1958), a number of dentate forms were recognized. One sherd of Jack's Reef Dentate-collared was recovered (Plate I, Q) which Ridley explained as a carry-over of the cultural tradition of the Point Peninsula period. Ridley also defined Boys Oblique Dentate (p. 29) and Scugog Oblique Dentate (p. 31), and illustrated these types (Plates I, E, F, H, I). This material appears to be related, again in the generic sense, to Vase Dentate. These types are characteristic of the Boys site, and their near absence (only one Boys Oblique sherd) on the Barrie site is evidence of the transition from the Point Peninsula level to the Barrie-Uren level. Boys Oblique Dentate is completely absent from the Uren site suggesting that Uren might be *slightly* later than Barrie. Ridley used the first of a series of radio-carbon dates from the Snell site as a contributor date for the Boys site. Since then other dates for the Snell site have been published (Crane and Griffin 1958) which are about 500 years later than the date used by Ridley. The Snell site date of A.D. 787 ± 100 years (M-178, only one sigma) seems to be appropriate.

Since this type has similarities to both the earlier Wayne ware and the other, later, Riviere ware types, an intermediate temporal position is suggested. This material would be characteristic of the A.D. 800 to A.D. 1000 occupation, although continuity on both sides of these extremes is a possibility.

There are several variants of the type Macomb Linear. These are Macomb Linear-corded (Plates XIII, XIV, and XV) and Macomb Interrupted Linear (Plate XVI). These variants may have temporal significance, but from their distribution at the Riviere au Vase site there is no basis for separation. This type has an extremely coarse temper, and has a strong tendency toward being collared and castellated. The pattern runs parallel to the rim and along the collar. It is applied with either a cord-wrapped stick or cord, or by the interrupted-linear technique, where the impressions are made with a tool on wet clay. This latter has been referred to as "stab and drag" or "push and pull."

McPherron (1936) suggested that this type of material (his "second readily distinguishable ware": p. 573) appears sometime after A.D. 1070 ± 75 years (M-1140 at the Juntunen site. He suggested that examples of this ware may be found at the Younge site, Riviere au Vase, the Wolf site and the Fort Wayne Mound. He illustrated a sherd (Figure 1, E) which is similar to Macomb Interrupted-linear forms. The Barrie site material (Ridley 1958) and some of the sherds from the Uren site (Wintemberg 1928) were mentioned as being similar to the material from this horizon at the Juntunen site.

Sherds similar to Macomb Linear-corded are illustrated in the Uren site report (Wintemberg 1928: Plates X, 12; XIV, 19; XV; XVIII, 5) and were defined as Uren Corded by MacNeish (1952: 19-20). MacNeish placed the Uren site at the bottom of the Neutral-Wenro developmental sequence, but noted its "Owascoid" affinities.

Horizontal cord impressions seem to be absent from the Boys and Barrie sites (Ridley 1958). Ridley has reported it (1954:47) as a rare variant in the Barrie-Uren Strata at the Frank Bay site.

This horizon is represented in the New York Owasco sequence by the type Owasco Corded-collar (Ritchie and MacNeish 1949: 112-14) which is a middle to late Owasco type.

Macomb Interrupted-linear (Plate XVI), while a minority variant at the Riviere au Vase site, seems to be representative of a wider horizon than Macomb Linear-corded. This is the type of decorative technique illustrated and noted at the Juntunen site by McPherron.

Interrupted-linear impressions were the most common rim decoration in the Barrie-Uren Strata at the Frank Bay site (Ridley 1958:42). Macomb Interrupted-linear is probably in generic relationship to the type defined as Iroquois Linear by MacNeish (1952:19) who stated, "This type is important because it appears to be a conclusive link between late Owasco and early Iroquois, as well as a time marker." In his Neutral-Wenro developmental sequence this form was limited to the Uren horizon. Ridley (1958:22-28) later suggested that the name Iroquoian Linear might be more appropriate. This was the most common type at the Barrie site although it was a minor component at the Uren site, again suggesting a slightly earlier temporal position for the Barrie site.

In the New York series the analogous form seems to be Bainbridge Linear (Ritchie and MacNeish 1949:115-16). MacNeish (1952:19) noted the similarity of this type to the Uren site Iroquois Linear and McPherron (1936:574) noted its similarity to the material from the post A.D. 1070 horizon at the Juntunen site. Ritchie and MacNeish suggested that this was a very late Owasco type.

Mr. Peter P. Pratt (personal communication) excavated material with a similar rim decorative technique from the Hicks site in New York. He believes this material to date to about A.D. 1150.

The two final types, Vase Tool-impressed and Vase Corded, appeared to be very closely related in our quantitative examination of rim sherds. They both had significant associations with castellations and medium to coarse tempering particles. They seemed to have a similar areal distribution throughout the site.

Vase Tool-impressed (Plate XVII) almost invariably has oblique impressions which appear to have been made in the wet clay with the edge of a tool. In some instances it looks like a pointed tool might have been used and trailed along the surface, but this is very rare. Although there is no quantitative basis for separating the forms at the Riviere au Vase site, it may be that the collarless vessels are earlier. This would be a type similar to Krieger Incised (Kidd 1954:167-68), and would be represented by the bottom right sherd in Plate XVII. At Riviere au Vase, however, the statistical examination suggests that this is a variant of the collared type. Further work in southeastern Michigan might well lead to further clarification of this type.

Vessels similar to Vase Tool-impressed were present at the Uren site (Wintemberg 1928: Plates IV, V, VI, VII, VIII). It appears to be similar in style to Ontario Oblique (MacNeish 1952: 18) and Uren Noded (1952:18). One sherd of this type was present in the Barrie-Uren Strata at the Frank Bay site (Ridley 1954: 47). Ridley (1958:29) referred to this type as Impressed Oblique, and emphasized the impressed rather than incised nature of the application of the design (which we have also noted). Ridley saw this as a development from his Scugog Oblique Dentate type with the substitution of a smooth tool for a dentate tool. This same development may be seen at the Riviere au Vase site. Ridley noted that a single sherd of this type was found at the Middleport site (Wintemberg 1948: Plate III, 13) which MacNeish has suggested is a later stage in the Neutral-Wenro sequence than that represented by the Uren site.

In the New York Owasco sequence Ritchie and MacNeish mention rare oblique tool impressions on Owasco Herringbone (1949: 110-11). This is an uncollared middle Owasco type that may have developed out of late Point Peninsula types. They also mention similar variants of Castle Creek Beaded (1949:114), a slightly collared middle to late Owasco type.

Vase Corded (Plate XVIII) is a type with both collared type A rims and uncollared rims. The decorative motif is oblique impressions which are applied to the wet clay with a cord-wrapped stick or cord-wrapped cord.

Forms similar to the uncollared sherds of Vase Corded are represented at the Krieger site where they are referred to as Krieger Stamped (Kidd 1954:168) although this type also includes forms similar to Vase Dentate which we have excluded. There are several sherds of a similar form which are apparently collared, illustrated in the Uren site report (Wintemberg 1928: Plate IV, 2-4) although MacNeish does not include this as a type in his study of the Uren material. Several of MacNeish's Uren Corded sherds might fall within the range of our Vase Corded type (MacNeish 1952: Plate V, 7, 8).

Similar forms are present at the Boys site where Ridley (1958:Plate I, N, P) calls them Owasco Herringbone and refers the reader to Ritchie and MacNeish (1949:110). Ritchie and MacNeish suggest that this is an early to middle Owasco type. They also suggest that it had a prototype in late Point Peninsula dentate-stamped forms.

A number of fragments of usually temperless miniature vessels were recovered from the Riviere au Vase site. These included decorated forms (Plate XIX), plain forms (Plate XXI) and a complete plain vessel (Plate XX). These are not particularly diagnostic. Most recently Wright (Wright and Anderson 1963:36) noted their common occurrence on almost all ceramic-bearing sites in the Great Lakes area. It still might be worth mentioning, in light of the parallel distribution of Vase Corded, Vase Tool-impressed and miniature vessels at the Riviere au Vase site, that there is a striking resemblance between the decorated miniature vessel rims (Plate XIX) and the miniature vessel fragments from the Uren site (Wintemberg 1928:Plate III). This too would seem to suggest that many of these fragments can be related to the last phase of the Riviere au Vase site aboriginal occupation.

Several aberrant sherds were noted from the site. These include a number of forms which were classed as "opposed" in the quantitative analysis. This is a very minor group, and further study may place these sherds with either the Macomb Interrupted-linear type or the Vase Dentate type depending on the technique of design application used in each instance. The three net or fabric-impressed rims from the site must be noted under aberrant ceramics. Their distribution is given in the section describing the pits from the site. This type is characteristic of later Michigan horizons and will be dealt with later.

There is one sherd (Plate XXII, A) which has cord-wrapped stick impressions on the lip and criss-cross incising below this. A similar sherd was found at the Root site (Griffin 1962:Plate I) which Leonard Griffin has suggested was occupied from Middle Woodland times to the contact period. More specific placement may come from the Verchave I site where an almost identical sherd (Plate XLIII, I) was recovered from Feature Number 4 which also contained two Vase Corded sherds.

Two sherds have a smooth surface and oblique or opposed incising (Plate XXII). These sherds may be trade sherds of Ontario Oblique and Uren Noded.

Three rim sherds (Plate XXII, E-G) have a rounded or rolled rim with oblique, rolled cord-wrapped stick impressions. The over-all effect is that of fancy icing on a cake.

Several points need to be made in regard to the body sherds from the site. It is very probable that the early occupation is represented by the cord-marked body sherds, particularly the thinner forms. The roughened body sherds are associated with later types, particularly with elongated vessels (Plate XIII, see also Lee 1958: Figure 7; Greenman 1939b:Plates IV, V). Simple stamping is found at Uren (Wintemberg 1928:Plate II), the Boys site (Ridley 1958: Figure 2, I, J) and the Middleport site (Wintemberg 1948: Plate II). These sherds may belong to the later phases of occupation at the site. The single-brushed body sherd *may* be related to the Illinois type Baehr Brushed, a late degenerate Hopewell type (Griffin 1952c:120). It was found in Trench B, the area of the site where the burials with Wayne Cord-marked were found. The simple-stamped sherds, on the other hand, seem to come from the opposite end of the site.

In brief, it can be said that the ceramics from the Riviere au Vase site can be placed in the transitional period between the Middle Woodland horizon and the later variants of Late Woodland in northeastern North America. There seems to be a development paralleling that taking place in the New York Owasco sequence (Ritchie and MacNeish 1949), the Southwestern Ontario Glen Meyer sequence (Lee 1951, 1952, 1958a), at the Boys and Barrie sites (Ridley 1958), the Frank Bay site (Ridley 1954) and in the Straits of Mackinac at the Juntunen site (McPherron 1963). These relationships are all of a generic rather than a specific nature, although several sherds from the Riviere au Vase site may be Uren types.

Lithic Material

Analysis of Chipped Stone

The analysis of chipped stone is, of necessity, rather restricted. Because of either the nature of the excavation or the nature of the site, little of the stone chippage was saved. There are more projectile points than flakes in the museum collection, so this analysis is more formal than processual.

The small sample size and wide range of describable chert and flint types also precludes an analysis of the raw material. The only cores from the site were found with burials, and these are a banded chert. The banding and range of quality and color on these few cores includes almost the entire range of cherts described for individual artifacts. The one type not covered by the range of these banded cores, a white brown-mottled chert, is found in an insignificant amount among all classes of artifacts. While an examination of chert types, possible sources and correlation with artifact types would be desirable, the nature of the sample makes it impossible.

The largest category of chipped-stone artifacts from the site is projectile points. There are thirty-eight points and basal sections, and an additional eight blade fragments used in this examination. The largest group of points are triangular. The triangular points, in turn, were easily segregated into two groups, one of large points and a second of small points.

The larger triangular points (Plate XXIII) fit into Ritchie's (1961:31-2) classification of Levanna points. In New York this point type is first found in complexes dating around A.D. 700. It became common during the transitional period into Late Woodland, around A.D. 900, but tended to disappear after A.D. 1350. This point type is characteristic of the Owasco occupation in New York. The metric data for the sixteen Levanna points from Riviere au Vase is given in Table 22.

TABLE 22

METRIC AND NONMETRIC ATTRIBUTES OF LEVANNA POINTS

(In Centimeters)

UMMA Catalog No.	L	W	T	B	Provenience
23150	3.2	2.3	.5	C	Tr. E, Burial V101
23156	3.5	2.8	.4	C	Tr. E, Section 9
23157	3.9	3.1	.6	C	Tr. E, Pit 2
23162	?	2.5	.6	C	Tr. D, Pit 14
23164	3.4	2.9	.5	C	Tr. E, Burial V58
23165	3.8	2.4	.5	C	Tr. E, Burial V58
23167	?	2.6	.5	C	Tr. E, Burial V58
23168	4.4	2.8	.5	C	Tr. E, Burial V58
23169	3.9	2.4	.7	C	Tr. E, Burial V58
23169	?	3.0	.5	C	Tr. E, Burial V58
23170	3.8	3.1	.5	S	Tr. E, Burial V58
23171	2.8	2.2	.5	C	Tr. E, Burial V58
20941	4.0	2.6	.5	C	Tr. E, Burial V72
20971	3.6	2.2	.5	S	Tr. A, Burial V10
21000	3.6	2.4	.5	C	Tr. A, general
No number	3.8	1.8	.5	C	General site
Mean	3.7	2.6	.5		

L = length, W = width, T = thickness, B = basal configuration, C = concave, S = straight, ? = point base only.

The second type of triangular point is the type referred to as the Madison point (Scully 1951:14, Ritchie 1961:33). This point is smaller than the Levanna point (Table 23; Plate XXIV) and there is a significant difference in basal concavity. The Madison points tend to have straighter bases than the Levanna points. This is shown in Table 24 where a chi-square value of 7.418 is obtained demonstrating that this difference is significant at the .01 level. This type of point is generally considered to be a very late type. Ritchie believes that, in New York, Madison points replaced Levanna points around A.D. 1350. He (Ritchie 1961:34) feels that, in New York, it is a distinctively Iroquoian point type.

Since the majority of triangular points are found in Trench E, it is interesting to note the associations within this area. No Madison points are found with burials in Trench E; they are found only in the loose topsoil material. Of the sixteen Levanna

TABLE 23

METRIC AND NONMETRIC ATTRIBUTES OF MADISON POINTS
(In Centimeters)

UMMA Catalog No.	L	W	T	B	Provenience
23146	?	2.0	.5	S	Tr. E. Section 3
23147	2.4	1.3	.4	S	Tr. E, Section 43
23149	2.6	2.0	.4	S	Tr. E, Section 49
23151	2.5	1.8	.5	C	Tr. E
23153	?	2.0	.5	S	Tr. H, Burial VV22
23158	?	1.6	.7	S	Tr. E, Section 11
23160	3.0	1.7	.4	C	Tr. D, Pit 7
23161	3.1	1.5	.4	S	Tr. D, Pit 12

L = length, W = width, T = thickness, B = basal configuration, C = concave, S = straight, ? = point base only.

TABLE 24

BASAL CONFIGURATION OF TRIANGULAR POINTS

	Straight Base		Concave Base	
	Observed	Expected	Observed	Expected
Levanna points. . . .	2	5	14	11
Madison points . . .	6	3	2	5

$\chi^2 = 7.418$; dF = 1; $p < .01$.

points, twelve are from Trench E. One is found in a pit, one is from the general area, and eight of these ten are found in one ossuary, Burial Number V58, which strongly suggests that these points were made by one group. The fact that Madison points are spread over the surface, and are never with the burials in this area suggests that they are later. The sample is, unfortunately, much too small for a quantitative demonstration of this association. It does appear to conform to the New York sequence where Madison points replace Levanna points after A.D. 1200.

There were eight point tip and blade fragments (Table 25). For the most part these appear to be broken triangular points. The size of the fragments would place them within the Levanna range. The observation that two fragments (UMMA Catalog Nos.

TABLE 25

LOCATION OF POINT FRAGMENTS

UMMA Catalog No.	Provenience
20933	Tr. B, Pit 14
20942	Tr. B, Pit 20
20945	Tr. B, Pit 20
20957	Test Tr. 2, historic pit
23148	Tr. E, Pit 16
23159	Tr. D, Pit 1
23166	Tr. E, Burial V 58
23173	Tr. E, Burial V 58

TABLE 26

METRIC AND NONMETRIC ATTRIBUTES OF JACK'S REEF CORNER-NOTCHED POINTS

(In Centimeters)

UMMA Catalog No.	T.L.	B.L.	T.W.	H.W.	T	Provenience
20886	2.5	1.7	1.8	1.2	.6	North of Tr. A
20917	?	2.9	2.6	1.6	.5	Tr. B, Burial 1, II
20952	2.8	1.7	1.8	1.2	.8	Tr. B
20972	2.5	1.7	2.0	1.3	.7	Tr. A
23143	2.8	2.0	2.4	1.4	.6	Tr. B, Burial 2, II
23143	2.7	2.0	2.1	1.1	.4	Tr. B, Burial 2, II
23143	3.6	2.8	2.0	1.3	.5	Tr. B, Burial 2, II
23143	4.0	3.0	2.5	1.3	.6	Tr. B, Burial 2, II

T.L. = total length, B.L. = blade length, T.W. = total width, H.W. = hafting width, T = thickness, ? = fragmentary point.

23166 and 23173) were found with Burial V58 strengthens this position.

The next largest group of points is a corner-notched type (Table 26, Plate XXV). These points, eight in number, may be assigned to the type, Jack's Reef Corner-notched (Ritchie 1961: 26-7). Ritchie has suggested that these points are Late Middle Woodland and Early Late Woodland. They are found with the Carpenter Brook complex, an Owasco complex which has been dated at A.D. 905 ± 125 years (M-176, Crane 1956:668). It can be noted that six of the eight points are found with burials in Trench B. One additional point was found in the general excavation of Trench A and another was found to the north of Trench A. This is significant since no Madison or Levanna points were found in Trench B, no Madison points were found in Trench A and only two Levanna points were found in Trench A. No Jack's Reef Corner-notched points were found in Trench E which produced two-thirds of all of the triangular points from the site.

There are three other series of projectile points represented by two occurrences each. These are large side-notched points (Plate XXVI, A), ovate points (Plate XXVI, C) and large corner-notched points (Plate XXVI, B). The metric attributes of this material are given in Table 27. These points form groups which

TABLE 27

METRIC AND NONMETRIC ATTRIBUTES OF LARGE SIDE-NOTCHED LARGE CORNER-NOTCHED, AND OVATE POINTS

(In Centimeters)

UMMA Catalog No.	T.L.	B.L.	T.W.	H.W.	T	Provenience
Large Side-notched Points						
20970	?	?	2.9	2.0	.6	Tr. A
23163	5.3	4.3	2.8	2.2	.7	Tr. D
Large Corner-notched Points						
20939	3.8	2.9	2.6	.9	.5	Tr. H, Pit 14
33154	5.3	4.3	3.5	2.1	1.6	Tr. H, Pit 14

Ovate Points

UMMA Catalog No.	L.	W.	T.	Provenience
20923	4.1	2.2	.6	Test Trench 1
20967	3.6	2.2	.5	Tr. B, Burial II

T.L. = total length, B.L. = blade length, T.W. = total width, H.W. = hafting width, T = thickness, ? = fragmentary point.

are too small to suggest types. Both large corner-notched points were found in Trench H, Pit 14. Although there is a size discrepency, the similarity of material, workmanship, and the association within a single pit suggest a single manufacturer. The ovate category does not hold together too well. It is strictly taxonomic for there are differences in material, workmanship, and a wide areal separation of these points.

There is a small series of nonprojectile point chipped-stone artifacts from Riviere au Vase. This series consists of drills, scrapers, perforators, and two retouched artifacts which are possibly crest blades from exhausted cores.

There are four drills and drill fragments. Three of these (Plate XXVII, B) are small expanding base drills made from the same grey-banded flint. They are typologically and metrically homogenous (Table 28). The fourth drill is represented by a much

TABLE 28

METRIC ATTRIBUTES OF EXPANDING-BASE DRILLS, PERFORATORS, SCRAPERS, AND CREST BLADES

(In Centimeters)

UMMA Catalog No.	L	B.W.	W	T	Provenience
Small Expanding-base Drills					
20935	2.8	.9	.6	.5	Tr. B, Burial 5, II
20959	2.9	1.6	.6	.5	Tr. B, Pit 1
23145	3.6	?	.6	.6	Tr. B, Burial 1, II
Large Expanding-base Drill Fragment					
23155	?	3.2	?	.5	Tr. D
Perforators					
20943	2.7	..	1.1	.5	Tr. B, Pit 20
No number	2.5	..	1.6	.6	General Site
Bifacial Scrapers					
20944	2.3	..	2.1	.9	Tr. B, Pit 20
20976	3.1	..	2.0	.5	Tr. A
23152	2.8	..	2.2	.5	Tr. E
Retouched Crest Blades					
20925	3.9	..	1.6	.5	Tr. B, Pit 20
V743	5.1	..	1.3	.5	Tr. E

L = length, B.W. = basal width, W = width, T = thickness, ? = fragmentary.

larger base which was apparently notched (Plate XXVII, A; Table 28). Here too, there is an interesting distributional pattern. The large base was found in Trench D. Two of the small drills were found with burials in Trench B; a third was found in a pit in Trench B. This might allow us to make an association of this material.

There were two pointed bifacially worked objects (Plate XXVII, C) which are tentatively classed as perforators (Table 28). It is very possible that they are projectile points that were discarded during manufacture.

There were three bifacially worked scrapers (Plate XXVII, D, Table 28). One would expect more of such implements on a site this size. The small number could be caused by either the sampling process used or to the specific nature (mortuary) of the site.

Two objects were identified as crest blades removed from exhausted cores (Plate XXVII, D; Table 28). These are both retouched and show signs of use. One was found in Trench B, Pit 20, the historic house site, along with a scraper and a perforator.

There are several burials in Trench B that contained cores and chippage as well as projectile points that give us some indication of possible methods of point manufacture. The terminology used is taken from White (1963) and Whithoft (1957).

Burial 1, II in Trench B produced a flake from a quartz crystal. All of one face and most of the second face show secondary alteration. There was a quartz crystal with this burial. There are two small cores of an amorphous shape with this burial, and one tabular flake of the same material as the smaller of the cores.

Burial 2, II produced two cores, a cache of six blanks, four broken blanks and a number of rather large chips. Two cores both show weathered cortex on the exterior surfaces suggesting a pebble source rather than the use of quarried flint. Both are fairly small and amorphous. The area where a flake had been removed served as the striking platform for the removal of the next flake. The cache of six blanks (Plate XXVIII) (Table 29) which were found with this burial are made of a blue-grey flint with white banding. Cortex is present on two blanks and there is an inclusion in one that would make it difficult for the blank to be finished into a projectile point. Little can be said about the nature of the flake from which these blanks were made. Bifacial working has removed the bulb of percussion and remanent of the striking platform on all but one blank. This blank appears to have been made on a large flat flake with the striking platform at the tip. Four artifacts, originally identified as "chips" were reclassified as broken blanks because closer examination revealed

TABLE 29

METRIC ATTRIBUTES OF A CACHE OF BLANKS FROM BURIAL 2, II

(In Centimeters)

UMMA Catalog No.	L	W	T	Provenience
20927.	4.2	1.6	1.1	Tr. B, Burial 2, II
20927.	4.2	1.9	.9	Tr. B, Burial 2, II
20927.	4.6	2.8	1.0	Tr. B, Burial 2, II
20927.	4.6	2.4	.9	Tr. B, Burial 2, II
20927.	3.6	2.6	.6	Tr. B, Burial 2, II
20927.	3.3	2.8	1.0	Tr. B, Burial 2, II

L = length, W = width, T = thickness.

bifacial percussion flaking. In three of the four, all made from the same grey-blue flint as the blanks, breaks were found along flaws in the flint. The fourth was made of a poor grade purple chert. There are two tabular flakes which were possibly removed from a core by free flaking. There are four expanding flakes, and two flakes which appear to be resolved flakes with a "hinge-out." These appear to have been removed during the final shaping of the blanks.

With burial 4, II there was an interesting series of flakes. There were two flakes, obviously freely flaked, which appear to have been removed from a core in preparing the striking platform. All other flakes were removed by flat flaking. There were three expanding flakes and six lamellar flakes. The most interesting association with this burial was a series of several bladelets. These were the only bladelets found at the site. No cores were found with this burial, but the uniform grey-purple nature of all the artifacts suggests a common source.

Burial 5, II produced six cores. These were of the same amorphous type as the cores associated with burial 2, II with each flake preparing the striking platform for the next flake. The most interesting thing about these cores is the range of chert variation on any one core, and the obvious intergradation from core to core. The range of cherts, as was mentioned in the introduction to this section, on the three largest cores from this burial would account for most of the material variation on the site. There is one bifacially worked broken blank with this material. It is made of the same poor quality purple chert as the broken blank with burial 2, II, suggesting that this material was very difficult to work. There are five large flakes removed by free flaking and five lamellar flakes removed by flat flaking.

All other chippage noted from the site was either free flaking or flat flaking. Most of the flakes are tabular, a few are expanding, and a small number of them are lamellar. As was stated before, the series outside of the burial groups mentioned above was so small that it was insignificant.

People living at Riviere au Vase, as far as we can tell, used nodual flint rather than quarry flint. They struck flat flakes from amorphous cores. For the most part these were lamellar flakes or expanding flakes. Any necessary preparation of the core was done by free flaking. Large flat lamellar and expanding flakes were bificially worked by the removal of flat flakes and, rarely, resolved flakes. Flat flaking was the modal technique. This was probably done by percussion flaking. Finally the blanks were finished into artifacts by pressure flaking.

Finished artifacts, other than projectile points, are very rare on the site. They consist of scrapers, perforators, and drills. The small expanding base drills are associated with corner-notched points.

There are six groups of points on the site. Three of these groups, large side-notched, large corner-notched, and ovate points are too small to say much about. Three other groups of projectile points fall within the range of variation of established point types in the northeastern United States. These types are Madison points, Levanna points, and Jack's Reef Corner-notched points. In other areas of the northeast these points are characteristic of horizons falling between A.D. 700 and A.D. 1400 with a sequence of Jack's Reef Corner-notched-Levanna-Madison being well established for what Ritchie sees as a development from Late Point Peninsula through Owasco to Early Iroquois. There is an areal separation of Jack's Reef Corner-notched and triangular forms at Riviere au Vase. There is, apparently, a vertical separation of Levanna and Madison in Trench E so it is possible to reconstruct a developmental sequence on this basis.

Analysis of Ground Stone

There are sixteen pieces of ground stone from Riviere au Vase that are included in this analysis. Several other possible "hammerstones" were in the collection, but their generalized nature makes it difficult to include them in this analysis.

There were several celts and adzes from Riviere au Vase (Plate XXIX, D, E; Table 30). There is one adze (UMMA Catalog No. 20919) which is larger than the other specimens. It has a rough surface, and may be unfinished. Like the other specimens it is made of diorite, but has more of a grey-brown cast than the other adzes and celts. It was found in 1927, supposedly in the area of the site, and donated to the museum in 1937. It does not fit in with the other material, and may not have come from the site.

TABLE 30

METRIC ATTRIBUTES OF ADZES AND CELTS

(In Centimeters or Grams)

UMMA Catalog No.	Tool	L	W	T	Wt	Provenience
*20919.	Adze	18.0	4.7	2.9	428	Surface
20958.	Celt	7.4	4.7	1.9	125	Tr. B, Pit 2
21337.	Celt	?	4.5	1.8	206	Tr. E
23139.	Adze	10.5	5.0	2.2	225	Tr. B, Burial 5, II
23140.	Celt	7.9	4.6	1.7	100	Test Tr. F

L = length, W = width, T = thickness, Wt = weight.

*This adze is not polished like the rest of the material from the site. Its appearance, coupled with the fact that it was found in 1927 and given to the museum ten years later, makes its origin uncertain.

One of the artifacts is classified as a celt although its working edge is missing. This object (UMMA Catalog No. 21337) appears to have been broken during its manufacture. The butt and one face are not completely smooth, although definitely were being worked when the object broke.

The two complete celts are fairly uniform in size and weight. They are much lighter than the adze which was found with Burial 5, II. This adze is battered around the bit and butt, and may have been ceremonially mutilated as a part of the burial custom. The fact that one celt was found in a refuse pit suggests a functional status for the celts.

There are two objects of sandstone from the site that have been classed as abraders (Plate XXIX; Table 31). They show numerous grooves on either face, and were possibly used as shaft smoothers. One was found in a pit in Trench B, and the other was found in the fill in Trench A.

There is a series of unfinished and finished gorgets and fragments that demonstrate the process of manufacture and ultimate

TABLE 31

METRIC ATTRIBUTES OF ABRADERS

(In Centimeters or Grams)

UMMA Catalog No.	L	W	T	Wt	Provenience
20960.	4.5	3.6	1.9	36	Tr. B, Pit 7
20966.	5.6	4.5	1.6	56	Tr. A

L = length, W = width, T = thickness, Wt = weight.

TABLE 32

METRIC ATTRIBUTES OF FINISHED AND UNFINISHED GORGETS

(In Centimeters or Grams)

UMMA Catalog No.	L	W	T	Wt	Provenience
Finished Gorgets					
20946	?	?	?	?	Tr. B
20951	?	3.4	.7	14	Tr. B, Burial 2, II
23142	9.1	?	.7	29	Tr. B, Burial 2, II
Unfinished Gorgets					
20913	?	?	.6	17	Tr. B, Pit 23
20914	?	?	.7	18	Tr. B, Pit 23
20930	9.1	4.6	.9	44	Tr. B, Burial 1, II
20947	?	6.1	1.1	71	Tr. B
20969	?	5.4	1.2	45	Tr. A
V410	?	?	.8	12	Tr. B, Pit 20

L = length, W = width, T = thickness, Wt = weight.

disposition of these items (Table 32). In the first stage of manufacture we have two pieces of slate which have been chipped into a roughly rectangular outline. Both of these fragments were broken. There is a smoothed rectangular end on an unfinished gorget and a smoothed face and edge on another of these items. One unfinished gorget has achieved its final shape and needs only to have one face ground evenly and the holes drilled. It will be ready for its ultimate disposition. Two of these objects at the Riviere au Vase site appear to have been ceremonially "killed" and placed with burials. The drilled forms in the University of Michigan collections are all broken, and the two best examples were found with a burial (Plate XXIX, A, B).

Plate XXIX, A, B shows the two gorgets found with Burial 2, II. They are very similar in size and workmanship. If the two fragments are superimposed, the holes match each other. One is broken across its width and the other along its length. The one that is broken along its length allows us to examine the method of boring the holes. It is obvious that two holes were drilled from opposite sides. In both gorgets, the alignment of the holes is off by more than half the diameter of the hole. This may have some cultural meaning since it would have been an easy matter to have the holes coincide. The evidence from the Riviere au Vase site is too scanty to shed light on this problem.

A nearly completed gorget was found near Burial 1, II, although not directly associated with it. None of the other unfinished fragments were found near burials. Several were found in refuse pits which might help in tying the refuse pits and burial groupings together. Note that all but one of these fragments were found in Trench B. Since the remaining form was from Trench A, the distribution of gorgets follows that of Jack's Reef Corner-notched points.

Other Aboriginal Artifacts

Copper

There were thirty-five copper artifacts found at Riviere au Vase. There was one awl which was 9.3 cm long. It was square in cross section with a .3 cm diameter. A fragment of copper-stained bone, possibly a handle for the awl (Greenman 1945:458) was found with the copper and is illustrated with the awl and beads in Plate XXX. The other thirty-four artifacts were beads. These beads (Table 33) are fairly uniform in size. They have a mean length of .99 cm and a modal length of 1.0 cm. They have a mean diameter of .47 cm and a modal diameter of .5 cm. They were apparently made by rolling thin sheet copper around some object. Flaking on some specimens reveals several layers of copper in the construction. All of the copper artifacts were found with Burial 1, II in Trench B, and are illustrated in Plate XXX.

Pipes

Fragments of thirty-three aboriginal elbow pipes and one complete elbow pipe were found at Riviere au Vase. There are

TABLE 33

LENGTHS AND WIDTHS OF COPPER BEADS FOUND WITH BURIAL 1, II

(In Centimeters)

Length	Width	Length	Width
1.0	.5	1.0	.5
1.1	.5	. .9	.4
1.4	.5	1.4	.5
1.3	.5	1.0	.5
.9	.5	.8	.6
1.4	.5	1.0	.4
.8	.5	1.3	.4
.8	.4	1.0	.5
.8	.3	.9	.4
.7	.3	1.0	.5
1.3	.5	.8	.5
1.1	.5	.9	.5
.9	.4	1.0	.5
.9	.5	.9	.5
1.0	.5	.9	.6
.8	.5	.8	.4
1.0	.5	1.0	.4

TABLE 34

METRIC ATTRIBUTES OF COMPLETE AND RESTORABLE PLAIN-BOWL ELBOW PIPES

(In Centimeters)

	UMMA Catalog No.	
	20973	20974
Stem length	6.2	6.2
Stem width	2.0	2.2
Stem thickness . . .	1.5	1.7
*Stem bore	.4	.4
Bowl length.	4.4	4.6
Bowl width	2.0	
Bowl thickness. . . .	1.9	
Bowl bore	1.1	1.2
Provenience	Tr. A V43	Tr. A

*The bore was measured by drill bits calculated to sixteenths of an inch. The fraction of an inch was converted to centimeters and rounded off to .4. Actually, specimen 20974 has a larger stem bore.

seventeen bowls which may be divided into five groups on the basis of decoration.

The largest category is plain-bowl pipes. The metric data on the complete pipe, and on one nearly complete pipe (Plate XXXI, A) is given in Table 34. It should be noted that the complete pipe was associated with a burial. The restorable pipe was broken during excavation, and, since this was an area of heavy burial concentration, may have been associated with a burial. The unbroken and unused condition of these pipes would be explained if they were mortuary offerings. The data on the fragmentary plain-elbow pipes (Plate XXXI, B) is given in Table 37. Only one of these fragments was found with a burial, and one additional fragment was from the burial area. All of the rest were found in pits.

It was possible to distinguish four types of decorated pipe bowls (Plate XXXII). This included one bowl with circular punctates, four fragments with very fine dentate stamping, two pipe bowls with raised bands and small incisions (banded), and one pipe that appeared to be engraved after it had been fired. Only two fragments were large enough to obtain metric data. These were specimen UMMA Cat. No. 23196, a fine dentate bowl which was 5.0 cm long, 2.1 cm wide, 2.1 cm thick, and had an interior bore of 1.2 cm; specimen UMMA Cat. No. 23199, banded pipe bowl which was 2.1 cm thick, 2.2 cm wide and had an interior bore of 1.1 cm. The provenience of the decorated pipe bowls is given in Table 35. With one exception the decorated-bowl pipe fragments are found in refuse pits. Only one fine dentate bowl was found with a burial.

There were seventeen stem fragments of aboriginal pipes from the site. For the most part they were similar to the stems

TABLE 35

PROVENIENCE OF DECORATED-BOWL PIPE FRAGMENTS

UMMA Catalog No.	Technique	Provenience
20938.	Punctate	Tr. B, Pit 18
21216.	Dentate	Tr. H, VV 20
23187.	Dentate	Tr. D, Pit 15
23190.	Dentate	Tr. D, Pit 13
23196.	Dentate	Tr. D, Pit 25
23198.	Banded	Tr. G, Pit 3
23199.	Banded	Tr. E, Pit 16
20929.	Engraved	Tr. B, Pit 5

TABLE 36

LOCATION OF ABORIGINAL PIPESTEM FRAGMENTS

UMMA Catalog No.	Provenience
20344	General Site
20463	Tr. B, Pit 20
20937	Tr. B, Pit 15
20952	Tr. B, Pit 22
20954	Tr. B, Pit 14
21016	Tr. A
21092	Tr. D, Pit 2
21198	Tr. DA, Pit 27
21334	Tr. D, Pit 12
21336	Tr. E
23185	Tr. D, Pit 17
23188	Tr. D
23191	Test Tr. F
23193	Tr. E
23196	Tr. D, Pit 25
23200	Tr. A, VV 17
23202	Tr. H

of the complete and restorable pipes. There were two variants, one round (UMMA Cat. No. 20344), and one with an expanding bit (UMMA Cat. No. 23188). The provenience of these fragments is given in Table 36.

There is no readily apparent distribution of aboriginal pipes and fragments. All that can be said is that there is a tendency for complete pipes to be found with burials and for pipe fragments to be found in pits outside of the burial area.

Harper (1945) described the physical properties of a small series of seven pipestems from the Riviere au Vase site.

Quartz was the most common tempering material with occasional fragments as large as 1.46 millimeters. Most of the tempering material was considerably smaller and, in several instances, it was absent. Small quantities of muscovite, biotite, magnetite, flint, sericite, and rock fragments were also present in the temper.

The pipes were brownish grey to buff in color, and it is possible that they were fired at a lower temperature than were the pots from the site. There are distinct differences in the process of manufacture, and Harper suggested that this might be caused by the women making the pots and the men making the pipes (Harper 1945:488).

TABLE 37

METRIC ATTRIBUTES OF PLAIN-BOWL PIPE FRAGMENTS

(In Centimeters)

UMMA Catalog No.	B.L.	B.W.	B.T.	B.B.	Provenience
20932	2.9	1.4	1.3	.6	Tr. B, Pit 14
21092		Fragmentary			Tr. D, Pit 2
21094	4.4	2.5	2.4	1.4	Tr. D, Pit 2
*23186	..	1.2	1.1	.4	Tr. D, Pit 17
23197	..	2.0	1.8	1.0	Tr. E
23201	4.3	2.6	2.5	1.2	Tr. A, Burial VV18
23203	3.6	1.6	1.8	.8	Tr. H, Pit 10

B.L. = bowl length, B.W. = bowl width, B.T. = bowl thickness, B.B. = bowl bore.

*This is a very small pipe. It is poorly made, and the hole to the stem is not bored through. It is possible that this is a toy.

TABLE 38

METRIC ATTRIBUTES OF BONE AWLS

(In Centimeters)

UMMA Catalog No.	Length	Width	Provenience
21231	3.1	.6	Tr. D, Pit 15
23175	10.0	1.3	Tr. D, Pit 13
23176	5.5	1.2	Tr. E, Pit over burial No. 66
23177	4.7	.4	Tr. D, Pit 23
23178	6.2	.9	Tr. D

Bone Artifacts

Five bone awls were recovered from the site (Plate XXXIII). These all show signs of use. It is interesting to note that they are found, for the most part, in Trench D. The metric data on these objects is given in Table 38.

There is one perforated turtle carapace which was found with burial VV29. It appears to have been altered either through heat or stress, and is presently in a fragmentary condition. It bears no evidence of engraving.

The only additional bone with possible cultural significance is a cache of nine Turkey tarsometatarsus found with Burial 3, II, in Trench B. Charles Cleland of the University of Michigan Museum of Anthropology examined this material, and believes that five individuals are represented.

Clay Effigy

One small clay effigy figure (Plate XXXIV) was found at Riviere au Vase. The effigy (UMMA Cat. No. 21395) was found with Burial VV28, a child's skull that was found at the western edge of Pit 17 in Trench H. The head is broken and the remaining body is 3.0 cm long and 1.5 cm wide at the legs. There is no tail on the effigy, but there is a small hole between the rear legs which either represents the anus or once held a tail of organic matter. The object is poorly made, and finger prints are found in several places. It seems to represent a small mammal, perhaps an otter.

Historic Material

The historic material is to be divided into three main classes of objects with one residual category for purposes of this study. We shall deal in turn with ceramics and glass, kaolin pipes and fragments, metal objects, and other historic objects from the site. With the exception of a small number of artifacts, all of the historic material came from one feature, Pit 20 in Trench B. The remainder of the historic material came from Pit 26 in Trench B, or from the general Trench B collection.

Ceramics and Glass

There were 540 historic sherds recovered from the site. This material was identified by Dr. Arnold Pilling, director of the Wayne State University Museum of Anthropology. The most common type was a North Staffordshire white paste earthenware. There were 163 plain sherds of this ware. Many of these might have been body sherds of patterned material, but by themselves, they were nondiagnostic. The decorated North Staffordshire ware will be discussed before the other historic wares.

The most common decorated type was the Gaudy Dutch series. There were ninty-one sherds in this series. All had either floral or polka dot patterns. There were four subdivisions of Gaudy Dutch which are listed and discussed below.

Early Gaudy Dutch 3 sherds (Plate XXXV, A)

One of these sherds has a solid light blue and maroon flowered pattern; the other two have delicate blue and maroon painted patterns, and belong to the same vessel, probably a handleless teacup. This is a pre-1830 type in this area. It is among the earliest historic ceramic material from the site.

Painted Blue 5 sherds (Plate XXXV, B)

Painted Blue has a large floral pattern painted in blue on a white paste earthenware. It is a variant of Early Gaudy Dutch, and may be dated to the late 1820's and early 1930's.

Middle Gaudy Dutch 11 sherds (Plate XXXV, C)

This is characterized by a large floral pattern executed in four colors (green, blue, maroon, black). Sherds from Riviere au Vase have a black line around the interior rim. This became common during the 1930's. This is what is popularly known as Gaudy Dutch.

Gaudy Dutch Polka Dot 6 sherds (Plate XXXV, D)

This is a polka dot variant of Middle Gaudy Dutch. The same colors are used, but the interior rim has a narrower light blue band. It also was common during the 1830's. Two vessels, a cup and a saucer, are represented.

The following North Staffordshire type may be a descendent of the Gaudy Dutch series.

Sprig ware 66 sherds (Plate XXXV, E)

Sprig ware is a delicate four-color floral pattern on North Staffordshire white paste earthenware. Local variants were made in Ohio, but there is no record of any but local use. A number of handleless cups and saucers are represented. It is interesting to note that although the pattern is similar there are at least four styles of teacup present. This ware became common during the late 1830's.

There are a number of other North Staffordshire wares which will be listed individually.

Blue Edge 24 sherds (Plate XXXVI, A)

Here blue pigment covers a molded edge. There are five variants of this pattern, two variants have been named: Arrow and Wheat. The other forms are unnamed, but found in association at several sites in southeastern Michigan. All Blue Edge sherds are from plates. This material may be dated to the late 1820's and early 1830's.

Spatterware or Spongeware 25 sherds (Plate XXXVI, B)

This ware has a mottled pattern of blue, red, or green on a white paste earthenware. At Riviere au Vase there were twenty-three sherds of light blue and one of red. There was one sherd that has a larger pattern, and is an American variant of Spatterware. Its greatest occurrence was between 1825 and 1840.

Light Blue Banded 12 sherds (Plate XXXVI, D)

This material represents one handleless teacup and its saucer. One sherd is from Test Trench Number 1, while the remainder, including articulating material, is from Pit 20, Trench B. It is possible that this vessel is a mustard jar. This type has been placed between 1820 and 1840 at the Hotel Pontchartrain dump.

North Staffordshire Red Print 9 sherds (Plate XXXVI, C)

These appear to represent a cup and saucer. Similar material has been found in southeastern Michigan with an "Adams" manufacturer's mark. Early Red Print dates to the late 1820's, but it was popular for a number of years.

Red Print Meander 5 sherds (Plate XXXVI, E)

This is a distinct variant of North Staffordshire Red Print. This pattern has been found in blue at the Hotel Pontchartrain dump site. It probably became common in this area during the 1830's.

Flowing Blue 9 sherds (Plate XXXVI, I)

Flowing Blue or Blue Flow is a dark blue to light blue pattern. It was first made in the 1820's, and was made as late as the 1860's. It became common in the 1850's in this part of Michigan. It is the most recent of the historic sherds from the site.

Raised Glaze 5 sherds (Plate XXXVI, F)

Raised Glaze, also known as Mocha ware, is very rare in southeastern Michigan. It was made over a long period of time, but its maximum use was between 1825 and 1845. These specimens are a four-color ware with a very full design.

Blue Printed Willow — 3 sherds — (Plate XXXVI, G)

This is a dark blue willow pattern on white. It was used between 1825 and 1845 in this area with maximum occurrence in the late 1830's.

Old Blue — 2 sherds — (Plate XXXVI, H)

This is a printed medium blue on white. It is the oldest of the historic ceramics from the site, and dates to the early 1820's.

Brown Print — 3 sherds — (Plate XXXV, I, J)

This is a brown printed pattern on white. The highest occurrence of this material is in the late 1830's, but this particular vessel form was popular between 1845 and 1855 when the object was probably made. There are two distinct color variants from the Riviere au Vase site.

The non-North Staffordshire materials from the site are listed below.

Common Yellow — 1 sherd — (Plate XXXV, H)

Yellow covers the entire surface of this type. This material was common during the late 1840's.

Brown Glaze — 1 sherd — (Plate XXXV, G)

This is a highly glazed brown on yellow. It is similar to Bennington, and dates to the 1840's in this area.

Gilt Edge — 1 sherd — (Plate XXXV, N)

This is a white paste earthenware with a fine band of gilt on the rim. It is a luxury ware, and out of place with the rest of the material.

Molded ware — 1 sherd — (Plate XXXV, K)

One sherd was found with this molded pattern.

Majolica — 1 sherd — (Plate XXXV, M)

There is a single sherd of buff paste Majolica, probably of British or French manufacture. It is light green and white. Majolica does not usually occur on the site of so late a period.

Porcelain 1 sherd (Plate XXXV, L)

This single sherd is of an unusual shape, and may be a teapot spout.

There were sixty-seven sherds of Red Bisque earthenware. The only diagnostic forms are four sherds of a thin shiny glazed ware which has been found in late 1830's and early 1840's context at the Hotel Pontchartrain dump (Plate XXXV, F). Several vessels are represented, and one (Plate XXXVII) has been partly restored.

Six sherds of salt-glazed stoneware were present in the sample, all from a single vessel.

Four odd pieces are interesting. One is from a teapot spout, two are white paste earthenware handles, and one is an Ironstone handle. This latest object is of particular interest since Ironstone is commonly found in occupations dating to the 1850's or later.

Ninety-five sherds of glass were recovered. Most of this material was window glass or bottle glass. Almost all sherds showed evidence of heat alteration. Several specimens are illustrated here (Plate XXXVIII, C, D). There are four fragments of glass, two from one bottle, which have molded letters. This was not common until the 1840's. The two articulating sherds have the terminal letters. . .MENT (Liniment?) (Plate XXXVIII, D), while the small white glass sherd has the letters. . .ACKE. . . . Amber and white glass objects were probably lamp chimneys. The other glass items in the plate are included as part of a typical 1820 - 1850 assemblage.

There are fifty-six glass beads from Pit 20 in Trench B. Fifty-two of these are rosary beads. There are amber and blue forms, while the majority are white. The beads themselves are roughly round (Plate XXXVIII, E), and strung on a chain made of copper wire. A copper crucifix was found with them. There are also four hexagonal blue beads (Plate XXXVIII, F). Pilling has suggested that these are similar to trade beads, which he found in a nineteenth-century context in California.

Kaolin Pipes

There were eighty-nine kaolin pipe fragments recovered from Pit 20 in Trench B. Seventy of these were stem fragments, and the other nineteen were bowl fragments. We could determine the interior bore diameter on sixty-two of these fragments. An attempt to date this feature by means of the pipestem hole diameter formula proposed by Lewis R. Binford was a failure. The mean diameter was 5.2/64th which gave us a date of 1733.66 for the pipestems in this pit. This is completely incongruous with dating for the rest of the material. Binford, however, has pointed out that his formula does not apply after 1780 (Binford 1962), and most of our sample dates to the first half of the nineteenth century.

Included in the sample are four Kaolin pipestems which were glazed near the tip. According to Pilling this trait does not become common in southeastern Michigan until the 1840's.

Four of the pipestems bore inscriptions. There were two stems inscribed with "Henderson" and "Montreal." According to H. G. Omwake (n.d.) these were made in Montreal between 1848 and 1876. There are two variants of the Henderson mark at Riviere au Vase. One (Plate XXXIX) has small impressed letters with no border. This stem is also of interest because of its 6/64th hole diameter. The second Henderson stem (Plate XXXIX) has larger lettering and is enclosed in a dentate pattern. There is a rather elaborate pipestem with raised letters and oak leaves (?). One side has the word "Peter" (Plate XXXIX) and the other "Dorni" (Plate XXXIX). Omwake has written an article on "Peter Dorni" pipes, and suggests a date of 1850 to 1880. This stem may, from the rest of the material in this feature, be dated to the 1840's or very early 1850's, which means it may have been made by "Dorni" or Peter Dornier himself. After 1850 the pipemakers in Gouda, Netherlands, started making "Dorni" pipes and exporting them in large numbers. Omwake has suggested that the raised letter form with oak leaves may be the original Dorni product. A "Peter Dorni" pipestem was found at Fort Ridgley, Minnesota (Sackett 1943:77) with "In Gouda" inscribed on the reverse face. This is also done in raised letters. Fort Ridgley was occupied between 1853 and 1867, or slightly later than Riviere au Vase. It is suggested that the Riviere au Vase stem is an original Dorni, and that the Fort Ridgley Dorni is an early Gouda Dorni. There is one additional inscribed pipe. It bears the word "Glasgow" on one face. The second face is very worn, the entire pipestem is relatively soft, and the letters are barely legible. It is possible to make out the following "...-78 ??HITE...." This is, perhaps, a "W-WHITE" pipe which were made over a long period of time.

There were two complete bowls (Plate LX), one with an American eagle design. Four bowls, all with different designs, were present in fragmentary form. One of these bears the initials T. D. enclosed by thirteen stars. This is a type which was popular from the War of 1812 until the 1870's. An identical form was found at Fort Ridgely (Sackett 1943). One of the fragments appeared to have been part of a bowl base. It is massive when compared to the other bowls, and has been molded into scales. It may have been a dragon or mermaid form.

Metal

The most common metal artifacts from the historic occupation of the site were a number of knives and forks from Trench B, Pit 20. There were eight hoop iron table knives (Plate XLI, C), three four-tined forks (Plate XLI, E), one represented only by the handle, and two forks (Plate XLI, E) which appear to have only two or three tines. One of these has a scored handle. There are a number of scored- and plain-handled fragments (Plate XLI, Q). It is possible that these went with the hoop knives as well as with the three-tined forks. Each of the bone handled fragments is unique. The four-tined forks did not have bone handles. There are two pewter handles (Plate XLI, N); the longer of them is from a fork with the tines broken, and the smaller is nondiagnostic. There is one utility knife (Plate XLI, H) and one penknife (Plate XLI, G) which have the wood adhering to them. The handle is preserved on the penknife by copper guards on either side of the blade well. A second penknife did not fare as well, and is almost rusted away.

There were numerous pieces of iron corroded beyond recognition as well as buttons, hinges, broaches (?) (Plate XLI, A) and a pin and eye (Plate XLI, L). Many small pieces of lead or pewter were found. These may have been pewter utensils that melted during the fire that is in evidence on so much of the material. There were three copper thimbles (Plates XLI, F), two odd pieces of copper (Plate XLI, O, P), copper buckles (Plate XLI, B) and three ornamental pieces (Plate XLI, I-K), two of pewter or white metal and one, the first, made of copper.

Other Historic Material

There were numerous pieces of plaster and a few fragments of brick included in the University of Michigan collection. The lack of brick indicates a wood construction for the structure that existed in this area.

There were a number of other artifacts. These include clay marbles and a number of bone and ivory buttons (Plate XXXVIII, A). All that can be said about this material is that it is not incongruous with the rest of the historic material from the site. The small comb (Plate XXXVIII, B) is very similar to one found in association with Middle Gaudy Dutch ceramics at the Hotel Pontchartrain dump.

I originally identified three slate objects as "fish gouges" or "perforators." Dr. William Ritchie, New York State archaeologist, later pointed out that these were "slate pencils" so they are mentioned at this point. Two were found in Pit 20, Trench B, and the third is also from Trench B.

III

FAUNAL REMAINS

Charles Cleland of the University of Michigan Museum of Anthropology has examined the faunal remains from the site. He has identified the following animals.

Common Name	Scientific Name	Occurrence
Cottontail rabbit	*Sylvilagus floridanus*	7
Chipmunk	*Tamias striatus*	9
Red squirrel	*Tamiasiurus hudsonicus*	3
Grey squirrel	*Sciurus carolinensis*	4
Beaver	*Castor canadensis*	1
Meadow vole	*Microtus pennsylvanicus*	2
Muskrat	*Ondatra zibethicus*	18
Porcupine	*Erethizon dorsatum*	1
Raccoon	*Procyon lotor*	1
Mink	*Mustela vison*	1
Deer	*Odocoileus virginianus*	33
Elk	*Cervus canadensis*	2
Dog	*Canis familiaris*	24
Rat*	*Rattus rattus*	2
Pig*	*Sus scrofa*	25
Cow*	*Bos taurus*	8
Red fox*	*Vulpes fulva*	3
Unidentified mammal bones		325
Canada goose	*Branta canadensis*	2
Mallard	*Anas platyrhynchos*	1
Redhead	*Aythya americana*	2
Lesser scaup	*Aythya affinis*	2
Hooded merganser	*Lophodytes cucullatus*	6
Common merganser	*Mergus merganser*	2
Turkey	*Meleagris gallopava*	8
Chicken*	*Gallus gallus*	23
Unidentified bird bone		56
Sturgeon	*Acipenser fulvescens*	2
Bowfin	*Amia calva*	3
Northern pike	*Esox lucius*	1
Sucker	*Catostomus* sp.	1
Catfish	*Ictalurus natalis*	17
Large-mouthed bass	*Micropterus salmoides*	9
Walleye	*Strizostedion vitreum*	4
Yellow perch	*Perca flavenscens*	9
Drum	*Aplodinotus grunniens*	25
Unidentified fishbone		621

*Found in historic feature.

The percentages of fish, turtle, bird, and mammal bone are given below:

	Fish	Per cent	Turtle	Per cent	Bird	Per cent	Mammal	Per cent	Total	Per cent
Identified	65	33.3	0	0	35	16.9	97	49.7	195	23.9
Unidentifiable	234	37.7	6	.9	56	9.0	325	52.3	621	76.1
Total	299		6		89		422		816	
Per cent of total	36.6		.7		10.9		51.7			

The site shows no tendency toward a specific ecological adaptation. The large occurrence of fishbone in some of the aboriginal pits, particularly in Trench B, may indicate a seasonal type of exploitation. This will be discussed in more detail by Cleland at a later date.

IV

BURIALS

The earliest reports on the Riviere au Vase site were reports on the mortuary complex. For a site in Michigan this complex is, indeed, elaborate. The University of Michigan excavations in 1936 and 1937 uncovered 145 burial groupings containing approximately 350 individuals. Since 1937 a number of other burials have been excavated. Several of these have been reported by Mr. Jerry DeVisscher of Mount Clemens, and will be included in the discussion of his work. Mr. Bernard Trinity of the Trinity Neighborhood Library and Museum, which is located on Sugarbush Road slightly to the north of the Riviere au Vase site, reported that children had encountered burials on the site in the spring of 1963. They reportedly recovered a skull from an area approximately 300 feet to the east of the 1936 and 1937 University of Michigan excavations at the site.

For the past thirty years investigators have been impressed by both the number of burials and the variety of burials which were encountered. Table 39 is a summation of the information on burials contained in the field notes and maps drawn during the excavation of the site. No attempt will be made to illustrate the positions of these burials. The area of excavation was so extensive, and the number of burials so large that approximately 60 pages of line drawings or over 100 of photographs would be required for adequate illustration. The reader who is interested in this information is directed to the field notes from this site which are on file at the University of Michigan Museum of Anthropology.

I found it very difficult to determine the exact number of individual interments encountered at the site. The field notes were, for many of the burials, vague and many supernumerary bones were recorded. For the number of burials and the distribution of burial types, it is necessary to draw on the work of Alfred Guthe. Guthe had the advantage of participating in the actual excavations. The notes were in better condition, and the collections more intact fifteen years ago than they are today. Guthe (1948:51) reported the following burial types:

Extended	87
Flexed	28
Bundle	128
Torso	20
Rearticulated	2
Cremated	1
Skull only	4
Indeterminate	80
Total	350

The majority of burials were located in Trenches A, E, and J. These were the remaining high areas on either side of the area where sand had been removed. Smaller numbers were located in parts of trenches D, DA, and H. A single burial consisting of two apparently headless individuals was recovered from Trench F. A small, but highly significant, group of burials was recovered from Trench B.

A number of these burial groupings seem to be ossuaries. These would include Burial V 5, V 13, V 45 and V 54, all in Trench A; V 58, V 72 and V 77 in Trench E; and VV 18 in Trench DA. Levanna points, Macomb Linear-corded sherds and Vase Tool-impressed sherds are associated with these ossuaries. One ossuary, V 13, is described as an extended individual with eight disarticulated skulls placed in an oval around the body. Several bundle burials and torso burials were then placed over the main interment. There are a number of additional burials which have extra skulls. These have been interpreted as trophy skulls and many seem to be located in the pelvic regions of the individuals with which they occur. The explanation of the location of these skulls is that they may have been suspended in some manner from a belt.

The single cremated individual, part of Burial VV 24, was found in what might have been an ossuary in Trench H. In addition to this cremation a number of extended individuals with extra skulls were found with Burial VV 24.

Although not classed as a cremation the extra skull with Burial V 33 also showed signs of having been burned.

The five burials in Trench B were described in detail by Greenman (1945). It is this group of burials that served as the base for the definition of the second or "Hopewellian" component at the Riviere au Vase site. Greenman (1945:457-58) divided the five into a group of three and a group of two burials in Trench B. He described them in the following manner.

"Two of the three, Numbers 2 and 5, consisted of adult skulls at depths of sixteen and nineteen inches in the light-gray sand of the site. Both skulls were brittle, white, and badly pitted and flaked, and large portions were missing as a result of disintegration. The other, Number 1, a torso of a young child, accompanied by the mandible and a humerus, lay at a depth of 30 inches. There was little left of the vertebrae besides cancellous tissue, but the surfaces, if present, were white and brittle, which was true of the humerous also. Two remaining burials, Numbers 3 and 4, were in refuse pits which apparently belonged to the Owasco component. Number 4, an adult skull at a depth of only six inches, was in the same condition of decay as numbers 1, 2, and 5. The only artifacts were a pot and eight chips of gray flint. Number 3 consisted of the pelvis and articulated leg bones of an adult, flexed, with a few ribs, hand bones, a radius and two lumbar vertebrae, at a depth of twenty inches. With this deposit were a pot (Pl. I, Fig. 5) and six pieces of split bird-leg bones. There is some doubt whether these two burials belong to this group. They are included because of their proximity to the others, and because of the woodland type of vessel found with each one, though since they were in refuse pits the association is questionable in both cases."

This same advanced state of decay was noted by DeVisscher (1957) who recovered only dental caps while excavating burials in this area of the site. Another point of interest is the occurrence of altered long bones, perforated crania, the removal of skull disks and the presence of clay in the faces of skulls removed from the Riviere au Vase site. This complex of characteristics is noted along with other information in Table 39. A summary of the perforated skulls and skulls with disks removed is to be found in Table 40. This table was used by Guthe (1948:55) and was prepared by Greenman from the field notes and an examination of the skulls. No report on the subject will be presented here since the Physical Anthropology Division of the University of Michigan Museum of Anthropology is preparing a detailed report on the skeletal material.

TABLE 39

BURIALS FROM RIVIERE AU VASE

Burial		Number of Individuals	Type of Interment	Trench	Age			Sex		Altered Long Bones	Altered Crania	Clay in Skull	Remarks and Associations
Series	Number				Adult	Juvenile	Infant	Male	Female				
V	1	1	Fragment	A	X								
V	2	2	Bundle	A	X						X		Two Vase Dentate vessels, Macomb Interrupted Linear.
V	3	1	Flexed	A	X				X		X		Vase Dentate.
V	4	1	Fragment	A									
V Group Group Group	5 1 2 3	 2 4 6	 Bundle Fragment Fragment	A							X	X	10 skulls.
V	6	2	Extended	A	X		X						Under burials V2 and V4.
V	7	1	Flexed	A	X				X				
V	8	1	Flexed	A	X								
V	9	2	Flexed	A		X							
V	10	7	Flexed Extended	A	X						X	X	Levanna point.
V	11	1	Extended	A	X								
V	12	4	Extended	A	X		X						Vase Dentate.
V	13	11	Bundle Torso Extended	A									Eight skulls are arranged around one individual.
V	14	1	Extended	A	X								Wayne Cord-marked.
V	15	1	Flexed	A	X								
V	16	1	Fragment	A		X							
V	17	1	Fragment	A		X							

V 18	1	Fragment	A									
V 19	2	Extended	A	X								Vase Dentate.
V 20	3	Flexed	A	X								Extra skull.
V 21	1	Extended	A	X								
V 22	1	Bundle	A									
V 23	5	Flexed Extended	A	X								
V 24	5	Extended	A	X						X	X	
V 25	3	Bundle	A	X						X		
V 26	8	Bundle	A									
V 27	8	Fragment	A	X	X	X			X			
V 28	9	Bundle	A	X						X		
V 29	1	Flexed	A									
V 30	1	Extended	A	X								
V 31	3	Flexed	A									
V 32	7	Bundle	A								X	
V 33	3	Extended Fragment	A									Skull burned.
V 35	2	Bundle	A							X		
V 36	3	Extended	A								X	
V 37	3	Fragment	A									
V 38	1	Extended	A									
V 39	3	Extended	A	X		X				X		
V 40	3	Bundle	A	X	X		X		X			
V 41	1	Extended	A	X								
V 42	1	Extended	A	X								Extra humerus.
V 43	1	Extended	A	X								Elbow pipe.
V 44	3	Extended	A	X	X		X		X	X		
V 45												
Group 1	2	Bundle										
Group 2	5	Bundle	A	X					X	X	X	Macomb Linear-corded
Group 3	2	Bundle	A									
Group 4	2	Skulls										Trophy skulls (?)

TABLE 39 *(Cont.)*

Burial		Number of Individuals	Type of Interment	Trench	Age			Sex		Altered Long Bones	Altered Crania	Clay in Skull	Remarks and Associations
Series	Number				Adult	Juvenile	Infant	Male	Female				
V	46	1	Bundle	A	X								
V	47	1	Skull	A	X			X					
V	48	3	Fragment	A									
V	49	1	Extended	A									
V	50	2	Extended	A	X			X					Extra skull.
V	51	2	Fragment	A	X								
V	52	3	Extended	A	X	X					X		
V	53	1	Bundle	A		X							
V	54	10	Bundle Flexed	A	X	X	X						
V	55	4	Extended	A	X			X	X	X	X	X	
V	56	1	Torso	E	X			X			X		
V	57	4	Extended	E	X		X	X			X		
V	58	6	Extended	E	X								Eight Levanna points.
V	59	1	Fragment	E									
V	60	2	Fragment	E	X	X							
V	61	1	Extended	E	X			X					Vase Dentate
V	62	1	Fragment	E									
V	63	2	Fragment	E		X	X						
V	64	1	Fragment	E									
V	65	1	Extended	E		X							
V	66	2	Bundle	E	X		X						Refuse pit (?), Wayne Cord-marked Vase Dentate.
V	67	?	?	?									No notes, prints, or maps.
V	68	2	Fragment	E	X		X						Foetal skeleton.

V	69	3	Extended Fragment Bundle	E	X								
V	70	2	Fragment	E	X								Extra skull.
V	71	1	Torso	E									
V	72	12	Ossuary	E	X		X			X	X	X	Disturbed by Pit 10, Levanna point.
V	73	2	Extended	E	X		X						
V	74	1	Extended	E	X				X				
V	75	1	Bundle	E		X							Edge of Pit 11.
V	76 78	3	Fragment	E	X		X						In Pit 12.
V	77	6	Ossuary	E	X		X	X	X		X		Vase Tool-impressed.
V	79	3	Extended	E	X	X			X			X	
V	80	2	Torso	E	X		X	X			X	X	
V	81	3	Extended Flexed Skull	E	X		X						
V	82	2	Fragment	E		X	X						
V	83	4	Bundle	E	X		X						Vase Tool-impressed
V	84	3	Flexed Extended Fragment	E	X								Disturbed by Pit 13; Wayne Punctate.
V	85	4	Fragment	E	X								Edge of Pit 13.
V	86	3	Bundle	E	X	X	X						
V	87	1	Extended	E	X			X					Beneath Burial 85.
V	88	1	Skull	E	X								Disturbed by Pit 16.
V	89	1	Extended	E	X			X					
V	90	1	Extended	E									Feet cut by Pit 18.
V	91	1	Fragment	E	X								Cut by Pit 16.
V	92	1	Torso	E					X				
V	93	2	Extended	E									Extra skull.
V	94	2	Extended	E	X		X						
V	95	2	Extended	E									Cut by Pit 17.

TABLE 39 *(Cont.)*

Burial		Number of Individuals	Type of Interment	Trench	Age			Sex		Altered Long Bones	Altered Crania	Clay in Skull	Remarks and Associations
Series	Number				Adult	Juvenile	Infant	Male	Female				
V	96	2	Fragment	E	X								In Pit 18.
V	97	1	Fragment	E	X								
V	98	1	Fragment	E	X								
V	99	1	Fragment	E	X						X	X	
V	100	1	Flexed	E									
V	101	4	Ossuary	E	X	X				X			Levanna point, Macomb interrupted Linear.
V	102	1	Fragment	E	X								
V	103	1	Skull	E	X								
V	104	1	Bundle	E	X			X					
V	105	3	Flexed	E									Two extra skulls.
V	106	1	Skull	E	X								
V	107	1	Extended	E	X								
V	108a	1	Skull	E			X						
V	108b	2	Flexed	E	X				X				
V	109	1	Extended	E	X								
V	110	2	Torso	J	X								
V	111	1	Extended	J									
V	112	1	Flexed	J	X								
V	113	3	Extended	J									Disturbed by Pit 6.
V	114	3	Flexed	J	X		X		X				
V	115	1	Skull	J									
II	1	2	Flexed	B	X		X						Copper beads, copper awl, quartz, Jack's Reef Corner-notched points, expanding-base drill, etc.
II	2	2	Torso Skull	B	X								Four Jack's Reef Corner-notched points, cache of blanks, 2 gorget fragments.

II	3	1	Flexed	B	X								Wayne Cord-marked.
II	4	1	Bundle	B	X								Wayne Cord-marked (one Macomb Interrupted-linear vessel was found 10 inches above this burial).
II	5	1	Skull	B	X								Expanding base drill, adze.
VV	6	1	Extended	D		X							
VV	7	1	Extended	D	X				X				
VV	8	1	Extended	D	X			X					Pit 13.
VV	9	2	Torso	F	X		X						
VV	10	1	Torso	DA									
VV	11	3	Bundle	D	X	X	X						
VV	12	1	Fragment	DA							X	X	
VV	13	1	Bundle	DA									
VV	14	2	Extended	DA									
VV	15	1	Torso	DA									Cut by Pit 28.
VV	16	2	Skull	DA	X								Two skulls in a pit.
VV	17	18	Ossuary	DA									Pipestem.
VV	18	1	Torso	A									Plain bowl pipe fragment.
VV	19	1	Bundle	H									Pit 2.
VV	20	1	Flexed	H	X			X					Wayne Cord-marked, dentate pipe bowl.
VV	21	1	Torso	X			X						
VV	22	5	Bundle	H	X	X	X						Madison point.
VV	23	1	Bundle	H									
VV	24	6	Cremation Extended Skull	H	X		X				X	X	
VV	25	3	Bundle	H	X								
VV	26	2	Extended	H	X	X		X					Juvenile is microcephalic.
VV	27	3	Bundle	H	X								
VV	28	1	Skull	H			X						Clay effigy.
VV	29	1	Flexed	H	X								Perforated turtle shell.
VV	30	2	Extended	H	X		X						

TABLE 40

PERFORATED SKULLS AND SKULLS AND DISKS REMOVED

Field Catalog Number	One Drilled Perforation		Two Drilled Perforations	Disk over 3 cm Removed from Posterior	Burial Type			Burial Number	Sex		Remarks
	At Apex in Median Position	Elsewhere			Bundle	Extended	Skull only		Male	Female	
V172	X			X	X			V25 skull B			
V15	X			X	X			V5			Clay in face
V950				X				V99			Clay in face
V888			X			X		VV12		X	Clay in face
V48				X		X		V12			Disk found
V330		X			X			V40 skull A	X		
V318				X	X			V35 skull A		X	
V7	X			X		X		V44 skull B	X		
V167	X		X	X							Clay in face
V216	X				X			V28			
V727	X				X			V72 skull D		X	Clay in face
V839				X	X			V77 skull A	X		
V64	X			X	X			V13 skull F		X	
V56	X			X	X			V10 skull 1 or skull 5			Clay in face
V62		X		X		X		V13 skull B			
V4		X			X			V2 skull 2		X	

V

PITS

A large number of subsurface pits were uncovered during the University of Michigan excavations at the Riviere au Vase site in 1936 and 1937. The manner in which the information on these features was recorded caused some problems in analysis.

There are numbers for 144 refuse pits. There are artifacts, faunal remains, or recorded burials for 101 of these pits. The field notes mention only 63 of these pits and dimensions are given for less than half of them.

Some of these pits are listed as containing burials. It is possible that many of the "blank" pit numbers were pits which were found to contain burials and were later referred to solely by the burial number.

From the drawings of pit profiles it seems that these features were roughly circular, straight-sided pits similar to those reported from the Wolf site (Greenman 1939*b*:7), the Furton site (Greenman 1939*b*:18), the Younge site (Greenman 1937*a*:13-21) and a number of other smaller sites in southeastern Michigan which I have examined. They were distinguished from the yellow sand of the site by their darker coloration, the occurrence of ash lenses or flecks of charcoal and by the occurrence of cultural material. Many of these pits contained large quantities of bone suggesting that they were refuse pits. They appeared to range in size from a few feet in diameter and several inches deep to over 7 feet in diameter and over 3 feet deep.

One major exception was the feature referred to as Pit 20 in Trench B. This was the site of the ruin of a log cabin. The majority of historic artifacts from the site came from this feature. The historic material was mixed with aboriginal artifacts which seemed to be related to the entire span of aboriginal occupation.

This confusion of cultural material seemed to be true of other pits at the site. This is to be expected with an intensive, continuous occupation covering several hundred years. Pits will be dug into occupational areas, burials, and other pits; the fill for these pits will contain refuse of both the previous inhabitants of the site and the people who dug the pits. Greenman (1945:458) noted the problems involved in isolating the contents of these pits. The site rests on a loose sandy ridge, and material is easily mixed.

On the other hand, it is very possible that the association of all the pottery types in some of the larger features may indicate a cultural continuity throughout the aboriginal occupation of the site. The samples from individual pits are too small, in my opinion, to present a valid seriation of the contents.

Therefore, all we can do, with any degree of certainty, is to present a description of the material in the University of Michigan Museum of Anthropology collections which is cataloged as coming from the pits at the site. This is done in Table 41. Since the majority of the material from the site was ceramic, the rim and bodysherd types and categories are listed separately. Other information, such as the presence of burials or lithic materials, is given under the heading of "other material." The faunal remains from the various pits, which have been identified by Charles Cleland of the University of Michigan Museum of Anthropology, are also listed under this heading.

It is strange that although 55 burial groupings, 350 rim and body sherds, and over 1,500 sherdlets were recovered from Trench A, no pits were recorded. This unit was excavated late in the 1936 season, and it may be that in an attempt to salvage as many burials as possible, before abandoning the site to the ravages of the weather and to looters, only these features were recorded. It is possible that there were no pits in this trench. There were only 15 refuse pits in Trench E, the largest of the excavation units, which was only a few feet to the west of Trench A and interposed between Trench A and the rest of the site.

Trenches B, D and H contained the largest numbers of refuse pits. The numbering of pits in Trench D A was a continuation of the numbering system used in Trench D.

TABLE 41

REFUSE PITS FROM THE RIVIERE AU VASE SITE

Trench	Pit	Vase Tool Impressed	Vase Corded	Vase Dentate	Macomb Linear Corded	Macomb Inter-rupted Linear	Wayne Cord-marked	Other Wayne Varieties	Opposed	Net Im-pressed Rim	Miniature Vessel	Incised Shoulder	Cord-marked	Smoothed Cord-marked	Smoothed	Fabric	Roughened	Other Material
B	1		X	X	X		X				X	X	X		X	X		Expanding base drill
B	2	X	X	X	X		X			X		X	X	X				Celt
B	3	X	X										X		X			
B	4		X											X				
B	5	X	X	X	X			X			X	X	X		X	X		Engraved pipe bowl
B	6											X						
B	7			X	X						X							Sandstone abrader
B	8																	
B	9		X										X		X			
B	10			X	X					X		X						Hooded merganser, sucker, yellow perch, drum, large-mouthed bass
B	11	X	X										X	X	X			
B	12	X	X										X		X			
B	13				X									X				
B	14	X	X	X	X	X	X		X	X	X	X	X	X	X		X	Plain pipe bowl pipestem
B	15	X	X	X	X													Burial 3, II (grave goods, see burials), brushed bodysherd, drumfish, redhead
B	16						X											
B	17	X		X							X	X		X	X			

TABLE 41 (Cont.)

Trench	Pit	Vase Tool Impressed	Vase Corded	Vase Dentate	Macomb Linear Corded	Macomb Inter-rupted Linear	Wayne Cord-marked	Other Wayne Varieties	Opposed	Net Im-pressed Rim	Miniature Vessel	Incised Shoulder	Cord-marked	Smoothed Cord-marked	Smoothed	Fabric	Roughened	Other Material
B	18	X			X		X				X		X	X			X	Punctate pipe bowl, meadow vole, drumfish, yellow perch
B	19												X	X				Dog
B	20		X	X		X	X	X	X		X	X	X	X			X	Historic house site (see section on Historic Material), pipestem, perforator, scraper, gorget, etc., sturgeon, drum, chicken, brant, mallard, hog, cow, deer, rat, rabbit, dog, grey squirrel
B	21			X											X			Walleye, drumfish
B	22	X	X	X		X	X					X	X	X				Pipestem
B	23			X									X	X	X		X	
B	24	X	X	X			X				X	X	X	X				Two unfinished gorgets, grey squirrel, deer, catfish
B	25	X		X		X					X		X	X	X			
B	26			X														Historic ceramics
B	27	X		X								X	X	X	X		X	
B	28		X								X		X	X	X		X	
B	29												X		X			
D	1	X	X	X	X		X		X		X	X		X	X	X		
D	2		X	X		X	X	X			X		X			X		Pipestem, two plain pipe bowls, deer, red fox
D	3			X	X	X		X			X			X	X	X		

D	4	X	X	X			X						X	X				
D	5		X	X			X						X					Muskrat
D	6																	
D	7		X	X														Madison point
D	8					X	X						X				X	Historic sherd, red fox
D	9		X	X									X	X	X	X		
D	10			X	X			X					X				X	
D	11		X	X			X					X	X	X	X		X	Mink
D	12	X	X	X	X		X					X	X	X				Pipestem, Madison point
D	13		X	X	X		X				X		X	X			X	Dentate pipe bowl, bone awl
D	14			X							X		X					Levanna point
D	15	X	X	X			X				X	X	X	X	X			Dentate pipe bowl, bone awl, deer
D	16		X											X				Deer
D	17		X	X	X													Plain pipe bowl and stem
D	18		X		X	X	X											
D	19		X	X	X						X	X	X	X				
D	20		X		X								X	X				
D	21	X		X	X	X							X		X			
D	22																	
D	23	X	X	X					X			X					X	Bone awl, drum
D	24				X		X						X	X		X	X	
D	25				X							X	X		X			Dentate pipe bowl, plain pipe-stem
D	26		X	X									X					
E	1	X		X		X						X		X			X	
E	2			X			X				X			X			X	Levanna point
E	3																	Deer
E	4																	
E	5			X														
E	6																	
	7																	

TABLE 41 *(Cont.)*

Trench	Pit	Vase Tool Impressed	Vase Corded	Vase Dentate	Macomb Linear Corded	Macomb Interrupted Linear	Wayne Cord-marked	Other Wayne Varieties	Opposed	Net Impressed Rim	Miniature Vessel	Incised Shoulder	Cord-marked	Smoothed Cord-marked	Smoothed	Fabric	Roughened	Other Material
E	8																	
	9																	
E	10				X							X						Disturbs Burial V 72
E	11																	Burial V 75
E	12		X	X				X				X	X				X	Burial V 76
E	13																	Disturbs Burial V 84
E	14																	
	15																	
E	16		X	X											X			Banded pipe bowl, Disturbs Burial V 88
E	17													X				Disturbs Burial V 95
E	18				X													Disturbs Burial V 90
E	19	X		X								X	X	X	X		X	
E	?	X		X								X						Pit over Burial V 66, bone awl
F	1												X	X	X		X	
F	2		X															
G	1		X										X	X				Porcupine
G	2	X	X		X									X	X			Deer
G	3			X									X					Banded pipe bowl
G	4													X	X	X		Walleye, common merganser, northern pike, grey squirrel, hooded merganser, deer
G	5																	
G	6		X											X	X			

G	7																	
G	8												X					
G	9																	
G	10	X																Plain pipe bowl
G	11																	
G	12										X							
G	13	X	X	X	X							X	X	X				Simple-stamped bodysherds
G	14			X	X		X						X	X				
H	1	X	X	X														
H	2			X							X		X					
H	3 4 5 6 7 8																	
H	9			X								X		X				
H	10			X									X	X				
H	11 12 13																	
H	14		X	X										X	X			Large corner-notched points
H	15			X						X			X				X	Chipmunk, yellow perch
H	16		X		X		X					X	X	X			X	
H	17					X			X		X			X	X		X	
H	18			X	X										X	X	X	
H	19																	
H	20	X		X														Sturgeon
H	21																	
H	22				X								X	X	X		X	
H	23 24																	
H	25			X														
J	1	X	X		X						X	X	X	X			X	

TABLE 41 *(Cont.)*

Trench	Pit	Vase Tool Impressed	Vase Corded	Vase Dentate	Macomb Linear Corded	Macomb Interrupted Linear	Wayne Cord-marked	Other Wayne Varieties	Opposed	Net Impressed Rim	Miniature Vessel	Incised Shoulder	Cord-marked	Smoothed Cord-marked	Smoothed	Fabric	Roughened	Other Material
J	2 3																	
J	4										X							
J	5		X	X							X				X			
J	6	X				X									X			Disturbs Burial V 113
DA	27			X			X								X			Pipestem
DA	28 29 30																	
DA	31			X											X		X	
DA	32 33																	
DA	34	X		X										X	X		X	Deer
1	1													X				
1	2																	
1	3			X														
1	5 6 7 8 9 10 11 12 13																	
1	14		X															
2	1	X										X	X	X	X		X	

VI

OTHER EXCAVATIONS AT THE RIVIERE AU VASE SITE

At several points in this study I have mentioned the work of Mr. Jerry DeVisscher at the Riviere au Vase site. DeVisscher's paper, "Three Macomb County 'Copper and Mica' Burials," appeared in *The Totem Pole,* the journal of the Detroit Aboriginal Research Club. Since this journal has a small circulation and copies are not readily available, DeVisscher has given permission to reprint part of his report in the present study.

I have deleted references to illustrations which are not included here. Some editorial comment is also included, primarily on the identification of artifacts recovered by DeVisscher. Where such comment has been inserted it is in parentheses and identified by my initials. This identification is based on personal observations of DeVisscher's collection from the site made in January of 1963, photographs and drawings of the objects made by Ronald Mason in 1957 while this material was on loan to the Museum of Anthropology, the University of Michigan, and the drawings which accompanied DeVisscher's report.

On July 27, 1957, while digging in the vicinity of the old excavation of the University of Michigan in Chesterfield Township, Macomb County, I noticed a weak disturbance of the sandy soil below the three foot level. At 40 inches below the surface I came upon several potsherds of a type different from the Owascoid shards commonly found there near the surface (an illustration of a Wayne Cord-marked rimsherd is given. J.F.).

I carefully enlarged the excavation to a 5 by 6 foot pit, and went to work with trowel and whiskbroom, and soon found some well worn abrading stones. These proved to be part of an exceptional group of artifacts. . . . I have concluded that the shards first found were in the grave fill, but it is possible that previous investigators, ancient or modern, had recovered some additional shards of this pot, as the earth was considerably disturbed down to that point, and a shallow refuse pit containing Owascoid shards such as shown in illustration X (Vase Tool-impressed rimsherd. J.F.) was only three feet away.

I had carefully excavated near this same area in 1955, and previously I had found conditions identical with some previous digging near the surface but with occasional slight disturbances, scarcely noticeable, below this level. Dr. E. F. Greenman had reported, in 1945, that two different cultures had occupied this area and had found such evidence near this dig.

On June 26, 1955 at approximately 48 inches in depth, close to this latest find, I disinterred a whole pot (this is a Wayne Cord-marked vessel. There are impressions of a cord-wrapped stick running horizontally around the shoulder, but the rim type is still the same. J.F.). The earth was only very slightly disturbed at this depth and I was pleased to find fifteen dental caps in a cluster near the pot, all that remained of an ancient burial.

This burial contained over 150 copper beads (similar to those found in the University of Michigan excavations. J.F.), mostly just below the teeth with two smaller groups lower and at either side, possibly armlets. I also recovered two copper awls and a large copper band, curved as though part of a head-piece. Near the Molar caps was pot D, only three inches in diameter (a decorated miniature vessel of a rare type in the University of Michigan collection. It has broad incisions over cord marking. There are only two such forms in the University of Michigan collections. J.F.). It contained twenty-three small smooth pebbles, and was perhaps a rattle. The little pot has two perforated castellations, probably for suspension, and is decorated with a horizontal band of incised suns and crescent moons. Pot E was whole and undamaged (Wayne Cord-marked vessel previously described. J.F.) and heavily coated with charcoal on the exterior. It has lines of dentate stamping somewhat like cordmarking (cord-wrapped stick. J.F.) about the neck and is decidedly conical like pot D. A cluster of three celts, the smallest very sharp, lay near pot E.

Burial #2

Burial #2 was unearthed the same summer and was only a few feet from burial #1. It consisted of a cluster of nine dental caps representing the only skeletal remains. On either side of the teeth were the following items: one, two and one-fourth inches corner-notched blue-gray flint projectile point and a flint trianguloid knife. A thick mica slab, 4 by 7 inches, lay near three stone concretions, probably medicine stones.

One 6 inch pottery vessel accompanied this burial, crushed by the weight of the overburden. It is decorated around the neck with dentate lines, resembling "cord-wound stick" impressions (a Wayne Cord-marked Vessel. J.F.). The body is deeply impressed with heavy cord marks. This burial was 50 inches below the surface and showed faint evidence of red ochre having been sprinkled upon the offerings. All pottery is grit tempered with no evidence of coiling.

Burial #3

This most recent find is perhaps the most interesting, but contained only one copper piece, an awl 2 inches in length. Beginning with the cluster of twenty dental caps, and very close to the right, were 13 fine, thin projectile points of black and brown flint. All are corner notched and quite wide, a typical Goodal Focus, middle Woodland type (Jack's Reef Corner-notched projectile points. J.F.). A long-barbed spear-head lay four inches from the orderly group of smaller (two inches average) points.

Ten inches from the points was a slate gorget three and one-half inches long. It is partly embedded in what seems to be a ball of hardened "paint" of yellowish color, and is accompanied by a flint scraper made from a broken point. The gorget is bi-conically drilled with one hole and bears a deep sharpening groove, also fine end notching.

Eight inches to the left of the teeth lay a close packed assembly of tools suited for working wood and flint. These include abrading stones, two small flint drills, flint scrapers, a flat piece of bone and two antlers flakers.

Two feet, four inches below the teeth was a small crushed pot. It is dentate stamped in horizontal and oblique rows and very slightly castellated on two opposite sides of the rim. The body is semi-conical with a smooth lower half. (This vessel is an early, collarless variant of Vase Corded. J.F.).

Near the gorget is a section of badly disintegrated human bone, probably a tibia, which might indicate that the burial had been flexed. A copper awl was also found.

About ten inches below the teeth was a fine slate crescent or quarter moon, three and one-quarter inches long and about three-eights inches thick at the heaviest portion; edges are nicely tapered. This was four inches from a wide black corner-notched point one and three-quarters inches long.

None of the material found with these burials showed any evidence of having been ceremonially broken or "killed."

DeVisscher's excavations were in the general area of the University of Michigan Trench B. Small quantities of plaster, similar to that from Pit 20 in Trench B, were recovered, but he has stated that he did not find the large quantities of historic artifacts noted in the University of Michigan excavations. This seems to suggest that his pits were to the west and south of the earlier University of Michigan excavations.

DeVisscher and other interested people have donated portions of their collections from the Riviere au Vase site to the Wayne State University Museum of Anthropology. These sherds, supplemented by the surface collections from the site made by Wayne State University field parties provided an additional sample of approximately 1,500 rim sherds and body sherds. I examined these sherds, but no attempt at quantification was undertaken. No new types were identified, and there was no information on the location of these finds on the site which might have been used in the distributional study.

VII

OCCUPATIONAL HISTORY

A discussion of the occupational history is limited by lack of information on the stratigraphic relationship of the cultural materials. Outside of pits, the only depth measurements were taken on artifacts in Trench A. This was an area with a large number of burials suggesting a great deal of disturbance. Only thirty-eight rimsherds were recovered, and all of the types from the site occurred in all levels, so the resultant information was meaningless.

In several instances, pits cut into burials or information was recorded on materials superpositioned over burials. This proved to be of some help.

Burial V 72, an ossuary with twelve individuals which contained a Levanna Point, was cut by Pit 10 in Trench E. This pit contained sherds of Macomb Linear Corded and an incised shoulder fragment.

Burial V 84, which contained a sherd of Wayne Punctate, was disturbed by Pit 13 in Trench E. This pit contained four fragmentary interments (Burial V 85) but, unfortunately, no cultural material. This pit was also superimposed over Burial V 85, an extended individual.

Burial 88 was cut by Pit 16 in Trench E which contained Vase Corded and Vase Dentate rim sherds, smoothed body sherds and a banded pipe bowl.

Pit 18 in Trench E cut into Burial V 90, an extended burial. The pit contained a Macomb Linear-corded rimsherd.

Trench J Burial V 113, three extended individuals, was cut by Pit 6, which contained Vase Tool-impressed and Macomb Interrupted-linear sherds.

In Trench B, Burial 4 II was found at the bottom of a refuse pit. Fragments of a Macomb Interrupted-linear vessel were found 10 inches over this burial which was associated with Wayne Cord-marked sherds.

DeVisscher reported finding Vase Tool-impressed sherds over Wayne Cord-marked during his excavations.

In summary, Wayne Cord-marked is never found stratified over other types; Vase Dentate is found in one pit cutting into a burial; and Vase Tool-impressed, Vase Corded, and Macomb Linear variants are, in several instances, found in later pits cutting into earlier features.

At several points an areal separation of material has been noted throughout the site. The western parts of the site contained the fewest burials and the largest number of refuse pits. Trench B, which produced the burials with Wayne Cord-marked vessels, also produced larger than expected amounts of Vase Dentate, another possible early type. Adjoining Trench D produced the greatest discrepancy between observed and expected frequencies of Wayne Cord-marked vessels. Two and one-half times as many Macomb Linear vessels were found in Trench E as we would expect if chance alone were operating on the distribution.

Trench E also produced considerably larger amounts of roughened body sherds than we would expect. In several instances roughened surfaces are known to be associated with Macomb Linear vessels (Plate XIII). Trench E also had the greatest number of ossuaries. Macomb Linear sherds and Levanna points were found in several of these ossuaries.

The distribution of the other major groupings of body sherds is hard to interpret, but the relative distribution of the earlier brushed type in Trench B and the later simple-stamped types in the eastern trenches has already been noted.

We have also noted that, in terms of both actual count and area excavated, greater numbers of smaller sherdlets were found in Trenches B and D. These may be contrasted to the larger sherdlets in the eastern trenches, but there is an intergradation through Trench D.

Three main groups of projectile points were identified at the site. The earliest type was Jack's Reef Corner-notched. Trench B accounted for 75 per cent of the Jack's Reef Corner-notched points from the site. This is a transitional type found on late Point Peninsula and early Owasco sites in New York. In New York it is found with those ceramic types which are most similar to Wayne Cord-marked and Vase Dentate: Jack's Reef Corded and Jack's Reef Dentate.

Levanna points, the large triangular forms with a tendency toward concave bases, were found in greatest numbers in Trench E, particularly with ossuaries in this Trench. This type of point has been dated as early as A.D. 700 but is most common on sites in the northeast dating between A.D. 900 and A.D. 1100. Here again we have ceramic forms, Vase Corded, Vase Tool-impressed, and Macomb Linear, in Trenches A and E which have analogies at Ontario and New York sites falling in this period.

The third major point type, Madison points, tends to appear after A.D. 1300 in New York. They do, however, appear earlier in early Middle Mississippi sites. It is possible that they entered

Michigan at an earlier date than they entered New York. In any event, the distribution of these points on the Riviere au Vase site suggests a very late position in the depositional sequence.

Most significant of the other chipped-stone artifacts were the small expanding base drills. Two of these were found with burials in Trench B along with Jack's Reef Corner-notched points and other grave goods. The third was found in Pit 1 in Trench B with Vase Corded(uncollared), Vase Dentate (both collared and uncollared), Macomb Linear-corded (uncollared) and Wayne Cord-marked sherds. This seems to provide some continuity between the burials and the occupation debris.

Most of the ground stone is of little diagnostic value. It can be duplicated in sites in surrounding areas ranging from the Krieger horizon to the Uren horizon. The gorgets are of interest. The finished forms were found in Trench B with burials. Two fragments of unfinished gorgets were found in Pit 23 in Trench B, a pit which contained Vase Dentate sherds. This, again, links the burials in this area to the refuse pits.

The copper artifacts from the site were either from the University of Michigan excavations in Trench B or DeVisscher's excavations near Trench B. The occurrence of this material in such a limited form is, by itself, of no diagnostic value. The pipes also are of little diagnostic value. The forms present at the Riviere au Vase site are duplicated in other sites including Krieger, Younge, and Uren. The bone artifacts, likewise, are distinguished primarily by their generalized nature.

Altogether, a picture of the aboriginal occupation of the site begins to emerge. The first inhabitants of the site lived in this area during the very end of Point Peninsula or late Middle Woodland times. They occupied the western portions of the site, and, occasionally, buried their dead in this area. While they appeared to use Vase Dentate vessels most commonly as utility ware, they tended to bury with their dead Wayne Cord-marked vessels such as were included with the earlier Middle Woodland burials at the Fort Wayne Mount. They included grave goods of some forms with these burials. It is very possible that these were personal items: projectile points, a personal tool kit, raw materials, amulets, etc. Even this is an irregular practice and some burials show little attention.

The first phase of the occupation at the site might have begun as early as A.D. 600 although a date of A.D. 700 to A.D. 800 seems more likely in view of the continuity of the occupation as evidenced by the contents of the refuse pits.

A second phase of occupation is represented most strongly in the eastern part of the site. This is characterized by the occurrence of new ceramic types and the greater elaboration of old forms. Large triangular points replaced the corner-notched points and collars and castellations appeared on many more vessels. There was a tendency toward an elaboration of the mortuary complex. Instead of grave goods, which rarely occur, skulls were packed with clay, long bones and skulls were altered, and trophy skulls were included with these burials.

The common ceramic forms here were similar to those of the New York Owasco sequence and the transitional period between the Point Peninsula occupations and the early Neutral-Wenro materials in southwestern Ontario. This was, apparently, the main phase of the occupation at the Riviere au Vase site and provided the bulk of the material found. Developing out of the earlier cultural stage, it lasted from approximately A.D. 900 to approximately A.D. 1100 or 1200.

It might be possible to mark a terminal phase of occupation represented by the cultural material which is most like the Uren or Barrie material in Ontario. Some ceramic forms and some of the Madison points might have been left by sporadic post-A.D. 1200 occupations. Although the Uren site has been placed at the bottom of the Neutral-Wenro sequence, it is not felt that the occurrence of some Uren-like material necessarily implies an Iroquoian linguistic stock. Even the latest of the aboriginal cultural material from the site is far too early to attempt an identification with any ethnic group.

The aboriginal occupation of the Riviere au Vase site took place between A.D. 600 and A.D. 1300 with A.D. 800 to A.D. 1200 suggested as the period of most intensive occupation.

The historic material from the site is fairly homogeneous. The latest of the artifacts from the house site may be dated to the 1850's; and, since this is a minority of the material, it is suggested that the cabin burned down some time in the early 1850's. During the University of Michigan excavations Dr. Greenman found some of the older residents in the area, then in their seventies and eighties, who could remember the ruins of the cabin as far back as the 1860's although no one could remember when it had burned. It was said to have been occupied by a family named "Decahn" or Dequindre.

PART II

THE FULLER AND VERCHAVE SITES

VIII

UNIVERSITY OF MICHIGAN EXCAVATIONS IN MACOMB COUNTY IN 1962

In April of 1962, Dr. Arnold Pilling of Wayne State University contacted Dr. Richard Keslin of The University of Michigan, after a conversation at the Central States Anthropological Society meetings in St. Louis that year, about the location of several possible Early Woodland sites in Macomb County. In early June, James E. Fitting and Alan Babb went to several of these sites with Pilling and assessed the feasibility of excavation. It was felt that the remaining portions of the Fuller I site (20 MB 45) might warrant excavation.

On June 18, 1962, a field crew from the University of Michigan Museum of Anthropology, consisting of James E. Fitting, David Taggart, Fred W. Fischer, Henry Wright, Gary Wright, and Alan Babb, returned to the Fuller I site (20 MB 45). A period of one and one-half weeks was spent on 20 MB 45 and a locality about one-half mile to the north, also on the Fuller farm, which was designated Fuller II (20 MB 177).

Two and one-half weeks were spent at the Verchave sites in Harrison Township, Macomb County (20 MB 178, 181, and 182) and one and one-half weeks were spent at "D-40-A," a complex of three sites (20 MB 155, 156, and 157) in Sterling Township. Short periods were spent at the Brandenburg site (20 MB 32), the Holcombe site Locality I (20 MB 30) and Locality II (20 MB 171), the Davidson argillite site and the Zaborsky argillite site (20 MB 179). In this report the material from Fuller I, Fuller II, Verchave I, Verchave II, and Verchave III shall be considered. The material from the two localities of the Holcombe site will be covered in a report on that site by Keslin, and I will report on "D-40-A," which is primarily an Archaic site. The other sites lacked enough cultural material to permit analysis.

The work of the University of Michigan field party was aided by a number of individuals. The assistance given by Pilling has already been mentioned. Miss Nancy Edwards and Neil Johnson, students at Wayne State University, also assisted the University of Michigan field party. Mrs. Fuller of 50360 Callens Road, should also be thanked for granting permission to excavate several areas on the old Fuller farm. Lottie M. Schmidt, Inc., a Mount Clemens real estate company, gave us permission to excavate in areas to the south of Hooker Road at the Fuller site.

Mr. Bernard Trinity, of the Trinity Neighborhood Library and Museum at 47460 Sugarbush Road, deserves much credit for the success of the season. Trinity helped us establish pleasant contacts with the residents of the houses along Hooker Road by the Fuller site. It was he who suggested excavations in the area of Fuller II (20 MB 177), and the library was always open to us for shelter and work space.

Two families near the Fuller I site made our excavations more pleasant. The Halavans furnished our party with ice water on several hot days and the cheery disposition and ready wit of Col. Mathews and his family buoyed our spirits.

Mr. Jerry DeVisscher of Mount Clemens directed us to both the Verchave sites and "D-40-A," and obtained permission for us to excavate on "D-40-A." DeVisscher, who located and has excavated much of the Holcombe site, has aided both Wayne State University and The University of Michigan for a number of years. Mr. Edward Wahla of Roseville visited our excavations and contributed much to our understanding of Macomb County archaeology.

I should like also to express my appreciation for the exact and helpful geological commentaries on these sites furnished by Mr. David Taggart, assistant field director of the party, and for the detailed and useful field notes of Mr. Henry Wright and Mr. Fred W. Fischer.

All financial support for these excavations was furnished by the National Science Foundation.

IX

THE FULLER I SITE

The Fuller I site (20 MB 45) is located in the northwest quarter of the southwest quarter of Section 23, Chesterfield Township (T. 3N, R. 14E) of Macomb County, Michigan. It is on the farm of Mrs. Fuller of 50360 Callens Road. The site lies on a low sand ridge, about 585 feet above sea level which rises above the swampy meander scars cut into the former flood plain of the Salt River, which lies to the west. The greatest portion of the site was disturbed by bulldozing operations for the construction of the present Halavan, Mathews, and Depues houses (running from north to south) along Hooker Road. Parts of the site are still intact around the margins of these lots, on the remaining portions of the Fuller farm, and on parts of the same sand ridge across Hooker Road to the south (owned by Lottie M. Schmidt, Inc.). The Wayne State University collection from the site was obtained at the time of bulldozing operations on the site.

In the course of testing this site, the University of Michigan Museum of Anthropology field party made four controlled excavation units on the edge of the areas reported as productive (where houses are located today). A vacant lot to the north of the area of the reported concentration was tested by two units, a 5- by 10-foot unit and a 5- by 5-foot unit, and by three soil test pits. The opposite side of the road was tested by two additional 5- by 10-foot units. All of the excavated material was sifted through a one-quarter inch screen. The remaining portions of the site lie to the east of the houses in an area which is predominantely of low elevation and swampy in character. The area to the southeast of the houses may contain cultural material, but is very disturbed and irregular due to bulldozing and the collection of topsoil for gardens.

The excavation of these various units shows a uniform series of soil and stratigraphic zones. The basal deposit of the low ridge appears to be a grey lacustrine clay sloping upward from the swampy meander scar and riverside areas. It is covered by irregular deposits of sand which form low ridges parallel to the stream valley. The lower parts of these deposits show clear evidence of bedding and consist of fine sands mixed with clays followed by a thin series of banded medium to coarse sands. There are occasional thin lenses of clay followed by thin deposits of fine sand. Recent soil zones have developed on top of this. The series represents basic lake deposits with subsequent stream and dune deposition.

The cultural material from the site was so sparse that provenience units within excavation units are meaningless. There is some areal distribution of both historic and aboriginal material.

Cultural material from this site is found in collections in both the Wayne State University Museum of Anthropology and the University of Michigan Museum of Anthropology.

In both collections there are a number of sherdlets, approximately fifty, with both smoothed and cord-marked surfaces. The temper varies from medium, according to Riviere au Vase standards (1 to 2 mm) to fine, sandy material.

There were a total of five aboriginal rim sherds of possible diagnostic value. From the area of the University of Michigan excavations to the north of the Halavan house came two rimsherds with deep punctates (Plate XLII, C). These are very similar to the deep punctate sherds from the Furton site (Greenman

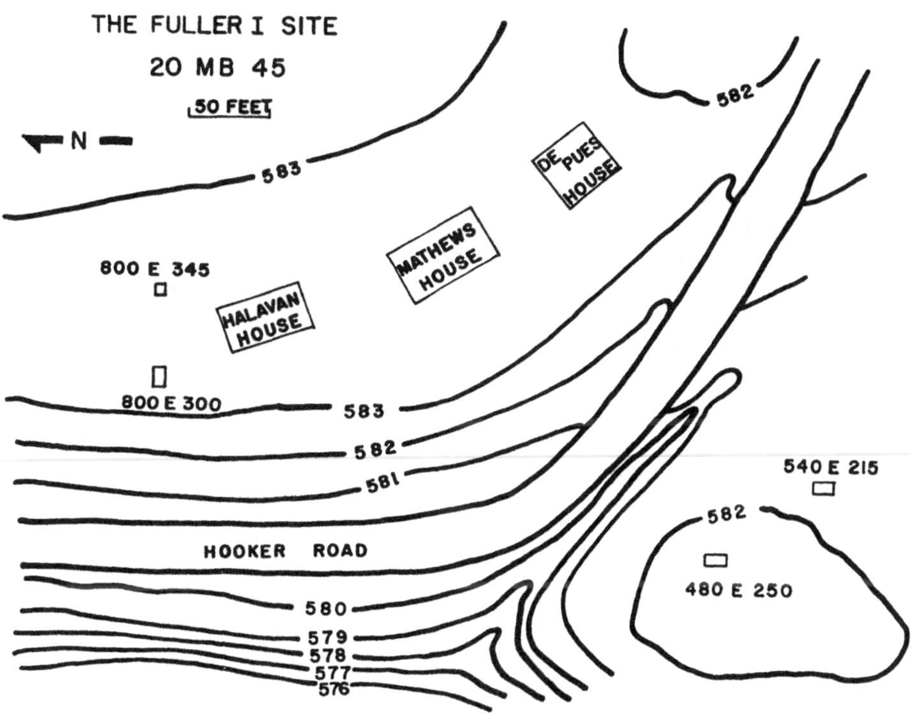

Fig. 9

1939*b*: Plate VI, Figure 2, h, i) which is located about 1 mile away from the Fuller I site. A rim sherd was located in the front yard of the Mathews house. This was a large sherd of a variant of Vase Corded (Plate XLII, D). It had a coarse temper (particles 2 to 4 mm), a slight collar, and was decorated with oblique cord-wrapped stick impressions. This sherd was in the fill of a flower bed. This fill had come from an area to the east and slightly south of the Mathews and DePues houses.

In the Wayne State University Museum of Anthropology collections, there were two rim sherds. These were collected during the bulldozing operations in the area of the Mathews and DePues houses. One sherd (Plate XLII, A) is a sherd of Vase Tool-impressed. The other is, at first glance, a sherd of Macomb Interrupted Linear (Plate XLII, B). It is, however, much finer, thinner, and harder than the majority of the sherds of Macomb Interrupted Linear which I have examined.

In addition to the number of flint chips in both the Wayne State University and the University of Michigan collections, there are several chipped-stone artifacts. Two stemmed points and one point tip (Plate XLII, E-F, H) were found in the area of the Halavan House by Wayne State University field parties. The University of Michigan excavated a stemmed scraper (Plate XLII, I) and a fragment of a stemmed point base (Plate XLII, G) in the area to the north of the Halavan house. A similar stemmed point was unearthed by Mr. Halavan while working on his yard.

The butt end of a dyorite plano-convex adze (Plate XLII, J) was found by the Wayne State Museum field party while the area of the Halavan house was being bulldozed. This is similar to the large adze from Riviere au Vase, which was found prior to excavation.

Certain differences may be noted in the historic material collected by The University of Michigan and Wayne State University. The University of Michigan field party found one fragment of a kaolin pipe bowl, one metal door hinge and several glass and brick fragments. The historic sherds consisted of four plain sherds of a white paste earthenware, four sherds of Sprig ware (late 1830's), three sherds of Blue Edge with a wheat pattern (late 1820's and early 1830's) and one sherd of North Staffordshire Red Print (late 1830's).

The Wayne State University collection consists of a number of glass fragments including two fragments of molded glass, four sherds of a very thick heat-altered blue glass and the neck of a bottle similar to the bottle illustrated for the Riviere au Vase site. There are four nondiagnostic sherds of a white paste earthenware and three sherds of an equally uninformative stoneware. The datable material consists of one sherd of Flowing Blue (1850's) and one sherd of Common Yellow (after 1840), two rose pattern sherds of a Late Victorian ware (late 19th century), one sherd of North Staffordshire white paste earthenware with a band of copper metalic luster (1880's) and part of a porcelain doll which can be dated to the 1870's or 1880's.

These collections came from different areas of the site. The University of Michigan material came from excavations to the north of the Halavan house where Wayne State had been unable to collect material because of the sod. The Wayne State collections came from the bulldozed area where the houses are today, or where excavations by the University of Michigan field party were impossible. The difference between these two collections is, however, interesting to note.

X

THE FULLER II SITE

The Fuller II site (20 MB 177) is located in the northwest quarter of the southwest quarter of Section 23 of Chesterfield Township (T. 3N, R. 14E) of Macomb County, Michigan. It is located one-half mile north of the Fuller I site (20 MB 45) and back of the Fuller house on 50360 Callens Road. It rests on a small bluff overlooking the Salt River, which is on the opposite side of Callens Road. There is a vacant lot to the west and south of the house which constitutes the excavatable area of the site.

The site is on the same sand ridge as the Fuller I site, and suggested itself because of its apparently greater elevation than the surrounding area. This proved to be relative, and the actual elevation was less than that of the Fuller I site. This area was also suggested as a possible area for excavation by Mr. Bernard Trinity, and Mrs. Fuller mentioned that her late husband had found numerous artifacts in the field behind the house.

Therefore, on June 25, 1962, while completing excavations on the Fuller I site, a small crew undertook a controlled test excavation on the Fuller II site. Only one excavation unit, a 5- by 10-foot unit, was opened. The elevation of the surface in this area was approximately 583 feet above sea level.

The soil horizons are basically similar to those of the Fuller I site. The basal clay is clearly bedded, much more so than at the Fuller I site, and has the appearance of varve formation. The basal clay is overlain by sand deposits and recent deposits of dark brown humus containing cultural materials. This site differed from the Fuller I site in that the sands show horizontal as well as vertical separation. One possible explanation for this is that the darker area closer to the present Fuller house has been more disturbed. This was partly substantiated by Mrs. Fuller, who remembered a brick kiln in an area slightly to the northeast of the excavation unit.

The cultural material from Fuller II (20 MB 177) was rather sparse, and consisted only of that material gathered during the University of Michigan excavation of the site. There were thirty-one sherdlets of aboriginal manufacture. Three of these fitted together, and represented the rim of a temperless miniature vessel with a few incisions over cord-marking. A number of chips were found, but no worked artifacts.

As was mentioned before, this area was slightly to the south of a former brick kiln, and numerous brick fragments were found. There also were coal and glass fragments, nails and fence staples, and one brass button of a late type.

XI

CONCLUSIONS

In examining this material, any conclusions must be tentative. Two aboriginal and two historic components seem to be represented at Fuller I (20 MB 45).

In the area to the north of the Halavan house The University of Michigan excavated material similar to that from the Furton component at the Furton site. The rim sherds in this area showed a pattern similar to the Furton punctate pattern. This ware is thicker than the Wayne wares, and lacks the fine, shallow, circular punctates which characterize Wayne Punctate. In this same area the University of Michigan field party excavated the base of a straight-stemmed point; Wayne State University field parties had found two more straight-stemmed points, and Mr. Halavan had found an additional straight-stemmed point. The University of Michigan stemmed scraper is not out of place with this material. The majority of the points from the Furton site are of a straight-stemmed type (Greenman 1939*b*: Plate I, i-k), while no straight-stemmed points have been reported from the excavations at Riviere au Vase or the Wolf site. The fragment of the plano-convex adze came from this area also. The generally finer temper of the sherds is a further suggestion of Furton affinities (Greenman 1939*b*:21). The closest relationship for this material seems to be the Furton site.

A second aboriginal component seems to be represented by the material in the area of the Mathews and DePues houses, and in the area of the southeast of these houses. The Wayne State University field parties found two rim sherds, and the University of Michigan field party found one, that would suggest a close relationship to the later phase of occupation at the Riviere au Vase site. This area of the site was either destroyed during bulldozing operations, or was very swampy so The University of Michigan was unable to test it in the summer of 1962.

The fact that there appears to be two concentrations of historic materials at the site which follow the distribution of the two aboriginal components of the site is suggestive. The land between the Salt River and Anchor Bay is all very low and swampy. Occupation, even today, is limited to naturally high or filled areas. If, prior to bulldozing, there had been two areas slightly higher, by even a foot or two, then the surrounding swamp, you might expect habitations on them. The closeness, yet distinctness, of the two historic and two aboriginal components suggests this "high ground" occupation.

The material from Fuller II (20 MB 177) furnishes us with even less information. At Riviere au Vase the distribution of miniature vessels parallels the distribution of later types. The aboriginal occupation at this site may have been contemporary with the late Vase component at Riviere au Vase and Fuller I.

XII

THE VERCHAVE SITES

In July of 1962 the University of Michigan Macomb County field party spent two weeks excavating a series of sites on the Verchave farm on North Clinton Road east of Mount Clemens. The farm is located in Harrison Township (T. 2N, R. 14E) of Macomb County, and is about one and three-quarters of a mile east of Mount Clemens. It is located on a spur along the north bank of the Clinton River. Mr. Jerry DeVisscher brought the site to the attention of the University of Michigan field party, and reported that a grooved stone axe and polished stone "pick" had been found along the river bank in this area.

The three most productive sites in this area occur on a nearly continuous sand ridge extending across the neck of a spur in the river and paralleling Clinton River Road (Figure 10). This ridge varies from 1 to 8 feet above the valley floor, and has a tendency to arch toward the Clinton River. A second ridge, which is barely perceptible, is found to parallel the first at about 100 yards to the south. These ridges consist of fine sand resting on a series of water-laid sands, silts, and clays upon which a blackish loamy sand topsoil and an orangish fine sand subsoil has developed. Cultural material is located in the topsoil and in pits dug into the lower subsoil. The rest of the low spur consists of a series of nearly imperceptible swells which occupy an intermediate position between the ridges and the present river channel. These probably represent older, filled channels of the Clinton River. The deposits in this area consist of stiff clays, silts and sands, and contrast sharply with the ridges. The stiff grey clay may be considered the basic deposit in this area, where it represents old lake formations and delta deposits, which have been slightly altered by the shifting channels of the Clinton River.

The main ridge on the north edge of the spur is separated on the basis of cultural material into three sites: Verchave I (20 MB 178), Verchave II (20 MB 181), and Verchave III (20 MB 182).

Verchave I is located on the easternmost section of the sand ridge examined by the University of Michigan field party, and extends onto the next farm. Cultural material was readily collected from the surface in this area, but became much sparser as one moved west toward Verchave III.

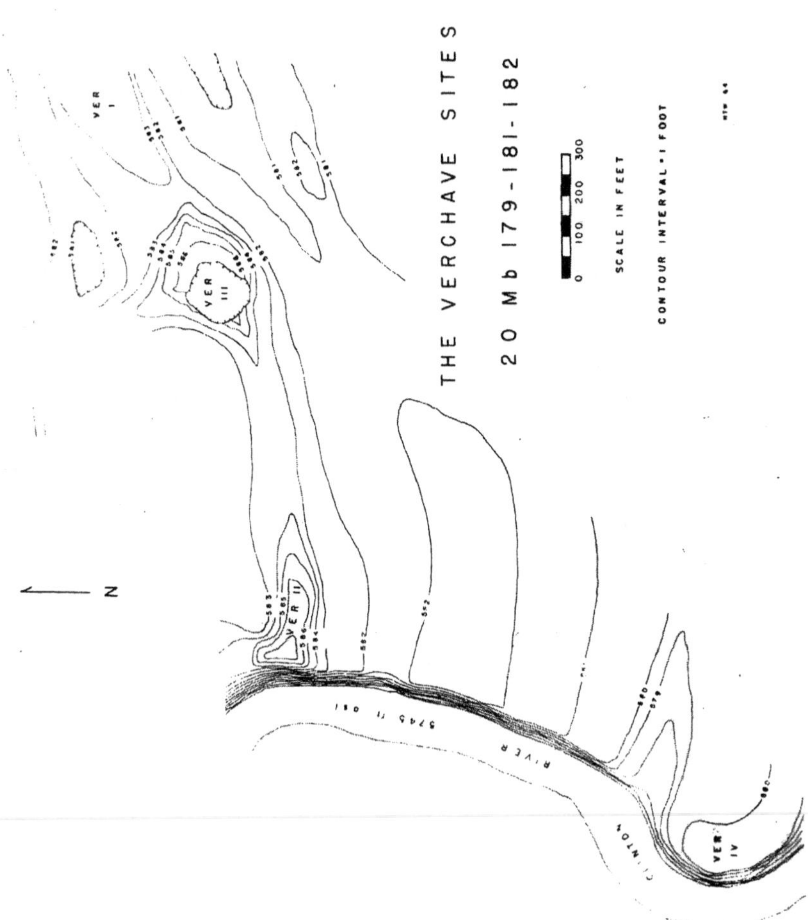
THE VERCHAVE SITES
20 Mb 179-181-182
0 100 200 300
SCALE IN FEET
CONTOUR INTERVAL = 1 FOOT
N
VER I
VER II
VER III
VER IV
CLINTON RIVER

Fig. 10

Verchave III was located on a prominent sand knoll in the center of the ridge behind the Verchave farm house and barn. The knoll was disturbed by sand removal, but both prehistoric and historic cultural material was in evidence in surface collections from the area.

Verchave II consisted of a high sand knoll at the western part of the sand ridge. This locality has been partly undercut by the Clinton River, and shows a sod cover over most of its area. The site contains a series of features overlain by a dense historic occupation. The intervening ridge to the east is barren of cultural materials, and this area is topographically distinct. It is possible that the concentrations of cultural materials continue into the heavily wooded northern and northwestern portions of the knoll.

Work at this site was greatly facilitated by the co-operation of the Verchave brothers who owned the farm. Usually we can thank property owners for permission to excavate. We can thank the Verchave brothers for actually aiding in the excavation by disking the easternmost field so that we might, by surface collection, locate concentrations of artifacts and areas for excavation. George Verchave, in particular, provided aid by furnishing us with ice water, and allowing us to eat lunch in the shade of the farm house. His friendly attitude and bountious stock of stories did much to sustain the morale of our field party. The Wildwood Bar in Harper Woods owned by the Verchave brothers, was always open to us as an unofficial field camp after working hours.

XIII

VERCHAVE I

Verchave I (20 MB 178) was the first of the sites in the Verchave complex to be located. Four 10- by 10-foot and one 5- by 10-foot excavation units were used to sample the site (Figure 11).

The first excavation unit was designated as 490 East 780 in the grid system established for the site. At the base of the plow zone, approximately 1 foot below the surface, a dark brown area was found in the basic yellow sand. This was designated as Feature Number 1. This brownish stain with flecks of charcoal proved to be a roughly circular and straight-sided pit, which was a little over 1 foot in depth below the plow zone, and about 2 feet in diameter (Figure 12). With the exception of the feature, cultural material was found only in the plow zone and at the base of the plow zone in this unit. The yellow sand became lighter with increased depth, and was light grey to white with orange staining

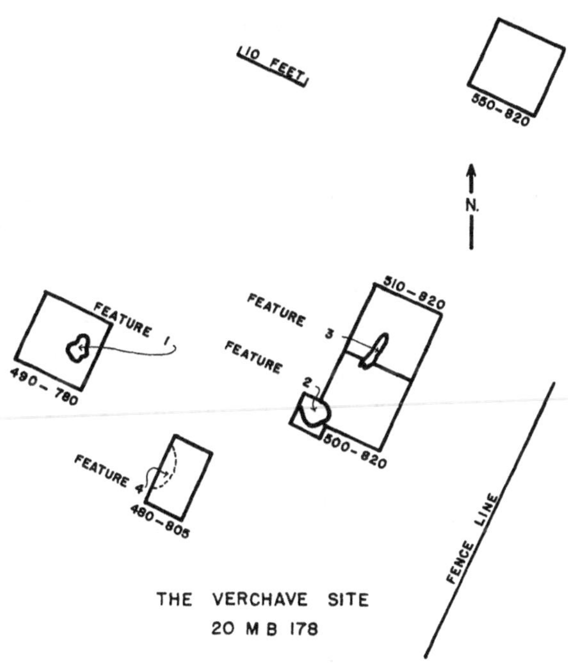

Fig. 11

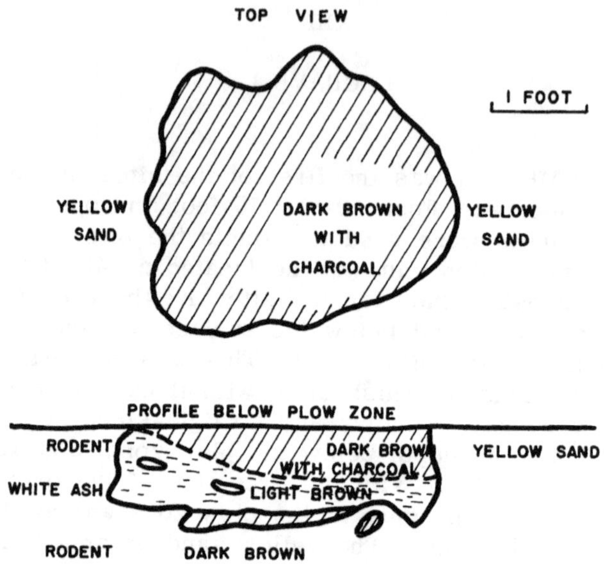

THE VERCHAVE I SITE 20-MB-178 FEATURE I

Fig. 12

at a depth of 4 feet. This proved to be the typical profile for much of this area.

The second unit, 500 East 820, was a 10- by 10-foot excavation unit. At a depth of approximately 1 foot, soil discolorations suggestive of features were noted in the southwest corner and in the center of the north wall. This area in the southwest corner consisted of a dark brown area in the yellow sand similar to Feature Number 1 in unit 490 East 780. It was designated as Feature Number 2. The area around this feature was extended, and at the base of the plow zone the outline of a second circular pit about four feet in diameter was detected. This was filled with charcoal, bone, sherds, and other cultural material. This pit was dug over a foot into the subsoil below the plow zone (Figure 13).

The disturbance in the north wall was designated as Feature Number 3, but further examination revealed that it was an extremely deep plow scar.

The eastern half of unit 500 East 820 appeared darker during excavation. It was, for a time, thought that this was a midden deposit. Careful troweling suggested that this darker area below the plow zone had also been plowed. Cinders, brick fragments,

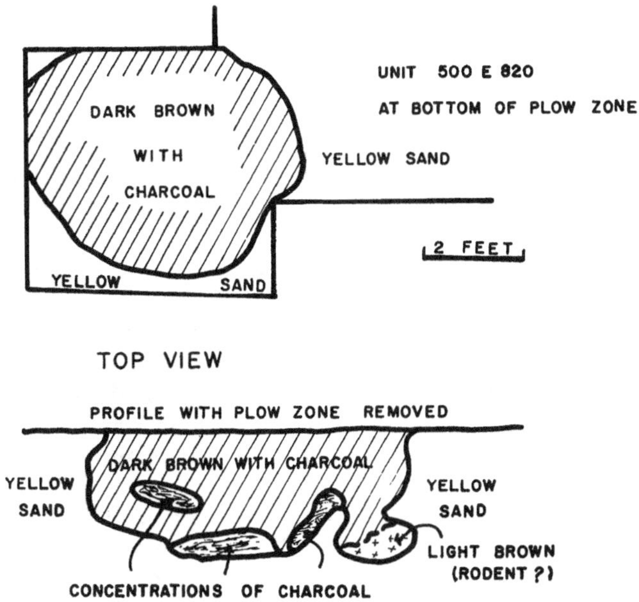

THE VERCHAVE I SITE 20-MB-178 FEATURE 2

Fig. 13

and nails were found in it. It was noted that sand was piling up against the fence line to the east. It is possible that wind-blown sand collecting against this fence to the east caused increased depth of humus deposits, and the plow no longer reached to the full depth of the former plow scars. The cultural material in this second plow zone was identical to that in the primary plow zone.

Two additional 10- by 10-foot squares were opened to the north of the two already described. These were 510 East 820 and 550 East 820. Here the plow zone rested on a mottled brown-yellow sand which contained no features and no cultural material. The cultural material from these units was more fragmentary, suggesting it had been carried from other areas by plow action. They apparently defined the northern boundary of the site.

One 5- by 10-foot excavation unit was opened to the south, and designated as 480 East 805. A darker area was noted at the west side of this unit. No feature number was given to this area in the field, but it was taken out as a separate provenience unit during excavation. Almost all of the cultural material from below the plow zone was from this area, so it is felt that a designation of Feature Number 4 for this area would be appropriate. It differs from the other features in that it lacks charcoal or evidence of fire, other than rare, small pieces of fire-cracked rock. Discoloration is slight, and the boundaries are vague, which could be explained if this area were used as a storage pit, and filled in with debris from the surface, rather than purposely being reused as a refuse pit.

This unit was excavated to the water table. It was found that the white mottled sand with ferric stains which were noted in unit 490 East 780 rested on cross-bedded, grey-brown, and brown silty sands at a depth below 3.5 feet. The area immediately above the water table, which was approximately 4.5 feet below the surface, was a coarse grey sand. This suggests that the sand ridge, at this point, has formed over an old channel of the Clinton River.

Over 900 sherdlets were recovered from Verchave I. These were fragments which were too small to determine with any degree of accuracy what the surface treatment of the vessel had been. They were quite numerous on the surface, and in the plow zone. Sherdlets were found below the plow zone in Features Number 1, Number 2, and Number 4. Feature Number 3 contained no cultural material.

A total of eighteen rim sherds were recovered from the site. It is unfortunate that fifteen of these rim sherds were found in the plow zone, or during surface collection of the site. Three of these rims were Parker Festooned (Plate XLIII, F), a type defined by Thomas E. Lee at the Parker Earthworks (1958*b*:15). This type postdates the entire Riviere au Vase sequence; indeed, it is completely absent from Riviere au Vase. These rim sherds have a square lip and medium temper.

Three additional rims (Plate XLVIII, A) were plain. These had a fine temper and an orangish paste, which was very distinct from the Riviere au Vase temper and paste. They had a rounded (type E) rim profile and are reminiscent of similar plain forms reported by Lee (1958*b*:17-8) in Ontario in association with Parker Festooned.

There were three rim sherds with a slightly everted (type B) rim profile and cord marking up to the lip (Plate XLIII, C, G). The lips were altered by cord-wrapped stick impressions running obliquely across the lip surface. In many ways they resemble the Wayne Cord-marked rims from Riviere au Vase. The paste and temper, however, seem to align them with the previously mentioned plain rims.

Miniature vessels were represented by four small fragments (Plate XLIII, B). The pattern of distribution of this form at Riviere au Vase suggested that they are found with later material. Since these fragments are all from the plow zone there is no indication of the temporal placement at Verchave I.

Two very interesting rim sherds seem to have opposed oblique interrupted-linear impressions below an everted (type B) rim profile (Plate XLIII, M). These seem to come from the same vessel, and present a very different total picture from the Macomb Interrupted-linear type.

Only three rim sherds were found below the plow zone in features. One rim sherd was found in Feature Number 2. This was a plain rim with a rounded (type E) rim profile (Plate XLIII, A). It is more excurvate than the relatively straight, plain rims found in the plow zone. It, too, has a distinctive orange paste, and a very fine, almost sandy, temper.

Feature Number 4 produced two typable rimsherds. These were two sherds of Vase Corded (Plate XLIII, H). These sherds had only slightly thickened rims, and lacked the typical collar (type A rim profile) of most Vase Corded sherds. The oblique impressions of a cord-wrapped stick occur below the lip protuberance. They belong to two distinct vessels.

Over 100 body sherds were large enough for me to make observations on the surface treatment. As with the rim sherds, the vast majority were from the surface collection, or from the plow zone. Out of the 93 bodysherds in the plow zone or surface collection, ten surface treatment techniques were noted. The largest group included a coarse cord-marked form represented by 30 body sherds. There were 27 plain-surfaced body sherds. An intermediate group was represented by 10 sherds which were thinner than the majority of the body sherds, and had a very fine cord-marked surface. Four body sherds (Plate XLIII, K) were obviously body sherds of Parker Festooned vessels. There were 3 sherds with interrupted-linear impressions (Plate XLIII, M), which are a part of the vessel with the oblique interrupted-linear designs on the rim. Two sherds had impressions of a coarse fabric. The rest of the material was represented by single occurrences, and included the following: tool impression, dentate stamping, crosshatching and one sherd with a roughened surface similar to that noted at Riviere au Vase and the Wolf site (Greenman 1939*b*:13). There was a single body sherd from the site with a plain surface, and a pattern of laminated hollow spaces in cross section, suggesting a leached shell temper. I have examined a similar sherd reported by Greenman (1939*b*: Plate II, Figure 2,d) from the Wolf site, and described by him as "cell" tempered (1939*b*: 12), and feels that it, too, has a leached shell temper.

Only fifteen body sherds were found below the plow zone in features. There were six plain surfaced, orange paste, finely tempered body sherds from Feature Number 2, which apparently go with the rim from this feature discussed previously. In addition to this material there was one thin, fine grit-tempered body sherd with a fabric-impressed surface. Two sherds show incisions, and are parts of an incised shoulder. There is one sherd with an interrupted linear pattern.

Feature Number 4 produced three coarse cord-marked body sherds. There was one sherd with three parallel incised lines that may be part of an incised shoulder, and one plain-surfaced body sherd.

Two aboriginal pipe bowl fragments and one pipestem were found at Verchave I. They all came from unit 480 East 805. A fragment of a dentate bowl (Plate XLIII, E) and a stem were found in the plow zone, and a banded bowl (Plate XLIII, D) was found in Feature Number 4.

A number of chipped-stone artifacts were recovered from Verchave I. These included seven Madison points (Plate XLIV, A), and two side-notched point fragments (Plate XLIV, B), which were found on the surface or in the plow zone. One of the Madison Points illustrated was found in Feature Number 2. The plow zone and surface collection from the site also produced one expanding base drill (Plate XLIV, C), a tip fragment of an additional drill (Plate LXIV, D), one bifacial scraper and five utilized flakes.

The chippage from this site was plentiful, and represented in all units and features. Because of the temporal range evidenced by the ceramics and the mixed condition of the site, no technological examination was undertaken.

One object of ground stone was recovered (Plate XLIV, E), which appears to be one-half of a longitudinally fractured hammerstone. It is battered on one end, and there is definite evidence of grooving on the narrow part of the body.

The historic material from the site was all from the plow zone. It represents no single occupation, and seems to contain mixed materials covering a long time span. Nails, cinders, brick fragments, and pieces of soft coal are numerous. There are a few pieces of glass and eight fragments of kaolin pipes, none of which have any diagnostic features or legends. Two twenty-two shells and the base of one shotgun shell were found. The only item of interest is what appears to be the lock of a child's toy cap-pistol (Plate XLIV, F).

The Verchave I site was apparently occupied several times. The single dentate sherd and the sherds which are similar to Wayne Cord marked suggest an early Late Woodland occupation, perhaps paralleling the early occupation at Riviere au Vase. Features Number 1 and 2 produced very little cultural material. It is quite possible that this last feature is related to the occupation which left the Parker Festooned sherds. The occurrence of a Madison Point in the feature does support this position. Feature Number 4 contains two Vase Corded rims, a banded aboriginal clay pipe bowl and an incised shoulder sherd. This suggests a temporal placement similar to the later material from Riviere au Vase. It is ironic that the feature from Verchave I, which can be best placed in the cultural sequence, is also the one feature that lacked enough charcoal to run a radiocarbon date.

The component represented by the Parker Festooned sherds is probably late.

Verchave I is a very shallow site which has been plowed for a long period of time. There appears to be no stratigraphy at the site, and the only unmixed cultural materials occur in occasional features. It is a typical Michigan archaeological site.

XIV

VERCHAVE II

The Verchave II site (20 MB 181) was discovered by Mr. Henry Wright while we were working at Verchave I. The area of the site on the western end of the sand ridge was covered with a thick sod so that no cultural material was present on the surface. While excavating a soil profile pit along this ridge, Wright found numerous sherd and bone fragments. This pit was designated as Test Cut Number 1, and was expanded into a 5- by 10-foot excavation unit, 300 East 200 in the grid system established for the site.

A second 5- by 10-foot unit, 320 East 200, was opened to the north around a second soil test pit designated as Test Cut Number 2. A third 5- by 10-foot unit, 280 East 200, was opened to the south of the original unit. The relationship of these units to each other, and to the slope of the ridge is given in Figure 14.

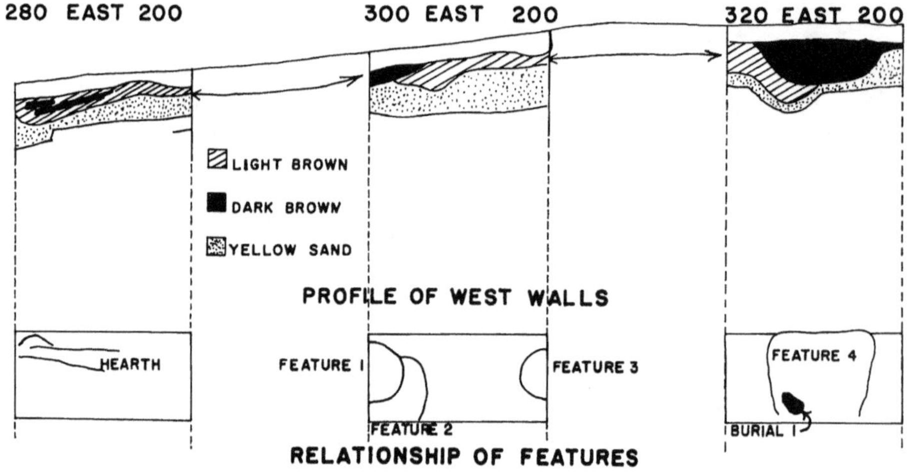

PROFILES & FEATURES OF VERCHAVE II
(20 MB 181)

Fig. 14

Only three 5- by 10-foot excavation units were used to sample this site. The dense sod cover, and the quantities of historic refuse, apparently associated with a house site, made excavation extremely difficult.

In the southernmost unit, 280 East 200, the bottom of the plow zone was reached at a depth of 1 foot. A great deal of brick, limestone, and plaster was found in the plow zone. This thinned out below the plow zone, although other historic material was present. Brick and plaster were found to a depth of 2 feet. There was no stratigraphic separation of historic and prehistoric material in this unit. The concentrations of brick and plaster in the plow zone also suggest that the house foundation is located in another area of the site.

The plow zone in the original unit, 300 East 200, was only .8 feet thick. Over 20 pounds of brick and tabular blocks of limestone were recovered from the plow zone in this unit. A concentration of brick, limestone, and plaster was noted at the south end of the unit, and was designated as Feature Number 1. This proved to be a pit of unknown dimensions (estimated to be 4 to 5 feet in diameter) dug into the subsurface deposits to a depth of a little over 1 foot below the plow zone. Twelve pounds of brick, tabular limestone, and plaster were recovered from this feature as well as many historic artifacts. This appears to have been the footing or pilaster of a building.

In this feature, as well as throughout the entire plow zone, large quantities of cow, sheep, pig, and chicken bones were found. This material was identified by Charles Cleland of the University of Michigan Museum of Anthropology.

To further complicate the situation, Feature Number 1 cuts into a larger prehistoric refuse pit, Feature Number 2. Thus, aboriginal and historic materials are mixed in the upper layers of the aboriginal pit. (See Figure 15 for the relationship of these two features.) Feature Number 2 was a light brown sand with well-formed lenses evident in some parts of the excavation. It ran to a depth of 2 feet below the plow zone. A grey sandy clay rested on the bottom of the pit and brown sand was found on top of this. Chert chips, fish, squirrel, muskrat, and bird bone came from this lens. This lens has so much fishbone that it was difficult to remove it. The volume was as high as 50 per cent fishbone in some areas.

Cleland of the University of Michigan Museum of Anthropology, has identified the bone from this feature. In the basal lens he found 1,150 fragments of unidentifiable fishbone of which 13 fragments were charred; 1 fragment of unidentifiable bird bone,

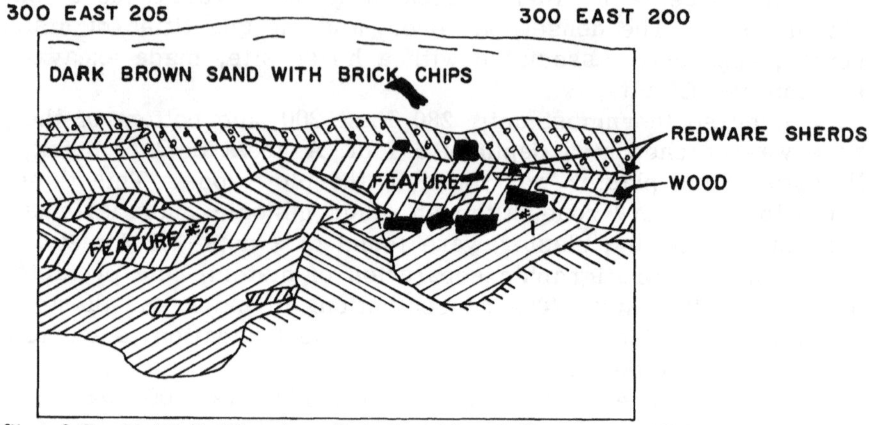

Profile of South Wall Showing Relationship of Features 1&2

VERCHAVE II (20 MB 181)

Fig. 15

9 fragments of turtle bone with 6 of these fragments charred; and 41 fragments of mammal bone with 36 charred fragments. Four species of animals and fish could be identified. The most common form was yellow walleyed pike with 164 bones representing at least 21 individuals. There were 2 bone fragments of drum fish or sheepshead representing 1 individual. Two small mammals, a grey squirrel and a muskrat, were each represented by 1 bone fragment. Cleland also noted the uniform size of the walleye remains. He found that 9 individuals were between 375 and 412 mm in length, 9 between 412 and 465 mm and only 3 over 465 mm. In a higher lens in the pit Cleland found 100 fragments of unidentifiable fish bone of which number 10 fragments were charred, 29 fragments of unidentifiable mammal bone of which number 26 were charred and 18 yellow walleyed pike bones representing 4 individuals.

Richard Yarnell, formerly at the University of Michigan Museum of Anthropology, identified the floral remains from the pit. He found large quantities of hickory nuts and smaller quantities of walnut, hazelnut, acorn, hawthorn, and grape. He also found corn in Feature Number 2.

By examining the fine-screen samples from this feature, Cleland and Yarnell were able to reconstruct portions of a seasonal exploitative cycle. The fishbone fragments were found in the basal lens and in a second lens separated from the first by an area of brown sand. The size and uniformity of size of the fish have lead Cleland to postulate that a spring fishing season is represented by these layers. The floral material examined by Yarnell, mature nuts and corn, seems to represent a fall deposition. This material was found in the light brown sand between the main lenses of dense bone concentration. Refuse was then deposited in this pit for at least two seasons. It is probable that there were additional layers, but these were obliterated by Feature Number 1.

A sample of charcoal from the fishbone layer at the base of Feature Number 2 was submitted to the University of Michigan Radiocarbon Laboratory in February of 1963.

A third feature, designated as Feature Number 3, was noted just below the plow zone in the northern part of 300 East 200. This proved to be a deep, steep-sided pit about 3 feet in diameter, and extending below the plow zone to a depth of several feet (Figure 16). This was an aboriginal feature although historic

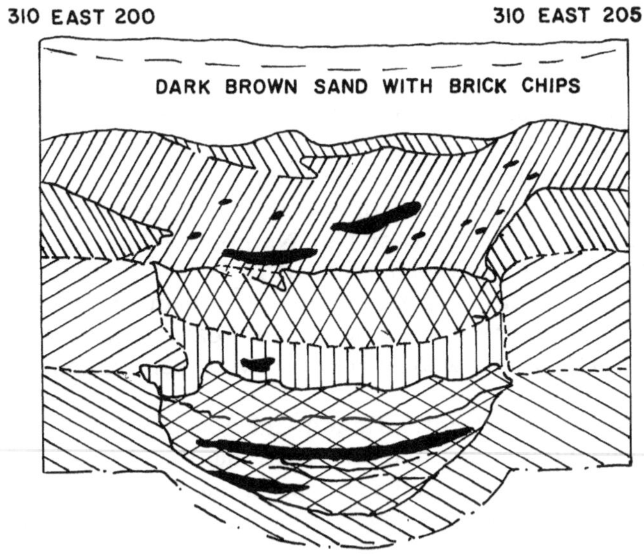

PROFILE OF NORTH WALL SHOWING X-SECTION AT FEATURE 3

VERCHAVE II

(20 MB 181)

Fig. 16

materials were found in the upper levels due to the intensive historic occupation. There was very little cultural material from this feature. The historic material was uniform throughout the site, while the aboriginal material, several sherdlets and chips, was of little help in cultural placement. Any involved discussion of the nature of the lenses in this feature would be pointless.

The features in this unit were dug into the orangish-yellow sand which forms the basic deposit along this ridge. Because of the complex nature of this unit, it could not be conclusively demonstrated that the soil was sterile below the plow zone in non-feature areas. The sparse quantity of cultural material found outside of the features, however, could easily have come from one of the several pits dug into this area.

At a depth of 5 to 6 feet below the surface, a distinct bedding of the sand layers was noted. This continued until the water table was reached at a depth of 8 to 9 feet. This suggests a situation similar to that at the Verchave I site with the sand ridge having formed over an old river channel.

In Test Cut Number 2 a number of human bones had been found, although in no apparent order. The 5- by 10-foot unit, 320 East 200, was opened around this test cut to see if a burial area was evident. It was immediately noted that there was less brick, limestone, and plaster in the plow zone (3 pounds) than in either of the other two units. The plow zone itself was .9 of a foot thick. At the base of the plow zone a large dark brown area was noted in the center of the unit. This contained charcoal and aboriginal ceramics. Test Cut Number 2 had penetrated into this darker area. At a depth of a little over 1.5 feet below the surface, a concentration of fragmentary human bone was encountered. The pit itself was designated as Feature Number 4, while the flexed burial which was uncovered was designated as Burial Number 1.

The burial was a tightly flexed old adult male. The head was oriented to the northeast, and the individual had been buried on his left side. The upper and rear portions of the skull, and most of the vertebrae, were scattered over an area several feet to the northwest of the burial. The soil configuration at this point suggested that a secondary pit, Feature Number 4, had been dug into a burial. The burial pit was obliterated except for traces around the articulated part of the burial. The second pit, Feature Number 4, dug into a part of the burial, and some of the bone material was scattered (that which was found in Test Cut Number 2 and the fill of Feature Number 4). Little cultural material and charcoal were found in the pit fill leading to the observation that the second pit was never utilized. It was, apparently, filled in after encountering the burial. This must have been during the aboriginal occupation, since no historic material was encountered in the pit fill.

Several units were opened a quarter of a mile to the south of Verchave II along the Clinton River. This area was designed as Verchave IV, although no site number was given to the locality. There was only one dubious feature in this area, and the cultural material from Verchave IV was also sparse. For this study it has been grouped for a comparison with the rest of the cultural material from the Verchave II site.

The diagnostic aboriginal cultural material from the Verchave II site was more scattered and sparse than the extensive system of features would indicate. It is very possible that there was considerably more material on the site, but the sod and dense layer of historic refuse made it impossible to continue excavation at that time.

There were approximately 300 aboriginal sherdlets from Verchave II, and an additional 100 from the nearby locality designated as Verchave IV. These were fragments which were too small to even ascertain the surface treatment. They have a medium (1 to 3 mm) to coarse (2 to 4 mm) granitic temper, although some few have a finer temper. This apparently finer temper could be caused by the extremely small size of the sherdlets.

In addition to the rounded base of a coarse-tempered, coarse cord-marked pot (Plate XLV) which Wright encountered in the first test cut, only thirteen coarse cord-marked sherds and one fine-tempered (almost sandy), thin, smoothed body sherd were recovered. This later sherd was found in Feature Number 1, the historic house pilaster. Verchave IV produced six smoothed body sherds, three smoothed-cord body sherds, and six coarse cord-impressed body sherds. This material fell within the medium to coarsely tempered group.

Three rim sherds were recovered from Verchave II (Plate XLVI, A, E, C) and one from Verchave IV (Plate LXVI, B). One Macomb Linear Corded rim (Plate XLVI, C) was found between 1.2 feet and 1.7 feet in depth in unit 320 East 200 in the undisturbed area around Burial Number 1. It has a typical type A collar, but no castellations are present. Feature Number 2 produced fragments of another Riviere au Vase type, a sherd of Vase Corded (Plate XLVI, E). The lip is broken, but the impression of a cord-wrapped stick is evident. Below this is a plain area with an incised shoulder design. Not enough of the incising is present to determine the nature of the pattern or the extent of the area covered. A matching sherd shows both a plain area with incisions and coarse cord marking suggesting that a coarse cord-marked body was associated with the Vase Corded rim (Plate XLVI, D).

One rimsherd, actually several contiguous fragments of a single rim, was discovered in Feature Number 4 (Plate XLVI, A). This rim belongs to a vessel of Parker Festooned, a type defined by Lee (1958*b*:17) at the Parker Earthworks near Corunna, Ontario. The rim is plain, thin (6 mm) and has a fine temper. The top 1.25 inches are plain. Then there is an area of applique with circular punctates. This sherd appears more closely related to one illustrated by Lee (1958*b*: Figure 9, 2) from Ontario than it is to any of the Parker Festooned sherds and vessels illustrated by Greenman (1939*b*: Plate V, Plate VI, 1, Plate VII, 2, g) from Michigan. A temporal difference may exist between the applique festooned and simple-festooned forms.

The fourth rim sherd is from the area of Verchave IV (Plate XLVI, B). It is a thin (6 mm), fine-tempered rim sherd with a square lip. It is similar to the larger Parker Festooned rim from Verchave I, except that it is smoothed horizontally rather than obliquely, and lacks the raised stamp area of the larger Verchave I Parker Festooned rim sherd. It is also similar to the upper portions of the Parker Festooned rim from Feature Number 4. Since the temper, paste, and thickness are similar, and it is broken short of the festooned area, it is possible that this is the upper portion of a Parker Festooned rim with the festooning occurring below the break. Lee (1958*b*:18-19) has reported similar fragments at the Parker Earthworks.

Two fragments of daub were recovered at a depth of between 1.6 and 2.0 feet in unit 300 East 200 suggesting wattle and daub house construction. Similar material was noted at Verchave I, and has also been reported from the Parker Earthworks (Lee 1958*b*: 15); from the Wolf site (Greenman 1939*b*: Plate VII), and the Riviere au Vase site.

The only aboriginal chipped-stone artifacts were projectile points. One is a very thin tip fragment of greyish chert (Plate XLVI, 6). This was found between several vertebrae in the disturbed area near burial Number 1. The tip itself is, of course, nondiagnostic, but its thinness may indicate a Madison or Levanna point. The second projectile point (Plate XLVI, F) is a poorly made side-notched point of a purple-grey material. It was found in the plow zone in unit 300 East 200.

One piece of negative evidence should also be noted. Almost no flint chippage was found in either Verchave II or Verchave IV excavations. This could not be due to poor sampling within the units since all of the material was screened, and that from the features was fine-screened. The lack of chippage and chipped-stone artifacts is reminiscent of the Wolf site and, in this instance, suggests that there was only a short period, perhaps seasonal, occupation.

The historic material from this site is extremely plentiful. Fortunately, it is almost identical to the historic component from Riviere au Vase, so most of it was readily identified. Dr. Arnold Pilling aided me in classifying some rare variants of common types, and Mrs. Kammer Aga-Oglu of the University of Michigan Museum of Anthropology helped in placing the porcelains from the site.

The historic ceramic material from Verchave II, as for Riviere au Vase, furnishes the best evidence for the age of the historic component. Approximately 1,400 historic sherds were recovered from the site. Most of this material can be readily analyzed. There were 380 sherds of glass, including several dozen that belonged to a mirror. With the exception of these mirror fragments, six sherds of blue gilded glass and nine fragments of small bottles, the sherds were window glass. Another 670 sherds were of a plain North Staffordshire White Paste earthenware. These may be plain fragments of vessels which are decorated, but, by themselves, are not too useful in pinning down the age of the site. Seventy sherds were of a red bisque earthenware. A number of glazes from shiny brown to tan were represented.

Approximately 200 sherds were of diagnostic wares and patterns. There were 14 different patterns on North Staffordshire White Paste earthenware. These fell within the Gaudy Dutch series including: Early Gaudy Dutch (pre-1830) represented by 9 sherds; Painted Blue (late 1820's, early 1830's), represented by 20 sherds; Middle Gaudy Dutch (late 1830's), represented by 22 sherds. Sprigware (late 1830's) was represented by 6 sherds. There were 41 sherds of Blue Edge (late 1820's, early 1830's), and 16 sherds of the closely related Green Edge pattern (1830's). There were 43 sherds of medium blue print which is associated with Sprig ware at the Hotel Pontchartrain dump site, so probably dates to the late 1830's in southeastern Michigan. There were 2 sherds of the large pattern American variant of Sponge ware (1825-1840). There were 2 sherds of Blue Willow (1825-1840), 3 of Red Print and Red Print Meander (1830's) and 2 sherds of Brown Print (late 1830's). Mocha ware, or raised glaze (1825-1840), was much more common at this site than at Riviere au Vase, and was represented by 21 sherds. The only material for which the date of greatest occurrence is later than 1840 is

Common Yellow, which is represented at the Verchave II site by 1 sherd.

There are two sherds of a salt-glazed stoneware and six fragments of porcelain. Four of the porcelain fragments are plain, and two are decorated with a fine red line, and one of these has a gilt tendril over the red line. This material was much more common in the eighteenth century.

With the exception of the porcelain and the single sherd of Common Yellow, the material is fairly consistant. A date of 1840 or shortly after is suggested for the abandonment of this occupation site.

There were nineteen stem fragments of kaolin pipes, and nineteen bowl fragments. Neither the stem or bowl fragments had any diagnostic characteristics or legends. No attempt was made to date the pipestems by bore diameter, because the sample was small, and there were ample indications that it dated to the nineteenth century, when bore dates are no longer operative. It might be noted, however, that two of the pipestems were whittled (Plate XLVI, H).

The most common class of metal objects recovered were square nails with 173 occurrences. In comparison to the area excavated and the material from a comparable time period at Riviere au Vase, this seems like a large number. It is not known if all the nails from Riviere au Vase were saved, but in any event the large number at Verchave II suggests some use of wood planking. This would be a very early date for the use of sawed timber for a house in this part of the state. There also were a number of hinge fragments.

There were nine copper buttons including one that can be dated to the military uniforms of the war of 1812. There were two objects that appeared to be copper disks, about three quarters of an inch in diameter, that had been plated with brass. These may have served as bases for cloth buttons. A brass ring slightly over 1 inch in diameter might have served the same purpose. There was a single bone button with one central perforation. Two objects had brass heads and iron points. These appear to have been upholstery brads. The eating utensils of the historic inhabitants of the Verchave II site are represented by two pewter fork handles and one iron fork handle. One plain bone fork handle and a fragment of a crosshatched bone fork handle, both similar to material from Riviere au Vase, were found at the Verchave II site.

Ten glass beads were recovered. Eight of these were round rosary beads, and two were hexagonal trade beads, which date to the late 1830's according to Dr. Pilling.

Two large gunflints of a grey-black material were recovered from the site. The regularity and uniform material suggest that these were imported forms.

A lead disk, about 1.5 inches in diameter with scalloped edges and two perforations was recovered. The use of this object is unknown, but it might have served as a child's plaything.

The bases of four shotgun shells found in the plow zone are presumed to have been left by recent hunters along the river's edge, and not the pre-1840 historic residents of the Verchase II site.

Several periods of occupation are suggested by the cultural material from Verchave II. The oldest is represented by the Vase material in Feature Number 2, and in the area of Burial Number 1 in unit 320 East 200, and in an area distinct from Feature Number 4, the intrusive pit in this unit. The collared Macomb Linear and early collarless Vase Corded forms suggest a time period comparable to the late period of the occupation at the Riviere au Vase site. The single burial in this area, and at this time period, raises some questions. Why would a single individual be interred here when a large mortuary area, the Riviere au Vase site, is located only a few miles away? The point fragment between the vertebrae suggests a violent death; perhaps representing either an outsider who was not particularly welcome, or a member of the group who met with foul play. This, however, is pure speculation.

The coarse cord-marked, coarse-tempered bodysherds are similar to bodysherds from the Riviere au Vase site. The yearly cycle observed by Cleland and Yarnell was practiced by this group, and the radiocarbon date should date the late Riviere au Vase occupation.

A second cultural group may be represented by the Parker Festooned material found in the fill of Feature Number 4 and at Verchave IV. This material has been found as a major component at a site in Southwestern Ontario, where it is associated with early Neutral trade sherds (Lee 1958*b*:25). Parker Festooned sherds have also been identified at the Lawson site. In Ontario, Lawson material is later than Barrie-Uren material (MacNeish 1952:84-5), which the late Riviere au Vase ceramics most closely resemble. Both Parker Festooned sherds and Riviere au Vase types, Macomb Interrupted Linear, Vase Dentate, Vase Corded, and Vase Tool-impressed, however, have been reported from the Wolf site (Greenman 1939*b*: Plate II-VII).

The final occupation of the site was in the first part of the nineteenth century. A house was built on the site, and was occupied between 1820 and 1840.

XV

VERCHAVE III

No systematic excavations were undertaken at Verchave III (20 MB 182), the high knoll in the center of the sand ridge behind the Verchave barn. Sand had been removed from this area, and it was reported that large numbers of human bones had been found. Some of these bones had been saved by the Verchave brothers, who donated them to the University of Michigan Museum of Anthropology. Examination of the sides of the area where the sand had been removed revealed coffin nails, some with wood adhering, fragments of shoe leather and additional human bones. A historic Indian chief was reputedly buried here with his musket and later removed. Since the material was all loose dry sand, no grave pits could be identified in the profile. Dr. Arnold R. Pilling and a group of students from Wayne State University located records which suggested that this cemetery was in use in the mid-1850's.

Stratified below the historic material, and intermixed with it, were traces of aboriginal occupation. These consisted of concentrations of sherds, chips, charcoal, and calcined bone. One projectile point was located at Verchave III (Plate XLVII, E). This was a Satchell Complex point of argillite, and was discussed by Pilling (1963:15) in his survey of cultural materials from the old beach lines in Macomb County.

In the University of Michigan collections from this area there were thirty-three sherdlets collected from the site which were too fragmentary to accurately ascertain the surface treatment involved. There were three smoothed bodysherds and six sherds with roughened surfaces similar to those described from Riviere au Vase and by Greenman (1939*b*:13) from the Wolf site. All of these sherds have a coarse temper with occasional fragments of granitic material as large as 6 mm. The single cord-marked bodysherd from the site had a finer temper with a 2 mm size for the granitic temper.

A single-typed rimsherd was found. This is a Macomb Interrupted-linear sherd (Plate XLVII, D) of which two fragments were found. There is an additional rimsherd (Plate XLVII, G) with a thickened lip. This lip is rudimentary, and is perhaps an incipient collar. Unfortunately, the outer surface has been destroyed. There are tool impressions on the lip and interior of the rim suggesting that it might be an early variant of Vase Tool-impressed.

This is indefinite, but such a sherd would not be out of place in a collection with a Macomb Interrupted-linear form.

There were a variety of coffin fittings in the area. Some of these were collected, and are illustrated (Plate XLVII, A-C, F) in order to aid future researchers in the identification of mid-nineteenth century material.

At least three cultural periods are represented at Verchave III. The argillite point is suggestive of an Archaic component (see Peske 1963 for a discussion of the temporal placement of this material). A Late Woodland component is represented by the ceramic material, and a historic component by the coffin burials.

PART III

LATE WOODLAND CULTURES OF SOUTHEASTERN MICHIGAN

XVI

CULTURAL SUCCESSION IN SOUTHEASTERN MICHIGAN

While we are to deal primarily with the Late Woodland cultural sequence in southeastern Michigan we must also discuss its Middle Woodland base and develop a terminology for the cultures of this area.

The first of the Late Woodland sites in southeastern Michigan to be reported in detail was the Younge site in Lapeer County (Greenman 1937*b*). Greenman (1937*b*:96, 1939*a*:8) used this as the type site for defining the Younge Focus which also included sites at Riviere au Vase, Flat Rock, Farmington, and Gibraltar. There is certainly a continuity in this area which might be referred to as a tradition. Because of the priority of the Younge site report we shall refer to the dominant Late Woodland sequence in this area as the Younge Tradition.

Two other sites excavated by Greenman in southeastern Michigan, the Wolf and Furton sites, were excluded from the original Younge Focus (1939*a*:7-8). The Wolf site was placed in the Mississippi pattern and the Furton site in a phase of the Woodland pattern. The Wolf site has elements which differ from much of the other Younge sequence sites but these differences can be considered as part of a variation through time. The Furton site does present interpretational problems for the ceramics from the site differ from the Younge sequence material. Because of the small sample and the individuality of the artifacts from the site, we can say very little about it here.

The Younge Tradition is marked by such traits as collared and castellated ceramics with predominantly oblique or chevroned motifs; horizontal motifs are also common. There are a number of methods of executing these designs. The projectile points are predominantly triangular types. Many of the Younge Tradition sites are comparatively large with large mortuary areas suggesting a sedentary or semisendentary population with an agricultural base. There is a tendency toward multiple burials with such mortuary specializations as clay packed into the skull, altered long bones, perforated skulls, and skulls with disks removed.

There is a late Middle Woodland base from which the Younge Tradition developed. This is represented at the Gibraltar site, the Fort Wayne Mound, the great mound at the mouth of the River Rouge and, possibly, some of the early material from the Riviere au Vase site. The fact that these sites also show evidence of later Younge occupations was noted by Greenman (1945:463) a number of years ago and is significant. Greenman felt at the time that there was no connection between the Middle and Late Woodland elements at the Riviere au Vase site. Our analysis has suggested, however, that the occupation represented in the western parts of the Riviere au Vase site was *transitional* from late Middle Woodland to Late Woodland and that Riviere au Vase was continuously, or sporadically, occupied for several centuries.

The late Middle Woodland sites in southeastern Michigan seem to have some relationship, perhaps very distant, to the Ohio Hopewell sites. Greenman (1945:463, 1958:88) has noted the similarity of material from the Gibralter site in southeastern Michigan and the Esch Mounds near Sandusky, Ohio. He (Greenman 1945:461-63) reported such objects as large cache blades and platform pipes from the Gibraltar site located to the south of Detroit near the mouth of the Detroit River.

Certain specimens from this Michigan site have been donated to the University of Michigan Museum of Anthropology by several persons who excavated in this area. I examined the ceramics with the idea of making a quantitative comparison with other Middle and Late Woodland sites in the area. Unfortunately rimsherds were present for only sixteen vessels representing both Middle and Late Woodland occupations of the site. The distribution of types was as follows: two Wayne Cord-marked vessels, four Wayne Smoothed vessels, two Wayne Cord-impressed vessels, one Vase Dentate vessel, two Vase Corded vessels, two Parker Festooned vessels, one vessel of Krieger Dentate and a vessel of either Neutral Trianguloid or Lawson Opposed. Most of these types are described in the Appendix.

Wayne Cord-impressed is a variant of Wayne Cord-marked found at Gibraltar and the Fort Wayne Mound. The decoration is made by single cord impressions around the neck and shoulder of a Wayne Cord-marked vessel. Parker Festooned is a type defined by Lee (1958*b*:17-18) and Krieger Dentate, a variant of Krieger Stamped, was defined by Kidd (1954:168). Lawson Opposed is a developed Neutral type defined by MacNeish (1952:13) which is late in the Neutral-Wenro sequence. Ridley (1961:40) feels that this material is really LaLonde at the Lawson site and the real late Neutral forms are his Neutral Trianguloid type (Ridley 1961:39). In any event, this vessel from Gibraltar appears to be a very late type; much later, in fact, than any other aboriginal ceramics examined from southeastern Michigan in the course of this study.

The variants of Wayne ware suggest a position intermediate between the early occupation at the Fort Wayne Mound and the early occupation at the Riviere au Vase site.

The Gibraltar site must have been very extensive and rich. Stories are still heard about some of the burials. Quite recently another burial, excavated during the 1940's, was reported. "Here lay a skull with a copper plate on the top, under the lower jaw a slate pendant. On both the left and right of the skull lay a small pot. . . . Only the femur and forearm were left, and under it were 42 pieces of blue-black flint. Some were knives, one a drill, one a leaf shaped spear, several arrows and scrapers and the rest blanks. . . . On the forearm were a double row of copper beads near the wrist end and the salts of the copper preserved some of the leather thong that ran through them. . . ." (Wahla 1963).

Another series of closely related sites with extensive Middle Woodland occupations were the mounds near Fort Wayne several miles south of Detroit. The excavations at one of these mounds has been reported by Holmquist (1946) and interpretations of earlier accounts have been presented recently by Greenman (1958) and Pilling (1961*a*, 1961*b*). The present account of these sites is dependent on the detailed research and evaluation of early sources presented in the articles by Greenman and Pilling.

Pilling (1961*a*:17) found evidence that the earliest account of the mounds near Fort Wayne was published in 1817 in *The Western Gazetteer; or Emigrants Directory* by Samuel R. Brown. Three mounds were reported at *Belle Fountains* or Springwells south of Detroit. Pilling also found several other accounts from the early nineteenth century mentioning three mounds. One source reported that the one ". . .standing in the Fort was covered with oak trees, and had apparently been undisturbed for many generations." The other two mounds were covered with less vegetation and it was reported that local Indians were placing intrusive burials in one mound as late as the early nineteenth century (B. F. H. Witherell cited from Pilling 1961*a*:23-24).

Bela Hubbard (1887:219) reported on these mounds and mentioned that one mound had been destroyed and another damaged by "Pilferers of Indian Relics." Silas Farmer (1884:321) mentioned that the mound inside the Fort had been opened in 1837. Pilling has suggested that this excavation was actually made on the large central mound rather than on the mound inside the Fort (Pilling 1961*b*:37-78).

The central mound of the group was excavated by John T. Blois in 1837. His account, originally published in 1838, has been reprinted in the *Michigan Archaeologist* (Blois:1958). Blois reported "Arrowheads," quartz, red ochre, "the remains of an uncommonly large white marine shell" and "beads made of the same kind of a shell" which were described as "an inch in length, and half an inch thick, with a perforation through them in a longitudinal direction." The pottery was described as being "carved and marked with various fantastic figures on the exterior" (Blois 1958:75). The over-all impression is of a Middle Woodland site with Hopewell affinities.

The mound within the Fort was first excavated by Henry Gillman in 1876. This was reported in 1877 and his account was also reprinted in the *Michigan Archaeologist* (Gillman 1958). Gillman dug a single trench through the mound. Complete excavation of this mound was undertaken by the Detroit Aboriginal Research Club in 1944 and 1945. The notes on these excavations have been published by Carl E. Holmquist (1946) and the collections are on loan to the University of Michigan Museum of Anthropology. It is hoped that a complete report on the excavation of this mound will be prepared in the near future.

Personal examination of the loaned collections has revealed at least two periods of interment at the site. There may be a third occupation represented by certain thick interior-exterior cord-marked bodysherds from the base of the mound. This pottery is an Early Woodland type similar to Vinette I (Ritchie and MacNeish 1949) and Marion Thick (Griffin 1952:97). Greenman (1958:86) has recognized four components but his divisions of "a Middle Woodland that is not definitely Vine Valley nor Hopewellian" and "a later development of this Middle Woodland" can be grouped in this study.

Jack's Reef Corner-notched points and columella beads were found in the primary mound level. Wayne ware was represented by thirty vessels, some complete, some represented by rims, which were found with the primary mound-level burials. Several new variants of Wayne Cord-marked were recognized in this collection and are discussed with the variants of Wayne Cord-marked in the Appendix of this report. In addition to Wayne Cord-marked, Wayne Smoothed and Wayne Corded there was a variant with criss-cross incisions on the neck. This variant was represented by two complete vessels and rimsherds representing three additional vessels. There was also a variant with punctates made with a cord-wrapped stick. The punctates on this variant follow a similar pattern to those on vessels from the Riviere au Vase site but the tool used in application varies.

The Late Woodland level at the Fort Wayne Mound contains material which easily falls within the Younge Tradition. Vase Dentate, Vase Corded, Vase Tool-impressed, and Macomb Linear vessels are all represented in the collection. In addition to these types there are rimsherds of twenty-two distinct vessels with fabric or net-impressed, collared rims. We have already mentioned three such rimsherds from the Riviere au Vase site and six more were found in the Wolf site collections. Although this was a minimal sample it was felt that a new type should be established. This type was named Springwells Net-impressed after the early name for the site of these mounds. It is described in the Appendix (illustrated in Plate XLVIII). The temporal position of this intrusive occupation is, as we shall demonstrate, somewhere between the Riviere au Vase site occupation and the Wolf site occupation.

Another mound in the area, the great mound at the mouth of the Rouge River, was discussed by Bella Hubbard in 1887 in an article which has been reprinted in the *Michigan Archaeologist* (Hubbard 1958). He noted a duality of occupation with perforated crania in the intrusive burials. The ceramics illustrated by Hubbard (*ibid.* 1887:218) are an improbable lot. The vessel on the left looks like a good Wayne Cord-marked vessel. The large vessel in the center appears to have the same shape as some Weaver vessels (Griffin 1952*c*: Plate XXXVII, c) and Steuben vessels (Morse 1963: Plate XVII, Figure 1) which are late Hopewell or post-Hopewell in Illinois. It is my impression that this particular vessel form is rare in southeastern Michigan. The third vessel illustrated by Hubbard is certainly a rare form in southeastern Michigan. Its large diamondlike incised surface treatment is, as far as I know, unique for this area.

The last site with Middle Woodland affinities is the Riviere au Vase site. We have discussed the transitional nature of this material in detail so it needs no further description.

The degree of relationship can be established for several of these sites by comparing the ceramics. It has often been suggested that no other artifact class is as sensitive an indicator of time and space relationships (Griffin 1952*c*:95). There are certain limitations to this type of comparison. We are faced with a very small sample of Middle Woodland ceramics. Our Wayne ware series consists of only ninety-one vessels: thirty from the Fort Wayne Mound, fifty-three from the Riviere au Vase site and eight from the Gibraltar site. We have classified all of these as one type with several variants so all we can compare are the variants.

The Wayne ware variants from the Fort Wayne mound and the Riviere au Vase site are compared in Figure 17. We can note several trends. Wayne Crosshatched and Wayne Cord-impressed are entirely absent from the Riviere au Vase site. These are the variants, particularly Wayne Crosshatched, that show the greatest Hopewell influences. There is a slight increase in the number of punctate forms but it must be remembered that there is a qualitative difference in the punctations at these sites. The material from the Fort Wayne Mound exhibits cord-wrapped stick punctates while the sherds from the Riviere au Vase site have smooth tool impressions. There appears to be an increase of undecorated forms, Wayne Cord-marked and Wayne Smoothed, at the Riviere au Vase site.

Although the sample from the Gibraltar site is too small to include in this diagram, only eight vessels, the forms which are present are of some significance. Wayne Crosshatched is absent but there are two vessels of Wayne Cord-impressed. There are

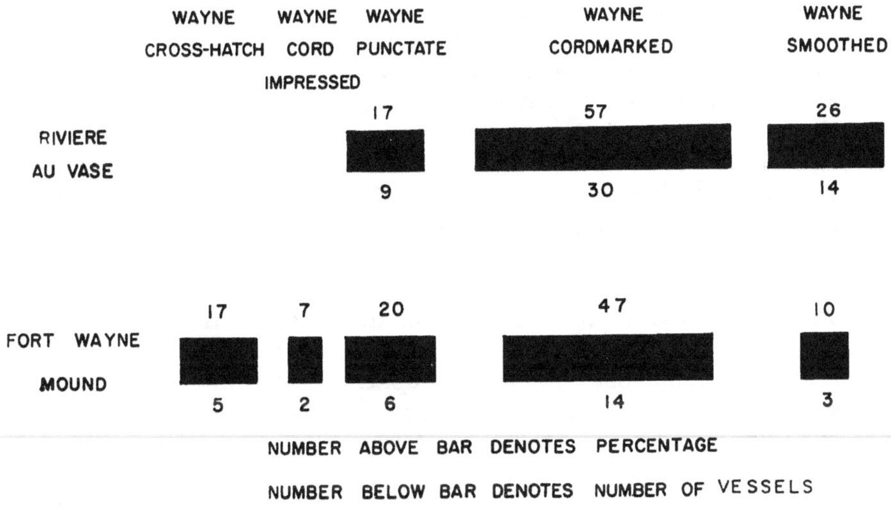

WAYNE WARE FROM SOUTHEASTERN MICHIGAN SITES.

Fig. 17

two vessels of Wayne Cord-marked and four vessels of Wayne Smoothed. The absence of Wayne Crosshatched and the increase in Wayne Smoothed suggest a position intermediate between the Fort Wayne Mound Middle Woodland level and the early occupation at the Riviere au Vase site.

Armed with the foregoing information we may attempt to establish a late Middle Woodland cultural sequence in southeastern Michigan. The sequence is only suggested and much more data will be necessary for its definite establishment. The earliest Middle Woodland material in this area might well be that recovered from the central mound of the Springwells group in 1837. Blois's description implies more Hopewell affinities than any of the other Middle Woodland sites mentioned. Since the developmental trend is away from Hopewell, this site would be the earliest in the sequence. Both the logic of this position, as well as the logic of basing such a position on an 1837 account, are inherently weak.

The Fort Wayne Mound, another mound in the Springwells group, is the first site where we can make any kind of positive evaluation. The Wayne Crosshatched variant is reminiscent of the Hopewell Crosshatched motif. Beads of marine shell are present and the corner-notched points seem to occupy an intermediate position between the large corner-notched points from the Norton Mounds near Grand Rapids and the Jack's Reef Corner-notched points from the Riviere au Vase site. They are closer to the latter type than to the former and have been classed with this type. The ceramics from the Fort Wayne Mound are not "carved and marked with fantastic figures" like the ceramics from the central mound. Although shell beads were found, no large marine shells were reported from the Fort Wayne Mound. This mound seems to postdate the central mound in the Springwells group and corresponds to the post-Hopewell developments within the Scioto Tradition in Ohio.

Many Hopewell traits were found in material from the Gibraltar site. The over-all impression is, however, of a late Middle Woodland or transitional period occupation. Quimby (1952:104) placed this material in the transitional period between Middle and Late Woodland and suggested that it was slightly earlier than the material from the West Twin Lake mounds. The West Twin Lake material is from Montmorency County, slightly to the north of the area under discussion, so I have not placed the site in our sequence. I have, however, noted the similarity of some of this material to that from the Riviere au Vase site which is discussed below.

From the ceramic sequence (Figure 17) and the complete lack of diagnostic Hopewell elements, the early occupation at the Riviere au Vase site seems to represent the terminus of the late Middle Woodland in southeastern Michigan. Because of the strong association of Wayne ware in features with early Late Woodland ceramics (Vase Dentate) it is even better to call this transitional Woodland.

What we have proposed is a development from the mound level of the central mound at Springwells, to the Fort Wayne Mound, to the Gibraltar late Middle Woodland and finally to the early occupation of the Riviere au Vase site. There are trends in ceramic decoration, stonework and the inclusion of exotic objects with burials that tend to validate this sequence. This sequence is, however, tentative and presented for the sole purpose of showing the late Middle Woodland base out of which the Late Woodland Younge Tradition developed.

Out of the six sites which Greenman (1939*a*:8) included in the Younge Focus only two, Younge and Riviere au Vase, provide enough material for a quantitative comparison. To this we will add the intrusive pits in the Fort Wayne Mound which were excavated after Greenman's article on cultural relationships of archaeological sites in this area appeared. Greenman (1958:86), although he did not place this material within the Younge sequence, he did note the resemblance of the Fort Wayne intrusive burials and the later Riviere au Vase occupation.

We shall also include the Wolf site in our discussion of the Younge Tradition. Greenman (1939*a*:7-8, 1939*b*:25-26, 1958:91) has maintained that the Wolf site should be placed in a different taxonomic group from the other Younge Tradition sites. In our examination of the Wolf site ceramics it was found that 58 per cent of the Wolf ceramics were Riviere ware types.

There are several smaller sites, including those mentioned by Greenman, and the Fuller and Verchave sites, which are too small for quantitative evaluation. Some, such as the Verchave site, seem to contain middle to late Younge Tradition elements. They have been analyzed on the basis of individual artifacts. Because of the size of the samples this was the only possible method.

Because ceramics are the most sensitive indicators of time and space relationships we have again chosen them as our basis of comparison. They also form the largest artifact class from these sites. Here again, the basic unit of comparison will be the vessel or the minimal number of vessels represented by the rim sherds from the site. Whenever it is possible the relationship of pipes and projectile points will also be considered.

We have noted the transitional nature of the early part of the occupation at the Riviere au Vase site. The ceramic sample from the site is also greater than the total sample from all the other Late Woodland sites in this area. An occupation of several centuries has been suggested and this should be kept in mind when comparing Riviere au Vase with the other sites.

The various percentages and vessel counts for the various types of Riviere ware are given in Figure 18. All types were present at Riviere au Vase but the large percentage of Vase Dentate and the small percentage of Springwells Net-impressed are of interest.

The second site in our series is the Younge site (Greenman 1937*b*) in Lapeer County, Michigan. Although the relationship of the Younge and Riviere au Vase sites has been mentioned many times, there has been little attempt at quantification of this relationship. Guthe made an attempt at this type of analysis in his trait list comparison (1948:150-53) but no degree of relationship was established.

Since our unit of analysis was the vessel it was realized that such an examination would be difficult since only forty-eight

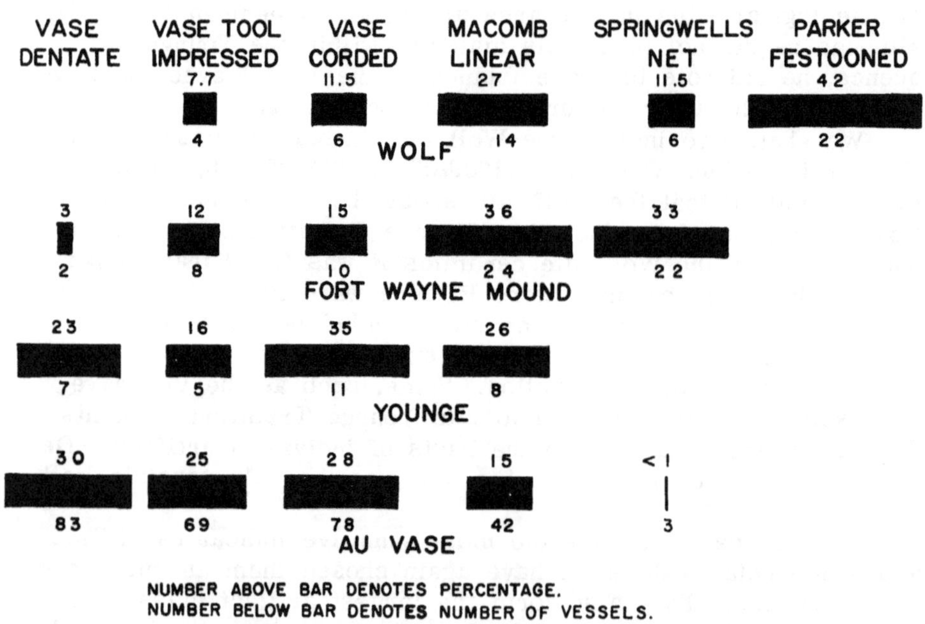

RIVIERE WARE FROM YOUNGE TRADITION SITES.

Fig. 18

rimsherds were found at the Younge site (Greenman 1937*b*:59). I was unable to locate several of these rimsherds; several were found to be rims of the same vessel; and a number of others were untypable, that is, the exterior surface below the lip had been obliterated. The results of this examination revealed thirty-one vessels representing four types of Riviere ware (Figure 18).

When the percentages were compared to the types at the Riviere au Vase site no marked differences were noted, though several trends were apparent. There was a decrease in Vase Dentate, a decrease in Vase Tool-impressed, a slight increase in Vase Corded and a large increase in Macomb Linear. The absence of Springwells Net-impressed is not surprising. Only three vessels of this type were represented in the much larger sample from the Riviere au Vase site.

There is a greater variation in pipe types from the Younge site than from the Riviere au Vase site. Both sites produced right-angled to slightly obtuse-angled elbow pipes. Incising and punctations are common bowl decorations at both sites.

The projectile points from the Younge site (Greenman 1937*b*: Plate XXII) are predominantly Madison points. There is a single Levanna point and several unusual forms.

The similarities in mortuary practice have already been noted. Perforated crania and crania with disks removed have been reported from both sites. At the Riviere au Vase site this was a characteristic of the later phase of occupation.

Altogether, the Younge site material seems most similar to the last part of the Riviere au Vase site occupation. It may have been abandoned shortly before the abandonment of the Riviere au Vase site. In Figure 18 we have placed it in a post-Vase position because of the ceramic trends and the predominance of late Riviere au Vase forms. It is again emphasized that the short occupation of the Younge site was contemporary with the later occupation of the Riviere au Vase site.

Carl E. Holmquist's (1946) report on the Fort Wayne Mound is a description of the excavations and presents no analysis of the artifacts. I examined the collections of ceramics on loan to the University of Michigan Museum of Anthropology in which at least 105 vessels were represented. Several of these were trade sherds which we will consider later. Thirty vessels fell in the Wayne ware series and have already been discussed. Fragments of sixty-six vessels from the intrusive pits in the Mound were classified as Riviere ware (Figure 18).

There was a marked decrease in the percentages of Vase Dentate and a slight decrease in the Vase Tool-impressed and

Vase Corded types. This is the site with the largest percentages of both Macomb Linear and Springwells Net-impressed vessels. More material of this intrusive burial phase at the Fort Wayne Mound will, no doubt, be excavated in the future in southeastern Michigan.

The last site in the area with sufficient ceramic material for a quantitative comparison was the Wolf site (Greenman 1939*b*). In the collections from this site, which contained material from the Museum excavations and material loaned to the Museum by Robert Schneider and Gwynne Cushman, there was evidence of fifty-two complete and fragmentary typable vessels. Only four Riviere ware types were present (Figure 18). Vase Dentate, a type which is evidently early, was completely absent from the collection. The trend toward decreased percentages of Vase Tool-impressed and Vase Corded continued. The relative amounts of Macomb Linear and Springwells Net-impressed also declined when compared to the intrusive pits at the Fort Wayne Mound.

The significant observation about the ceramics from the Wolf site is the appearance and high proportion of vessels of the Parker Festooned type. This is what led Greenman to separate this site from the other Younge sequence sites. There is evidence in southwestern Ontario that Parker Festooned is later than the types most similar to the Riviere ware series (Lee 1958*b*).

As Greenman noted (1939*b*:11) artifacts other than ceramics were very rare at the Wolf site. There were no pipes in the collections from the site and the only projectile point from the University of Michigan excavations appears to be a broken point reworked as a scraper. Therefore, ceramics are the sole artifacts which can be used for temporal placement of the site.

We are now in a position to suggest a development within the Younge Tradition. The unit which we have selected for constructing this sequence is the phase (Willey and Phillips 1962:22). The first phase might be referred to as the Riviere au Vase Phase from the early materials in the western part of the Riviere au Vase site. This is really a transitional period from the southeastern Michigan late Middle Woodland to the Younge Tradition Late Woodland. The Riviere au Vase Phase is characterized by the presence of some Wayne ware and a large percentage of Vase Dentate. There is a tendency toward single burials with grave goods of older types during the first part of this phase. This gradually gives way to rare grave goods, multiple burials and burials with later ceramic and projectile point types such as Macomb Linear vessels and Levanna points.

The Younge site material is similar to the middle to late occupation at the Riviere au Vase site. This might be referred to as the Younge Phase. It is characterized by a decrease in the frequency of Vase Dentate and Vase Tool-impressed vessels and an increase in Vase Corded and Macomb Linear types. It should also be noted that Wayne ware, which was found with Riviere ware at the Riviere au Vase site, was completely absent from the Younge site. This suggests that the transitional period was complete by the Younge Phase at the Riviere au Vase site.

Pipe forms and decorations remained relatively constant, but Madison points tend to replace Levanna points during the Younge Phase at both sites.

The next phase is represented by material from the intrusive pits at the Fort Wayne Mound. Since the mound itself was constructed during the Middle Woodland period this phase has been called the Springwells Phase after the old place-name for the mounds. The lithic assemblage is still unknown for this phase. There is a decrease in the frequency of Vase Dentate, Vase Tool-impressed and Vase Corded forms. The increase in Macomb Linear vessels and Springwells Net-impressed vessels is significant. Springwells Net-impressed serves as the marker for this phase.

The end of the Younge sequence is marked by the Wolf Phase. Vase Dentate is absent in this phase and the other Riviere ware types are found in decreased frequencies. The principle characteristic of this phase is the introduction of Parker Festooned. This is a readily recognizable type and has a wide-spread distribution which will allow us to make some connections with material in other areas.

XVII

RELATIONSHIPS WITH ADJACENT AREAS

In an early synthesis of Upper Great Lakes Archaeology published by Greenman (1939*a*:4), it was suggested that the cultural connections of the Michigan "Owasco" were to the south and east. Greenman later (1953:177) elaborated on this position with the statement, "the whole southeastern part of the lower peninsula of Michigan appears to me to have been an extension of the province of Ontario in late pre-columbian times. This Michigan 'Owasco' is present at sites not yet well known, notably at Riviere au Vase just north of Mount Clemens, the Tessmer site near Rochester, in the upper levels of the Gibraltar site and at other points south of Detroit along the River and Lake Erie shore. From conversation with Wilfrid Jury I believe that the Clearville and Younge sites are closely related."

In the most recent summary of Western Great Lakes archaeology, Quimby (1960:98) takes the position that Michigan Owasco is the westernmost extension of Iroquoian culture. Greenman (1956:12, 1958:90) has suggested that some of the material from southeastern Michigan was actually left by Iroquoian speakers. The writer was inclined toward this position until a re-examination of the literature revealed numerous instances of "Iroquois" pottery being made and used by non-Iroquoian speakers (Griffin 1952*b*:364, Ridley 1957, Ridley 1958:32). We must, however, look toward southwestern Ontario, an area historically occupied by Iroquoian speakers, for analogies to the southeastern Michigan Younge sequence.

The Canadian archaeologist, W. J. Wintemberg, recognized a developmental sequence in the Neutral area in Ontario at a very early period. After his death in 1941, a memorandum on this was found in his papers suggesting a Uren-Middleport-Southwold-Lawson sequence (Alcock 1948). Griffin had suggested that the Iroquois culture was an *in situ* development (1944:368). This position was later re-affirmed by Kidd (1952:82) and by Ritchie and MacNeish (1949:121).

MacNeish (1952:10) felt that the Neutral-Wenro sequence was the best for any Iroquoian group. Since this is the center of Iroquoian concentration which is geographically closest to our area of discussion, it is no accident that this Neutral-Wenro series is similar to the Younge sequence.

In our examination of the ceramics from the Riviere au Vase site we found many similarities to ceramics from the Uren site, the Barrie site and the Barrie-Uren strata at the Frank Bay site. These ceramic similarities were from the later, or Younge Phase, occupation at the Riviere au Vase site. Greenman noted these correspondences in his original Younge site report (1937*a*:96) and Kidd noted this linkage again (1952:75) in his summary of Ontario archaeology. The Younge Phase appears to be at a similar time level to the Uren site. Uren Noded ceramics were actually found at Riviere au Vase where they stood out in sharp contrast to the Riviere wares with similar patterns of decoration.

To my knowledge there are no net-impressed rims similar to those found with the intrusive burials from the Fort Wayne Mound from Ontario. We then must examine the Springwells Phase material from Michigan for possible Ontario connections. Among the trade sherds, or "aberrant sherds" as MacNeish calls them (1952:7), there is a form which appears to be similar to Pound Blank (MacNeish 1952:15-16). This is a type found only at the Pound site (Nash 1939) and the Southwold Earthworks (Jury 1946).

On the other hand, the Parker Festooned of the Wolf Phase is a type with wide connections. This type was defined by Lee (1958*b*) after the appearance of MacNeish's report. MacNeish illustrated a sherd of Parker Festooned (1952:Plate V, 10) which he suggested was a variant of his Uren Corded type from the Lawson site. In his seriation table for the Neutral-Wenro area, however, he did not list Uren Corded as being present at the Lawson site. The complete absence of this variant at the Uren site (Wintemberg 1928) coupled with its high occurrence at the Lawson site (Wintemberg 1939: Plate IV, 8-20) suggests that it is a late type. This type was found at the Wolf site and is the marker for the Wolf Phase which suggests that the Wolf Phase is on a similar time level to the Lawson site in Ontario.

We are able to correlate the last three phases of the southeastern Michigan Younge Tradition with the developmental Neutral sequence in southwestern Ontario. The Younge Phase is the temporal equivalent of the Uren site, the Springwells Phase is contemporary with the Pound and Southwold sites and the Wolf Phase may be placed in approximately the same time period as the Lawson site occupation. In southwestern Ontario the order of this series has been validated by stratigraphy (MacNeish 1952:12-13).

Since MacNeish's 1952 study, actually completed several years earlier (Alcock 1951:10), a number of other studies have appeared which shed additional light on the sequence in this area. MacNeish mentioned the work of Lee on the pre-Iroquoian material in Ontario (1952:81). Lee (1951, 1952, 1958*a*, 1960) has published several brief accounts of his Glen Meyer Focus but its extent is not very clear.

In 1951 Lee designated material found between Port Rowan and Wheatley as the Glen Meyer Focus. He suggested that it fell between Owasco and Uren and that, "statistical analysis has demonstrated trends toward Uren. . ." (1951:45). An additional site was located in a later survey and "sherds and one vessel showing close linkage to Uren" were found (Lee 1952:65). In 1958 Lee spoke of Glen Meyer as a development from ". . .Owasco, as represented at the Krieger site, toward Uren;. . ." (Lee 1958*a*:40). In a paragraph following this statement there are indications that Lee wished to push this material back to a position contemporary with Hopewell.

Ridley (1958:39) suggested that the Boys site, which Lee (1958*a*:39) would call Glen Meyer, was occupied around A.D. 400. We have already pointed out that this was based on the first of a series of dates for the Snell site in New York for which all subsequent dates were considerably later. Ridley's position that the Boys and Barrie sites, and Glen Meyer are contemporary with Owasco in New York (Ridley 1958:38, Lee 1960:53) seems to best fit the evidence. I have the impression that much of the material which falls into the Glen Meyer Focus would fall into the same temporal horizon as the Riviere au Vase and Younge Phases of the southeastern Michigan Younge sequence.

We have noted the correspondences of Kidd's (1954) Krieger site and the Riviere au Vase Phase material from southeastern Michigan. The greater elaboration of ceramic forms in Ontario, which is most marked during later periods, is already evident at the Kreiger site. Cultural connections between these areas are demonstrated by a sherd of Krieger Dentate from the Gibraltar site. Although the entire Younge Tradition is represented in the ceramic collections from Gibraltar, most of the material may be referred to either the Riviere au Vase Phase or the immediately preceding period.

Wilfrid Jury of the University of Western Ontario has excavated a number of sites in southwestern Ontario that bear on our discussion. In the opening paragraph of this section we cited Greenman's statement on the relationship of the Younge site and the Clearville site. The Clearville site (Jury 1941) was stratified and MacNeish (1952:13) believed the early level to be of the same age as the Uren site. An examination of Jury's illustrations suggests a very close similarity to the Parker Earthworks near

Corunna (Lee 1958*b*). The ceramics which Jury illustrated (Jury 1941: Plate III) are duplicated at the Parker Earthwork (Lee 1958*b*: Figure 9), even to the fragment of Parker Festooned (Jury 1941: Plate III, Figure 5). This would place the early occupation at Clearville on a level with Lawson and the Wolf site rather than the Younge and Uren sites.

Jury equated the Crawford site (1948) with the Uren site. He (Jury 1948:8) suggested that Crawford predated the early occupation at Clearville and decided that it was the earliest "Proto-Neutral" site in the area. The Crawford site would be the temporal equivalent of the Younge Phase in southeastern Michigan.

One of the most significant of recent excavations in Ontario was Lee's (1958*b*) work at the Parker Earthwork, only two miles from the St. Clair River. This site has some similarities with sites in both Michigan and Ohio. Lee tentatively suggested (1958*b*: 25) that this material was earlier than Lawson. It would seem, on the basis of Neutral trade sherds at the site and the Parker Festooned sherds at Lawson, that the occupation, or one of the occupations, at these sites fell within the same time period.

Cultural materials similar to those from southeastern Michigan extend south along the shore of Lake Erie into Ohio. Unfortunately much of this area is a "cultural blank" for the Late Woodland period. There is little published information until we reach the Cleveland area.

Greenman (1939*a*:7, 1939*b*:26) noted the relationship of Michigan material and the Whittlesey Focus in Northern Ohio. The Whittlesey Focus was named by Greenman (1937*b*:351) and most of the sites were excavated by him (1935*a*, 1935*b*, 1937*a*). One additional important site, Fairport Harbor, was reported by Morgan and Ellis (1943).

I examined 1,638 rimsherds from the South Park, Tuttle Hill, Reeve, and Fairport Harbor sites. This material was in the collections of the Ohio State Museum in Columbus and was viewed through the courtesy of Mr. Raymond Baby, Curator of Archaeology at the Museum.

Out of the 1,638 rimsherds 1,572, or 96 per cent, fell into four large groups or types. This furnished a basis for a comparison of these four sites which will be presented in another paper dealing with northern Ohio. The remaining 66 rim sherds fell into several categories. Only one of these categories contained material characteristic of the Younge sequence. This was the Parker Festooned type which was represented by 15 rimsherds, 12 of them from the South Park site. This was less than 1 per cent of the total sample from these sites and can be contrasted to the 17 per cent Parker Festooned rim sherds present at the Parker Earthworks and the 42 per cent Parker Festooned rim sherds from the Wolf site.

Greenman (1939*b*:25) mentioned a sherd from the Wolf site which was very similar to a form common in Northern Ohio sites (1939*b*: Plate II, Figure 3, *a*). This sherd has a strip of applique added below the lip which has been notched. I have already referred to this sherd in connection with the Verchave site report. It has a leached shell temper; shell temper is present at all the Whittlesey sites. Variants of this type constitute up to 83 per cent of the ceramics from some of the Whittlesey Focus sites.

There is a single collared rim sherd from the intrusive pits at the Fort Wayne Mound which is duplicated on the Whittlesey sites. This lacks the extreme notching of much of the Whittlesey material but it is duplicated at all of the Ohio sites examined. It is well within the type range for the particular group of Whittlesey ceramics which it most closely resembles. There is an overlap of Whittlesey and Younge material, then, in both the Springwells and Wolf Phases.

In 1939 Greenman (1939*a*:7) placed both the Uren site and the Wolf site in his Whittlesey group. We have already seen that Uren is developmental Neutral or perhaps furnishes a base for both the Huron and Neutral-Wenro sequences. Since there is less than 1 per cent Parker Festooned on Whittlesey sites and less than 1 per cent Whittlesey material in the late Younge Tradition sites, a reinterpretation of this placement is necessary. Instead of placing these sites in a single group they represent contemporary but ethnically distinct groups. The minor components represent either trade between the groups, exchange of women or the products of captive women. There are three distinct cultural traditions surrounding the Lake Erie Basin at this time period and we would expect some cultural contact.

Greenman (1937*b*:351) did not believe that the Whittlesey material could be either Erie or Seneca. Lee (1958*b*:25), admittedly working under the handicap of not having actual sherd counts from the sites under consideration, placed the Wolf and Parker sites in the Whittlesey group and seconded Greenman's position on the lack of a basis for ethnic identification. Greenman, in an earlier publication, had suggested that the Whittlesey material was Erie (1935*a*:9). Morgan and Ellis (1943:57) and later Morgan (1952:97) proposed that this was the most logical identification. For our purposes these arguments mean only that the Younge tradition peoples *may* not have been Erie.

XVIII

DATING THE YOUNGE TRADITION

There is only one radiocarbon date which is directly associated with Younge Tradition material. There are, however, a number of radiocarbon dates from Northeastern North America which serve as contributor dates and can be used to bracket the Younge Tradition. These are given in Figure 19.

The date on Younge material is from the intrusive level at the Fort Wayne Mound and dates the Springwells Phase. This is M741 which places this material at A.D. 1159 ± 75 years (Crane and Griffin 1960, one sigma). Three other samples have been submitted to the University of Michigan Radiocarbon Laboratory for analysis. These should date the Riviere au Vase and Wolf Phases and serve to bracket the Younge Phase.

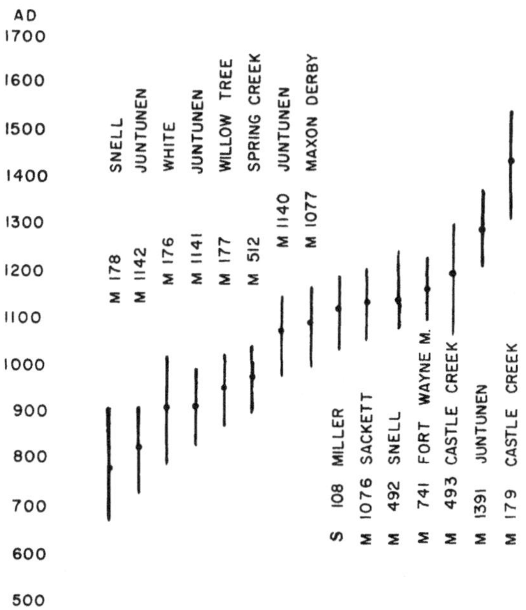

CONTRIBUTOR DATES FOR THE YOUNGE TRADITION.

Fig. 19

Several dates on Michigan material help in dating the Riviere au Vase Phase. Near Black Lake in Cheboygan County, Leonard Griffin (1963) found ceramics resembling the material from the first of the Late Woodland levels at the Juntunen site. This level at Juntunen has been dated to A.D. 835 ± 75 years (M1142, Crane and Griffin 1961, one sigma). The Black Lake collection contained some Wayne Cord-marked material and a few sherds resembling the material from the Spring Creek site. Spring Creek was excavated by George Davis and Edward Gillis of Grand Rapids. This site has a radiocarbon date (M512) of A.D. 967 ± 75 years. These two dates are taken to bracket the Riviere au Vase Phase which might be placed between A.D. 800 and A.D. 1000 with outside limits of A.D. 700 and A.D. 1100.

The other two early dates from the Juntunen site, M1141, A.D. 910 ± 75 years and M1140, A.D. 1070 ± 75 years, appear to date the same type of material (McPherron 1963). They fall within the suggested range and help to bracket this phase in southeastern Michigan.

The only date which might be used to date the Younge Phase is the date from the Miller site in Ontario. This date (S108) is A.D. 1115 + 70 years (MacCallum and Wittenberg 1962). We had suggested that Glen Meyer might be the temporal equivalent of the Riviere au Vase and Younge Phases. Since this is later than the suggested dates for the Riviere au Vase Phase it might date the Younge Phase. An examination of a limited collection of ceramics from the Miller site in the Ceramic Repository at the Museum of Anthropology of the University of Michigan has revealed stylistic elements similar to the late material from the Riviere au Vase site and the Younge site. This limited collection lacks the cord-marked rim sherds of the Riviere au Vase Phase.

In addition to the date from the Fort Wayne Mound, a date from the Juntunen site might be useful in placing the Springwells phase. This date (M1391, unpublished), A.D. 1330 ± 100 years is taken to date "push and pull" pottery at the Juntunen site. This material is related to Macomb Linear which occurs in its highest percentages in the Springwells Phase. These two dates serve as indicators of the span of this phase.

The dates for the New York Owasco sequence, although this material is, at best, distantly related to the Younge Tradition, help to limit the general time period with which we are dealing. There are four dates which circumscribe early Owasco material. These are M178, A.D. 787 ± 100 years (Crane and Griffin 1958, one sigma) for the Snell site; M176, A.D. 905 ± 125 years (Crane 1956, one sigma) for the White site; M177, A.D. 955 ± 125 years

(Crane 1956, one sigma) for the Willow Tree site and M492, A.D. 1157 ± 100 years (Crane and Griffin 1958, one sigma) which is also for the Snell site.

Two dates have been published on New York material described only as Owasco. These are M1077, A.D. 1090 ± 75 years for the Maxon Derby site and M1076, A.D. 1130 ± 75 years (Crane and Griffin 1962, one sigma) for the Sackett site.

Two dates have been published for the Castle Creek site which is a late Owasco site. These are M493, A.D. 1197 ± 100 years (Crane and Griffin 1958, one sigma) and M179, A.D. 1435 ± 100 years (Crane 1956, one sigma).

The relationship of these dates is given in Figure 19. They serve to limit the time period for the first three phases of the Younge Tradition.

A range of A.D. 1000 to A.D. 1200 is suggested for the Younge Phase with outside limits of A.D. 900 and A.D. 1300. The plus range for the material from the Fort Wayne Mound seems to fit more favorably with the other dates as an indicator for the length of the Springwells Phase. A range of A.D. 1200 to A.D. 1400 does not seem unlikely for Springwells Phase of the Younge Tradition. It would not be surprising to have radiocarbon dates for this phase fall anywhere between A.D. 1100 and A.D. 1500. The length of these phases is, of course, unknown. We might be very wrong in assigning equal time spans to each. The beginning and the end dates for this sequence, however, do appear to be fairly well established.

The Wolf Phase has not been directly dated. By a process of elimination it would seem that this material appeared in Michigan some time after A.D. 1400. From the evidence at hand it would all be prehistoric. The Parker Earthworks were prehistoric (Lee 1958*b*) as was the Lawson site (Wintemberg 1939). Greenman established the Whittlesey Focus because he could find no connections with any historic group.

The fact is, we do not know who was living in Michigan in the early historic period. As Bald has pointed out, "Before 1669, no white man had ever visited the Lower Peninsula of Michigan; at least no one had ever reported having been there" (Bald 1954: 33).

A nur ber of attempts have been made to reconstruct the population patterns in Michigan as of A.D. 1600. Quimby (1960: 109) believed Michigan to have been inhabited by Miami, Pottawatomi, and Ottawa; Fenton (1940:178) found evidence for Potawatomi and Mascouten; and Callander (1962:2) believed that the area was occupied by Sauk, Fox, Potawatomi, and Kickapoo.

Kinietz found evidence for refugee groups of Huron in Michigan after A.D. 1649 (1940:2) and for Ottawa (1940:227) and Chippewa (1940:316) being in the lower peninsula at other times during the seventeenth century.

The actual situation was summarized by Greenman (1961:25) in his statement, "The lower peninsula of Michigan was for the most part a sort of no man's land, an empty buffer zone between the Iroquois to the east and the Algonquian tribes—the Potawatomi, Sauk, Fox, Menominee, Mascoutens, and Miami—in eastern Wisconsin. Rumors and legends current after 1670 hint that some of these same tribes had lived in the lower peninsula before 1650, and that they had been driven to the other side of Lake Michigan by the Iroquois."

Since none of the cultural material which we have examined can be dated to the historic period, we have no means of identifying the people who left the Younge sequence material. Any attempt at speculation without detailed examination of the early historic sources would not be productive at present.

Addendum

In July of 1964, after submission of this manuscript for publication, I learned the results of the radiocarbon determination on material from Feature Number 2 at the Verchave II site (20 MB 181). This date (M-1431) was 865 B.P. ± 100 years or A.D. 1085 ± 100 years. In the analysis of Verchave II material I suggested that the material from Feature Number 2 duplicated the later phase of occupation at the Riviere au Vase site. In this chapter, I suggested that the late Riviere au Vase occupation and the entire Younge Phase fell between A.D. 1000 and A.D. 1200.

XX

SUMMARY

The dominant sequence in southeastern Michigan during the Late Woodland period was the Younge Tradition. The type site for this tradition was the Younge site in Lapeer County although more identifiable material was recovered from the Riviere au Vase site where most of the Riviere ware types were defined. Springwells Net-impressed was only represented by three vessels from the Riviere au Vase site, but a large sample from the intrusive pits at the Fort Wayne Mound allowed us to describe this type of Riviere ware.

Four phases were recognized within the Younge Tradition. The earliest is represented by the transitional material from late Middle Woodland to Late Woodland at the Riviere au Vase site and has been called the Riviere au Vase Phase. The second is an early Late Woodland Phase lacking any Middle Woodland elements. This has been referred to as the Younge Phase and is represented at the Younge site and the Riviere au Vase site. The third phase, called the Springwells Phase, is represented by the intrusive level at the Fort Wayne Mound. This is a middle Late Woodland occupation. The fourth phase is the Wolf Phase represented by the Wolf site and several smaller sites. This is a Late Woodland occupation but is still definitely prehistoric.

Trade sherds found at several of these sites allowed us to tie the Younge Tradition to the developmental sequence in Ontario and Ohio.

There is a developmental sequence in southwestern Ontario which parallels that in southeastern Michigan. We have been able to ascribe roughly the same temporal horizon to the Krieger site, some of the material which has been called Glen Meyer, and the Riviere au Vase Phase of the Younge sequence. The Barrie, Uren, and Crawford sites appear to be roughly contemporary with the Younge Phase. On less firm ground we suggested a contemporaneous position for the Springwells Phase and the Middleport-Pound-Southwold level in Ontario. There is fairly good evidence for the temporal equation of the Lawson site, the Parker Earthworks, and the Wolf Phase.

In discussing the archaeological material from Southwestern Ontario, Kidd (1952:75) made the statement, "stronger bonds, no doubt, exist between them (the Clearville, Lawson, and Uren sites) than between any single one and any more distant culture, such

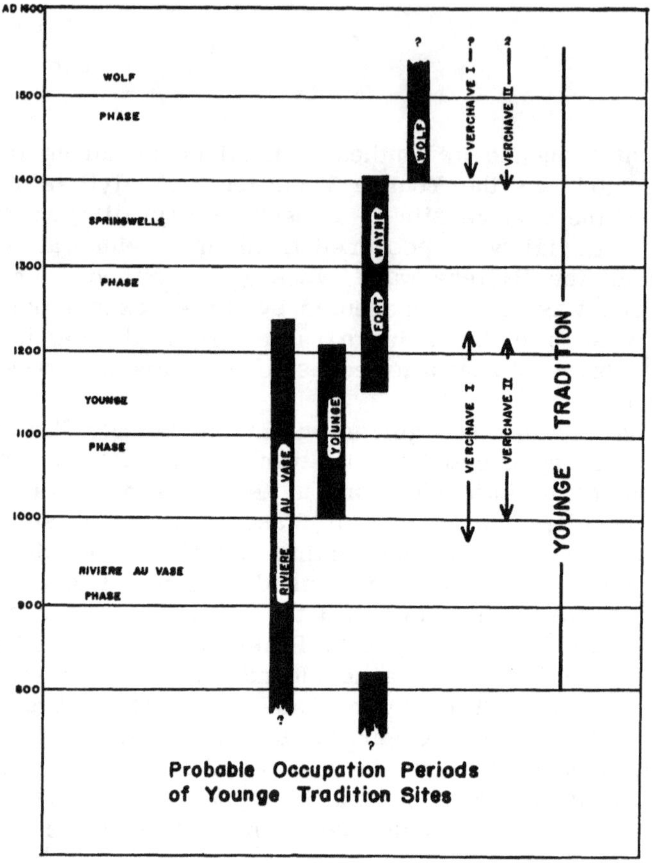

Fig. 20

as the Younge site manifests, despite many apparent link-traits." The reverse is just as true. The sites within the Younge Tradition in southeastern Michigan are closely linked and more similarities are present among these sites, even on different temporal horizons, than between any single site and any surrounding cultural group.

Very little work has been done on Late Woodland material from northern Ohio. The most recent papers on the Whittlesey Focus appeared over twenty years ago. Personal examination of collections from four large Whittlesey sites revealed less than 1 per cent of Younge Tradition ceramic types. Correspondingly less than 1 per cent of Whittlesey types were present in the southeastern Michigan sites which we have discussed.

A re-examination needs to be undertaken of the Late Woodland material in northern Ohio in order to determine its temporal placement. Its late prehistoric position is suggested by the occurrence of Whittlesey forms in Springwells and Wolf Phase sites in southeastern Michigan.

The Younge Tradition developed in southeastern Michigan out of a late Middle Woodland base between A.D. 700 and A.D. 800. A tentative dating is given as A.D. 800 to A.D. 1000 for the Riviere au Vase Phase, A.D. 1000 to A.D. 1200 for the Younge Phase and A.D. 1200 to A.D. 1400 for the Springwells Phase. The Wolf Phase started sometime around A.D. 1400 but there is no evidence that it lasted into the historic period. It was not possible to make an ethnic identification of the people who left the Younge Tradition material.

APPENDIX

SOME SOUTHEASTERN MICHIGAN POTTERY TYPES

The following list describes the ceramic types used and illustrated in this report. The number of vessels from each site refers to the minimum number represented by the rim sherds in the collection from the site. The two series, Riviere ware and Wayne ware, are described separately.

Riviere Ware

Vase Dentate	(Plates X, A, XI, XII; Greenman 1937*b:* Plate XVII, Figure 2, A, 1939*b*, Plate VII, Figure 2, d).
Sample:	Total, 93 vessels. (Riviere au Vase, 83; Younge, 7; Fort Wayne Mound, 2; Gibraltar, 1).
Paste:	(See Harper 1945).
Temper:	Sand and crushed granitic material. Some particles over 2.0 mm in diameter, predominently medium to coarse particles.
Texture:	Laminated and friable.
Hardness:	2.0 - 2.5.
Color:	Smokey grey and buff to light brown and cinnamon.
Surface Finish:	Cord-marked paddle and coarse fabric-wrapped paddle over entire surface. Shoulder area may be smoothed over.
Decoration:	
Design:	Oblique to vertical impressions along the rim. Several instances of herringbone.
Technique:	Impressions made with a dentate stamp or comb. In several instances these appear as a series of punctates but the regularity of the punctate pattern suggests that a wide-toothed comb or dentate tool was used. The lip and interior of the rim may be decorated with the same tool.
Form:	
Rim:	Collars are common but castellations are rare. Collared (Type A) and wedge-shaped (Type C) rims are most common. Rims are straight to slightly outflaring.
Neck:	Slightly constricted.
Lip:	Flat to outsloping.
Body:	Unknown. Probably globular to slightly elongated.
Base:	Unknown. Probably rounded to semiconoidal.
Geographical Range:	Known from several sites in southeastern Michigan. This type was completely absent in the available collections from northern and western Michigan.
Chronological Position:	Transitional period from Middle to Late Woodland (Type C rims ?) and Late Woodland (Type A rims ?).

Probable Relationship: This type represents a local variant of a horizon style which includes Jack's Reef Dentate Collar (Ritchie and MacNeish 1949:106), Boys Oblique Dentate (Ridley 1958:29), Scugog Oblique Dentate (Ridley 1958:31) and Krieger Dentate (Kidd 1954: 168).

Vase Tool-impressed (Plate XVII; Greenman 1937*b:* Plate XVIII, Figure 1, A, D, E, 1939*b*, Plate III, Figure 1, e, h).

Sample: Total 86 vessels. (Riviere au Vase, 69; Fort Wayne Mound, 8; Younge, 5; Wolf, 4).

Paste: Same as Vase Dentate.

Surface Finish: Cord-marked, fabric-impressed and roughened or washed examples are known.

Decoration

Design: Oblique to vertical impressions along the rim. Several instances of herringbone.

Technique: The impressions are made with a solid tool. The modal technique is a single impression with a wide tool. There are instances which look as though a pointed tool has been trailed along the surface, but this variant is rare. The lip and interior rim may be decorated with the same tool or with a cord-wrapped stick or paddle edge.

Form

Rim: Castellations are to be expected. Collared (Type A) rims are most common but other types are encountered. Rims are straight to slightly outflaring.

Neck: Slightly constricted.

Lip: Flat.

Body: Unknown. Probably slightly to greatly elongated.

Base: Rounded to semiconoidal.

Geographical Range: Southeastern Michigan and, probably, adjacent areas of Ontario and Ohio.

Chronological Position: Late Woodland. Uncollared variants may be early and collared variants late.

Probable Relationship: This type appears to be part of a widespread horizon. Uncollared forms have parallels in Krieger Incised (Kidd 1954: 167-68), rare variants of Owasco Herringbone (Ritchie and MacNeish 1949:110-11) and Castle Creek Beaded (Ritchie and MacNeish 1949:114). Generically related forms are found in the Barrie-Uren Stratum at the Frank Bay site (Ridley 1954: 47). Also similar to Ridley's Impressed Oblique (1958:29) and MacNeish's Ontario Oblique and Uren Noded (1952:18). Ridley sees this as a development out of Scugog Oblique Dentate with a smooth tool substituted for a dentate tool. This is not at all incompatible with the observed Michigan sequence.

Vase Corded (Plate XVIII; Greenman 1937*b*: Plate IV, Greenman 1939*b*: Plate XVII, Figure 1, F, Figure 2, C).

Sample: Total, 107 vessels. (Riviere au Vase, 78; Fort Wayne Mound, 10; Younge, 11; Wolf, 6; Gibraltar, 2).
Paste: Same as Vase Dentate.
Surface Finish: Predominantly roughened or washed with several instances of coarse cord marking or fabric impressions.
Decoration
Design: Oblique to vertical impressions along the rim. Occasional herringbone.
Technique: The modal technique for executing this design is a cord-wrapped stick or the edge of a cord-wrapped paddle. Several examples bear the impression of a cord-wrapped cord or cord-wrapped twigs. One example may have been a knotted cord. The same type of impressions are common on the lip and interior of the rim.
Form
Rim: Predominately castellated. Both collared and uncollared variants were present. These perhaps have temporal significance.
Neck: Slightly constricted.
Body: Elongated.
Base: Rounded.
Geographical Range: Southeastern Michigan and, possibly, adjacent areas of Ontario and Ohio.
Chronological Position: Late Woodland. Uncollared variants may be early and collared variants late.
Probable Relationship: This type has a limited geographical distribution. Uncollared examples might be related to Krieger Stamped (Kidd 1954: 168) and some of the sherds which MacNeish has classified as Uren Corded (1952:19).

Macomb Linear (Plates XIII, XIV, XV, XVI; Greenman 1937*b:* Plate XVII, Figure 1, C, D, E, Plate XIX, Figure 2, D, E; Greenman 1939*b:* Plate II, Figure 2, a, e, g, h, Plate VII, Figure 2, c, h).
Sample: Total 88 vessels. (Riviere au Vase, 42; Fort Wayne Mound, 24; Wolf, 14; Younge, 8).
Paste: (See Harper 1945).
Temper: Sand and crushed granitic material with particles up to and over 2.0 mm in diameter. Medium to coarse particles common with the latter predominating.
Texture: Laminated and friable.
Hardless: 2.0 - 2.5.
Color: Smokey grey and buff to light brown and cinnamon.
Surface Finish: Predominately roughened, some smoothed over cord and rarely cord-marked or coarse fabric-impressed.
Decoration
Design: Horizontal impressions interrupted by occasional triangles. These impressions may run parallel to the base of the collar but in many vessels there is a tendency toward following the castellations.

Technique: Two variants were observed which might prove to have temporal or cultural significance although none was noted in this study. Because of the small size these have been grouped into a single type.
Variant: Macomb Linear Corded (Plates XIII, XIV, XV). The horizontal design, in this instance, is executed with either a cord-wrapped stick, cord-wrapped cord or, very rarely, a knotted single cord giving an impression similar to that of a cord-wrapped cord.
Variant: Macomb Interrupted-linear (Plate XVI). Here the horizontal design is executed by means of short, overlapping incisions. This has been called "push and pull" or "stab and drag." There is a strong tendency toward interior rim and lip decoration with the same tool.

Form
Rim: Almost all vessels examined showed evidence of castellations. Collared (Type A) and squared (Type D) rims dominated the sample.
Neck: Constricted.
Lip: Flat.
Body: Elongated to extremely elongated.
Base: Rounded to semiconoidal.

Geographical Range: Southeastern Michigan and adjacent areas into the northern part of the lower peninsula of Michigan. Some of the Juntunen site vessels are of this type. It seems to be absent in western and southwestern Michigan.

Chronological Position: Late Woodland. This seems to be a middle to late Late Woodland type in this area.

Probable Relationship: This material is similar to McPherron's ". . .second readily distinguishable ware" (1963:573). Generic similarities might be noted to some of MacNeish's Uren Corded (1952:19-20) and Iroquois Linear (1952:19) and Ridley's Iroquoian Linear (1958:22-28) as well as Ritchie and MacNeish's Owasco Corded Collar (1949:112-14) and Bainbridge Linear (1949:115-16).

Springwells Net-impressed (Plate XLVIII).
Sample: Total, 31 vessels. (Riviere au Vase, 3; Fort Wayne Mound, 22; Wolf, 6).
Paste: Same as Vase Dentate.
Surface Treatment: Only roughened and smoothed cord-marked surfaces have been noted.

Decoration
Design: Fine to coarse or netlike loosely woven fabric.
Technique: Probably applied with a fabric-wrapped paddle although some sherds look like the fabric or net was stretched over the moist unfired rim.

Form
Rim: All known rims are collared (Type A) and many are castellated. The rims are straight to slightly outflaring.

Neck: Constricted.
Body: Unknown. Probably elongated.
Base: Unknown. Probably rounded to semiconoidal.
Geographical Range: Southeastern Michigan and, possibly, adjacent areas of Ontario and Ohio.
Chronological Position: Late Woodland.
Probable Relationship: Unknown

Wayne Ware

Wayne Cord-marked (Plates III, IV, VI, X, A; Quimby 1941: Plate I, A; Greenman 1945: Plate I, 4, 5).
Sample: Total, 91 vessels. (Riviere au Vase, 53; Fort Wayne Mound, 30; Gibraltar, 8).
Paste (See Harper 1945).
Temper: Sand and crushed granitic material. Particles ranging up to 1.46 mm in diameter.
Texture: Laminated and friable.
Hardness: 2.0 - 2.5.
Color: Grey buff to grey, rarely orange to cinnamon.
Surface Finish: Impressions made by a cord-wrapped paddle are modal. Some smoothed over cord-marking and some examples seem to have been treated with fabric-wrapped paddles.
Decoration
Design: Most examples lacked specific decoration, but where present it consisted of horizontal or oblique impressions.
Technique: Normally the cord-wrapped paddle impressions are found up to the lip. A number of variants have been noted which may have temporal significance. The present sample is too small for the establishment of separate types.
Variant: Wayne Cord-marked (Plates III, IV, VI, X, A). This is the most common form with cord marking up to the lip.
Variant: Wayne Smoothed (Plates VII, VIII). Here the cord marking on the rim and upper portions of the body has been smoothed over.
Variant: Wayne Punctate (Plate IX). The cord-wrapped paddle impressions have been altered by punctation with a plain tool with a rounded or wedge-shaped tip.
Variant: Wayne Corded Punctate. Similar to Wayne Punctate but a cord-wrapped stick was used for punctation. This variant was present at the Fort Wayne Mound.
Variant: Wayne Cord-impressed. Here the otherwise plain cord-marked neck is altered with the impression of a single cord.
Variant: Wayne Crosshatched. The rim has been decorated with criss-cross incisions on this variant. Lip decoration, which is relatively rare, takes the form of cord-wrapped

stick or paddle edge impressions (the modal technique) and parallel to oblique or criss-cross tool impressions. Occasionally a single cord is impressed into the lip around the circumference of the vessel opening.

Form

Rim: Uncollared, no castellations, rare thickening appears as a "pseudo" or incipient collar on some forms. Rims straight to outflaring.

Lip: Predominantly rounded with minor occurrences of thickened outsloping lips.

Body: Globular to slightly elongated.

Base: Semiconoidal to rounded.

Geographical Range: Occurs as a dominant form in southeastern Michigan and, possibly, in adjacent areas of Ontario and Ohio. It is found as far north as Cheboygen County and as far west as Kent County, Michigan.

Chronological Position: Middle to late Middle Woodland. Some of the variants appear to have temporal significance.

Probable Relationship: This type may be related to the pottery from the Esch Mounds in northern Ohio (Greenman 1939*a*). It is on a temporal horizon with the late Scioto Tradition developments (Prufer: personal communication) and the later decorated ceramics from the Krieger site in Ontario (Kidd 1954). There are also generic relationships with the Intrusive Mound Culture in Ohio (Morgan 1952:93, Mills 1922) and late Point Peninsula forms such as Jack's Reef Cord-marked (Ritchie and MacNeish 1949:106) in New York.

REFERENCES CITED

Alcock, F. J.

1948 Preface to The Middleport Prehistoric Village Site. National Museum of Canada, Bulletin No. 109, p. v. Ottawa.

1951 General Activities of the National Museum of Canada. *In:* Annual Report of the National Museum of Canada for the Fiscal Year 1949-50. *Ibid.*, No. 123, pp. 1-23. Ottawa.

Bald, F. Clever

1954 Michigan in Four Centuries. New York: Harper & Brothers.

Binford, Lewis R.

1962. A New Method of Calculating Dates from Kaolin Pipe Stem Samples. Southeastern Archaeological Conference Newsletter, Vol. 9, No. 1, pp. 19-21. Cambridge, Mass.

Blois, John T.

1838 Gazetteer of Michigan. Detroit: Sidney L. Rod and Co.; New York: Robinson, Pratt and Co.

1958 Excavations of a Burial Mound near Fort Wayne, Detroit. Michigan Archaeologist, Vol. 4, No. 4, pp. 73-75. Ann Arbor.

Callender, Charles

1962 Social Organization of the Central Algonquian Indians. Milwaukee Public Museum Publications in Anthropology, No. 7. Milwaukee, Wis.

Crane, H. R.

1956 University of Michigan Radiocarbon Dates I. *Science*, Vol. 124, No. 3224, pp. 664-72. Lancaster, Pa.

Crane, H. R., and Griffin, James B.

1958 University of Michigan Radiocarbon Dates II. *Ibid.*, Vol. 127, No. 3306, pp. 1098-1105.

1960 University of Michigan Radiocarbon Dates V. *In:* American Journal of Science Radiocarbon Supplement, Vol. 2, pp. 31-48. New Haven, Conn.

1961 University of Michigan Radiocarbon Dates VI. *In:* Radiocarbon, Vol. 3, pp. 105-25. New Haven, Conn.

1962 University of Michigan Radiocarbon Dates VII. *Ibid.*, Vol. 4, pp. 183-203.

DeVisscher, Jerry

1957 Three Macomb County "Copper and Mica" Burials. The Totem Pole, Vol. 40, No. 4, unpaged. Detroit.

Dixon, Wilfrid J., and Massey, Frank J., Jr.

1957 Introduction to Statistical Analysis. New York: McGraw-Hill Book Co., Inc.

Dustin, Fred

1932 Report on Indian Earthworks in Ogemaw County, Michigan. Cranbrook Institute of Science, Scientific Publications No. 1. Bloomfield Hills.

Farmer, Silas
1884 The History of Detroit and Michigan. Detroit: Silas Farmer and Co.

Fenton, William N.
1940 Problems Arising From the Historic Northeastern Position of the Iroquois. *In:* Essays in Historical Anthropology in North America. Smithsonian Miscellaneous Collections, Vol. 100 (whole Volume), pp. 159-253. Washington, D. C.

Gillman, Henry
1877 Investigations of the Burial Mound at Fort Wayne, on the Detroit River, Michigan. Proceedings of the American Association for the Advancement of Science, 25th Meeting, pp. 311-25. Salem, Mich.
1958 Investigations of the Burial Mound at Fort Wayne, on the Detroit River, Michigan. Michigan Archaeologist, Vol. 4, No. 3, pp. 56-63. Ann Arbor.

Greenman, Emerson F.
1935*a* Excavation of the Reeve Village site, Lake County, Ohio. The Ohio State Archaeological and Historical Quarterly, Vol. 44, No. 1, pp. 2-64. Columbus.
1935*b* Seven Prehistoric Sites in Northern Ohio. *Ibid.*, No. 2, pp. 220-37. Columbus.
1937*a* The Younge Site: An Archaeological Record From Michigan. Occasional Contributions from the Museum of Anthropology of the University of Michigan, No. 6. Ann Arbor.
1937*b* Two Prehistoric Villages near Cleveland, Ohio. The Ohio State Archaeological and Historical Quarterly, Vol. 46, No. 4, pp. 305-66. Columbus.
1939*a* Cultural Relationships of Archaeological Sites in the Upper Great Lakes Region. Papers of the Michigan Academy of Science, Arts, and Letters, Vol. 24, Pt. 4, pp. 1-10. Ann Arbor: The University of Michigan Press.
1939*b* The Wolf and Furton Sites, Macomb County, Michigan. Occasional Contributions from the Museum of Anthropology of the University of Michigan, No. 8. Ann Arbor.
1945 The Hopewellian in the Detroit-Windsor Area. Papers of the Michigan Academy of Science, Arts and Letters, Vol. 30, pp. 457-64. Ann Arbor.
1953 Review of: Sixty Years of Ontario Archeology by Kenneth E. Kidd and the Archeology of the Upper Great Lakes by George I. Quimby. American Antiquity, Vol. 19, No. 2, pp. 176-77. Salt Lake City: University of Utah.
1956 The Woodland Culture in Michigan. Michigan Archaeological Society News, Vol. 2, No. 3, pp. 7-12. Ann Arbor.
1957 Riviere au Vase Site. A Preliminary Report. Michigan Archaeologist, Vol. 3, No. 1, pp. 9-11. Ann Arbor.
1958 Prehistoric Detroit. *Ibid.*, Vol. 4, No. 4, pp. 81-98.
1961 The Indians of Michigan. The John M. Munson Michigan History Fund Pamphlets, No. 5. Lansing.

Griffin, James B.
1944 The Iroquois in American Prehistory. Papers of the Michigan Academy of Science, Arts and Letters, Vol. 39, pp. 357-74. Ann Arbor: The University of Michigan Press.
1952*a* Archeology of the Eastern United States (editor). Chicago: The University of Chicago Press.
1952*b* Culture Periods in Eastern United States Archeology. *In:* Archeology of the Eastern United States edited by James B. Griffin. Chicago: The University of Chicago Press.
1952*c* Some Early and Middle Woodland Pottery Types in Illinois. *In:* Hopewellian Communities in Illinois edited by Thorne Deuel. Scientific Papers, Illinois State Museum, Vol. 5, No. 3, pp. 93-129. Springfield.

Griffin, Leonard
1962 An Interim Report on the Root Site. Michigan Archaeologist, Vol. 8, No. 2, pp. 10-15. Ann Arbor.
1963 The Eisen Site: A New Concept in Amateur Archaeological Endeavor. *Ibid.*, Vol. 9, No. 4, pp. 73-78. Ann Arbor.

Guthe, Alfred Kidder
1948 A Survey of the Woodland Pattern in Michigan. (Master's thesis.) University of Chicago.

Harper, Victoria G.
1945 A Ceramic Study of the Riviere au Vase Site in Southeastern Michigan. Papers of the Michigan Academy of Science, Arts and Letters, Vol. 30, pp. 479-91. Ann Arbor: The University of Michigan Press.

Hinsdale, W. B.
1930 Reports of Archaeological Field Work in the Summer of 1928 in Montmorency, Newago and Lake Counties, Michigan. *Ibid.*, Vol. 12, pp. 127-35.

Holmquist, Carl E.
1946 The Fort Wayne Mound. Aboriginal Research Club Bulletin. Detroit.

Hubbard, Bela
1887 Memorials of a Half-Century. New York and London: G. P. Putnam's Sons.
1958 The Great Mound at the Mouth of the Rouge River. Michigan Archaeologist, Vol. 4, No. 4, pp. 75-81. Ann Arbor.

Jury, Wilfrid
1941 Clearville Prehistoric Village Site in Oxford Township, Kent County, Ontario. Bulletin of the Museums, University of Western Ontario, No. 2. London, Canada.
1946 Southwold Prehistoric Earthworks. The Canadian Historical Review. Vol. 27, No. 4, pp. 391-93. Toronto, Canada.
1948 Crawford Prehistoric Village Site. Bulletin of the Museums, University of Western Ontario, No. 7. London, Canada.

Kidd, Kenneth E.
1952 Sixty Years of Ontario Archeology. *In:* Archeology of the Eastern United States, edited by James B. Griffin. Chicago: The University of Chicago Press.
1954 A Woodland Site near Chatham, Ontario. Transactions of the Royal Canadian Institute, Vol. 30, Pt. 2, pp. 141-78. Ottawa, Canada.

Kinietz, Vernon
1940 Indians of the Western Great Lakes. Occasional Contributions from the Museum of Anthropology of the University of Michigan, No. 10. Ann Arbor.

Lee, Thomas E.
1951 A Preliminary Report on an Archaeological Survey of Southwestern Ontario in 1949. In: Annual Report of the National Museum of Canada for the Fiscal Year 1949-50. National Museum of Canada, Bulletin No. 123, pp. 42-48. Ottawa, Canada.
1952 A Preliminary Report on an Archaeological Survey of Southwestern Ontario in 1950. *In:* Annual Report of the National Museum of Canada for the Fiscal Year 1950-51. *Ibid.*, No. 126, pp. 64-75.
1958*a* Appendix. *In:* The Boys and Barrie Sites by Frank Ridley. Ontario Archaeological Society Publication No. 4, pp. 40-41. Toronto, Canada.
1958*b* The Parker Earthwork, Corunna, Ontario. Pennsylvania Archaeologist, Vol. 28, No. 1, pp. 3-30. Honesdale, Pa.
1960 The Lucas Site, Inverhuron, Ontario. *In:* Contributions to Anthropology, 1958. National Museum of Canada, Bulletin No. 167, pp. 29-65. Ottawa, Canada.

MacNeish, Richard S.
1952 Iroquois Pottery Types: A Technique for the Study of Iroquois Prehistory. *Ibid.*, No. 124. Ottawa, Canada.

MacCallum, K. J., and Wittenberg, J.
1962 University of Saskatchewan Radiocarbon Dates III. *In:* Radiocarbon, Vol. 4, pp. 71-81. New Haven, Conn.

McPherron, Alan L.
1963 Late Woodland Ceramics in the Straits of Mackinac. Papers of the Michigan Academy of Science, Arts and Letters, Vol. 48, Pt. 2, pp. 567-76. Ann Arbor: The University of Michigan Press.

Mills, William C.
1922 Exploration of the Mound City Group. Ohio State Archaeological and Historical Quarterly, Vol. 31, No. 4, pp. 423-584. Columbus.

Morgan, Richard G.
1952 Outline of Cultures in the Ohio Region. *In:* Archeology of the Eastern United States, edited by James B. Griffin. Chicago: The University of Chicago Press.

Morgan, Richard G., and Ellis, H. Holmes
1943 The Fairport Harbor Village Site. The Ohio State Archaeological and Historical Quarterly, Vol. 52, No. 1, pp. 1-62. Columbus.

Morse, Dan F.
1963 The Steuben Village and Mounds; A Multicomponent Late Hopewell Site in Illinois. Museum of Anthropology, University of Michigan, Anthropological Paper No. 21. Ann Arbor.

Nash, Philleo
1939 The Pound Village Site, Elgin County, Ontario. Society for American Archeology Notebook, pp. 74-75.

Omwake, H. G.
1961 Peter Dorni White Kaolin Pipes. The Archeological Society of New Jersey, Bulletin Nos. 18-19, pp. 12-15. Trenton.
n.d. Report of Examination of White Kaolin Pipe Bowl and Stem Fragments from Various Sites on Isle Royal. (Manuscript in possession of Tyler Bastian.)

Peske, G. Richard
1963 Argillite of Michigan: A Preliminary Projectile Point Classification and Temporal Placement from Surface Materials. Papers of the Michigan Academy of Science, Arts and Letters, Vol. 48, Pt. 2, pp. 557-66. Ann Arbor: The University of Michigan Press.

Pilling, Arnold R.
1961*a* Six Archaeological Sites in the Detroit Area. Part I. Michigan Archaeologist, Vol. 7, No. 3, pp. 13-30. Ann Arbor.
1961*b* Six Archaeological Sites in the Detroit Area. Part II. *Ibid.*, No. 4, pp. 33-54.
1963 Cultural Material on the 585-foot and 605-foot Beach Lines of the Western Shore of Lake St. Clair. (Abstract.) *Ibid.*, Vol. 9, No. 2, pp. 15-16.

Quimby, George I. Jr.
1941 Hopewellian Pottery Types in Michigan. Papers of the Michigan Academy of Science, Arts and Letters, Vol. 26, pp. 489-94. Ann Arbor: The University of Michigan Press.
1943 The Ceramic Sequence within the Goodall Focus. *Ibid.*, Vol. 28, pp. 443-48. Ann Arbor.
1952 The Archeology of the Upper Great Lakes Area. *In:* Archeology of the Eastern United States, edited by James B. Griffin. Chicago: The University of Chicago Press.
1960 Indian Life in the Upper Great Lakes. The University of Chicago Press. Chicago.

Ridley, Frank
1954 The Frank Bay Site, Lake Nippising, Ontario. American Antiquity, Vol. 20, No. 1, pp. 40-50. Salt Lake City: The University of Utah.
1957 Cultural Contacts of Iroquoian and Plains. Pennsylvania Archaeologist, Vol. 27, No. 1, pp. 33-38. Honesdale, Pa.

1958 The Boys and Barrie Sites. Ontario Archeological Society Publication No. 4, pp. 18-42. Toronto.
1961 Archaeology of the Neutral Indians. Etobicoke Historical Society. Toronto, Canada.

Ritchie, William A.
1961 A Typology and Nomenclature for New York Projectile Points. New York State Museum and Science Service, Bulletin No. 384. Albany.

Ritchie, William A., and MacNeish, Richard S.
1949 The Pre-Iroquoian Pottery of New York State. American Antiquity, Vol. 15, No. 2, pp. 97-124. Menasha, Wis.

Sackett, Richard R.
1943 Historical Clay Pipes of the Minnesota Area. The Minnesota Archaeologist, Vol. 9, No. 3, pp. 68-82. Minneapolis.

Scully, Edward G.
1951 Some Central Mississippi Valley Projectile Point Types. Museum of Anthropology, University of Michigan. (Mimeographed.) Ann Arbor.

Spaulding, Albert C.
1960 Statistical Description and Comparison of Artifact Assemblages. *In:* The Application of Quantitative Methods in Archaeology, ed. Robert F. Heizer and Sherburne F. Cooke, pp. 60-83. Viking Fund Publications in Anthropology, No. 28. Chicago.

Wahla, Edward J.
1963 Chips from the Totem Pole, November, 1963. Detroit.

White, Anta M.
1963 Analytic Description of the Chipped-stone Industry from Snyders Site, Calhoun County, Illinois. *In:* Miscellaneous Studies in Typology and Classification. University of Michigan Museum of Anthropology, Anthropological Paper No. 19, pp. 1-70. Ann Arbor.

Wintemberg, William J.
1928 Uren Prehistoric Village Site, Greenville County, Ontario. National Museum of Canada, Bulletin No. 83. Ottawa.
1939 Lawson Prehistoric Village Site, Middlesex County, Ontario. *Ibid.*, Bulletin No. 94. Ottawa.
1948 The Middleport Prehistoric Village Site. *Ibid.*, Bulletin No. 109. Ottawa.

Willey, Gordon R., and Phillips, Phillip
1962 Method and Theory in American Archaeology. Chicago: The University of Chicago Press.

Witthoft, John W.
1957 The Art of Flint Chipping. Ohio Archaeologist, Vol. 7, No. 2, pp. 42-46. Columbus.

Wright, J. V., and Anderson, J. E.
1963 The Donaldson Site. National Museum of Canada, Bulletin No. 184. Ottawa, Canada.

PLATES

PLATE I

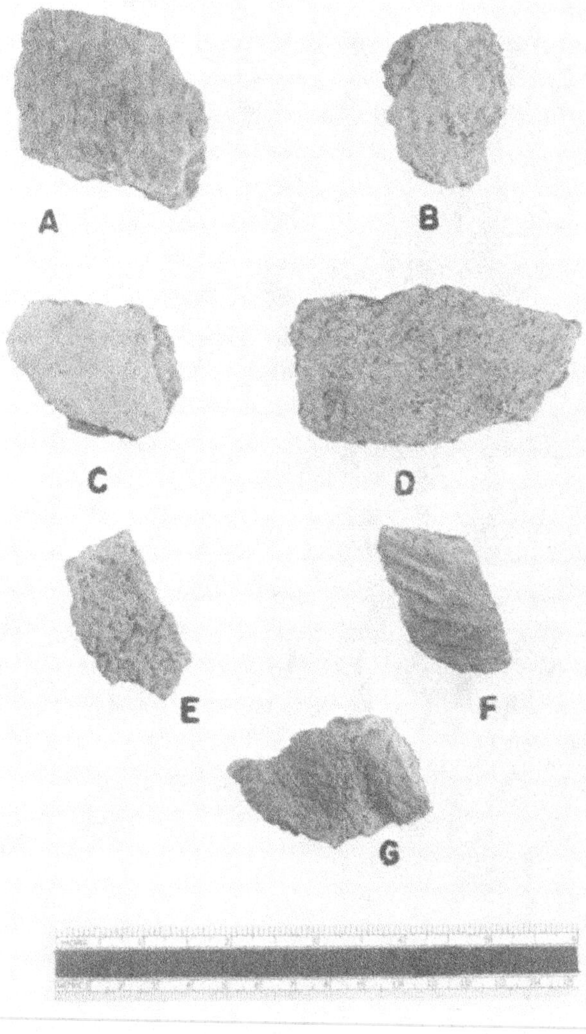

Types of surface treatment found on sherds from Riviere au Vase

A) cord-marked; B) smoothed cord-marked; C) smoothed; D) roughened; E) fabric-impressed; F) simple-stamped; G) brushed.

PLATE II

Incised shoulder fragments from vessel found near Flat Rock, Michigan

PLATE III

Wayne Cord-marked vessel from the Riviere au Vase site (20 MB 3)

PLATE IV

Wayne Cord-marked rim sherds from the Riviere au Vase site (20 MB 3)

PLATE V

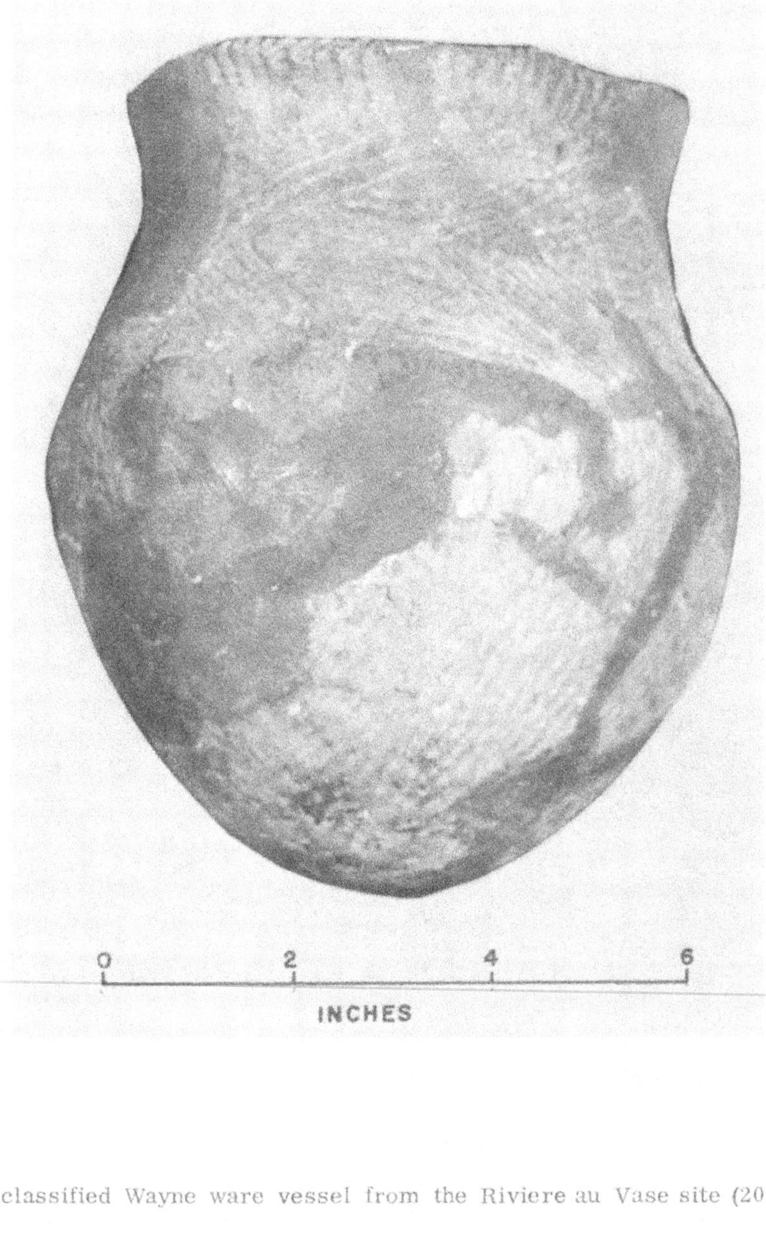

Unclassified Wayne ware vessel from the Riviere au Vase site (20 MB3)

PLATE VI

Wayne Cord-marked vessel from the Riviere au Vase site (20 MB 3)

PLATE VII

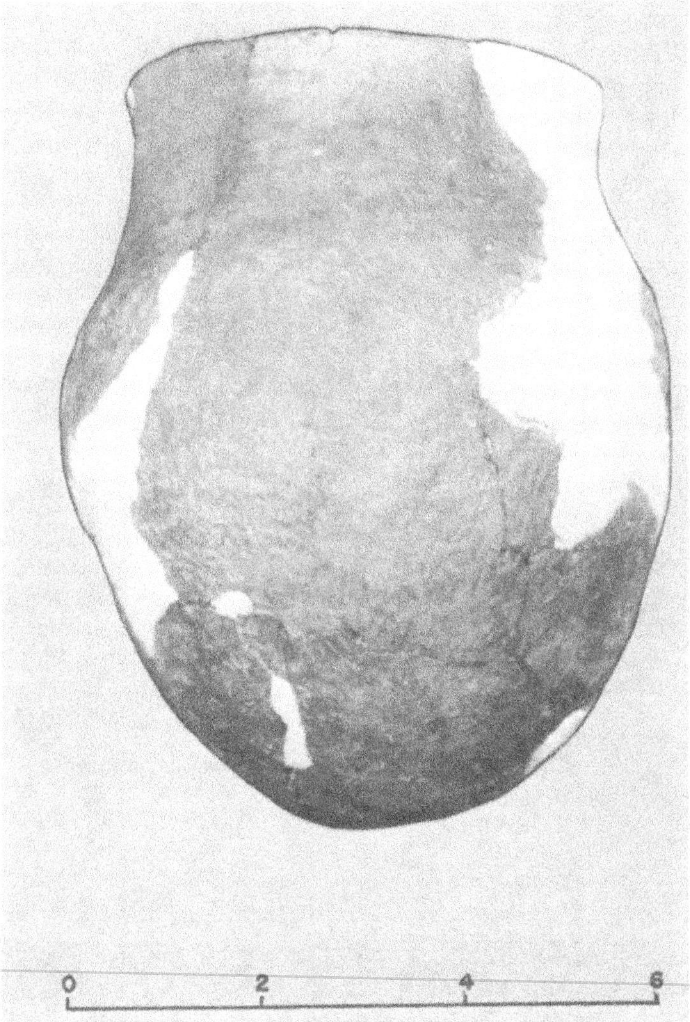

Wayne Smoothed vessel from the Riviere au Vase site (20 MB 3)

PLATE VIII

Wayne Smoothed rim sherds from the Riviere au Vase site

PLATE IX

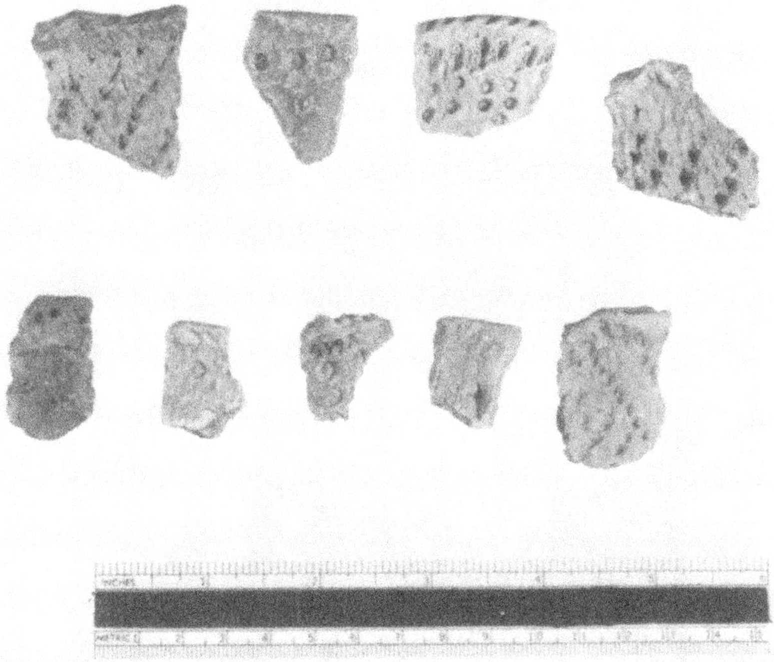

Wayne Punctate rim sherds from the Riviere au Vase site (20 MB 3)

PLATE X

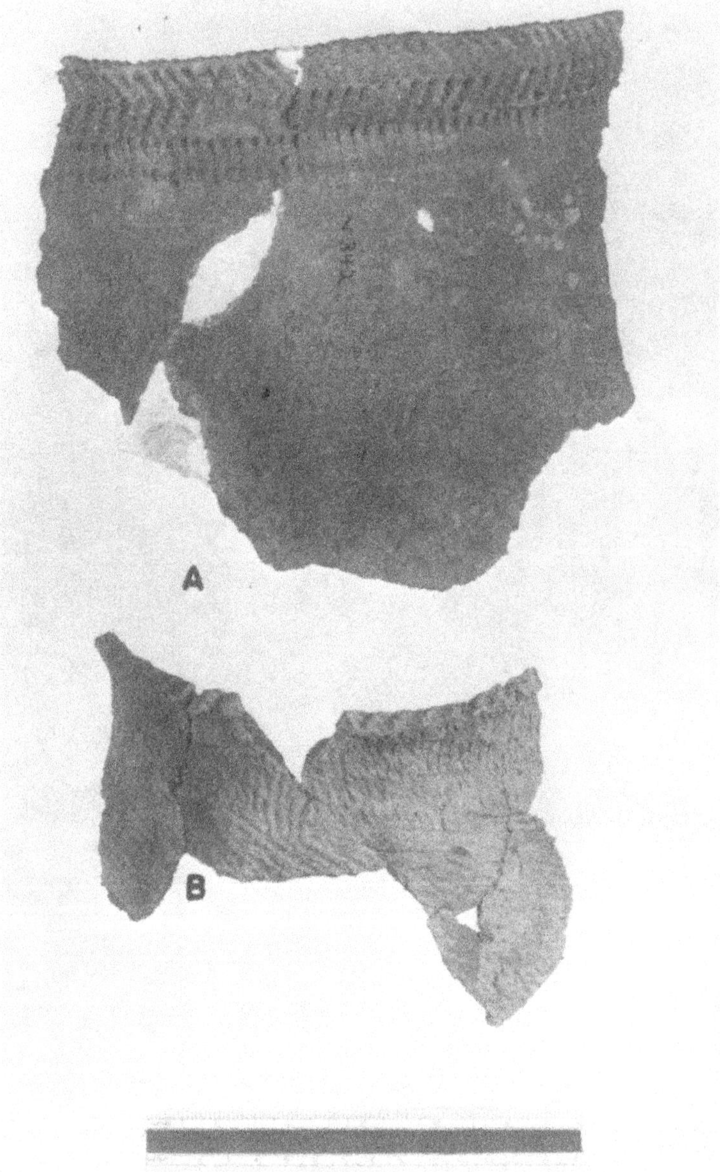

Rim sherds from the Riviere au Vase site (20 MB 3)
A) Vase Dentate; B) Wayne Cord-marked.

PLATE XI

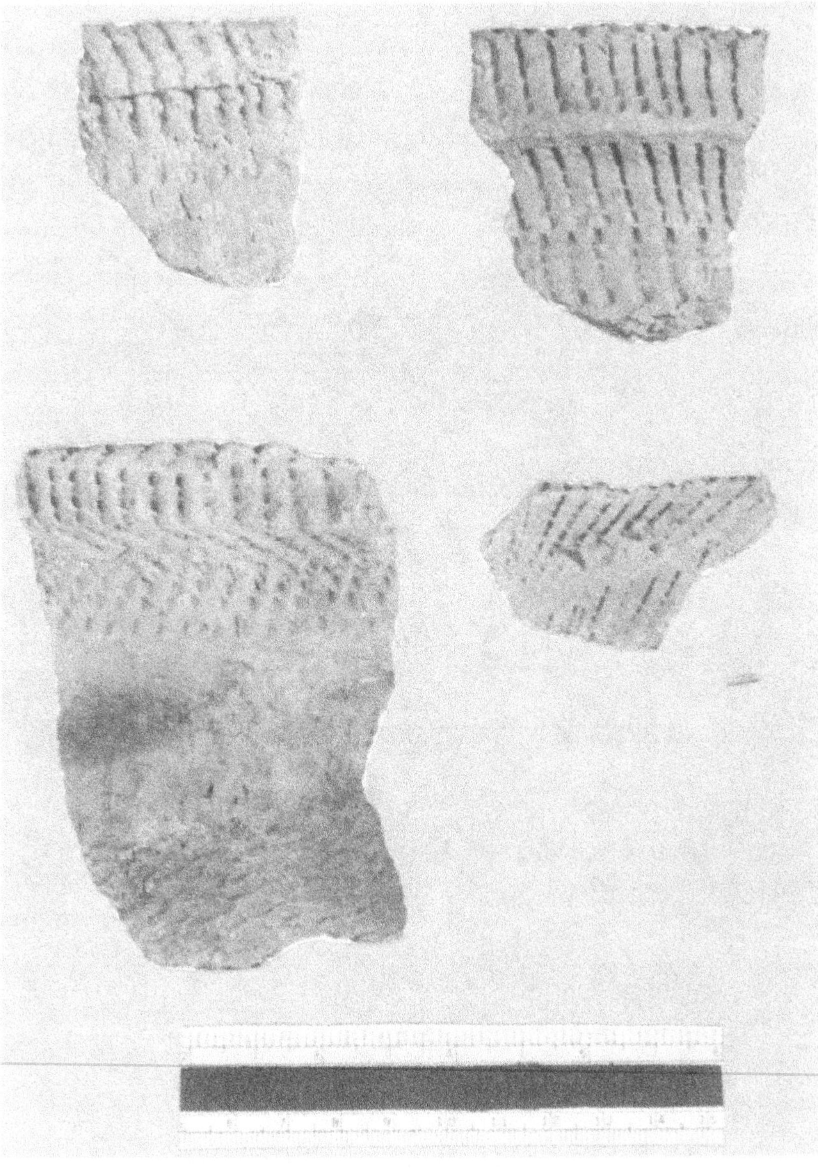

Vase Dentate rim sherds from the Riviere au Vase site (20 MB 3)

PLATE XII

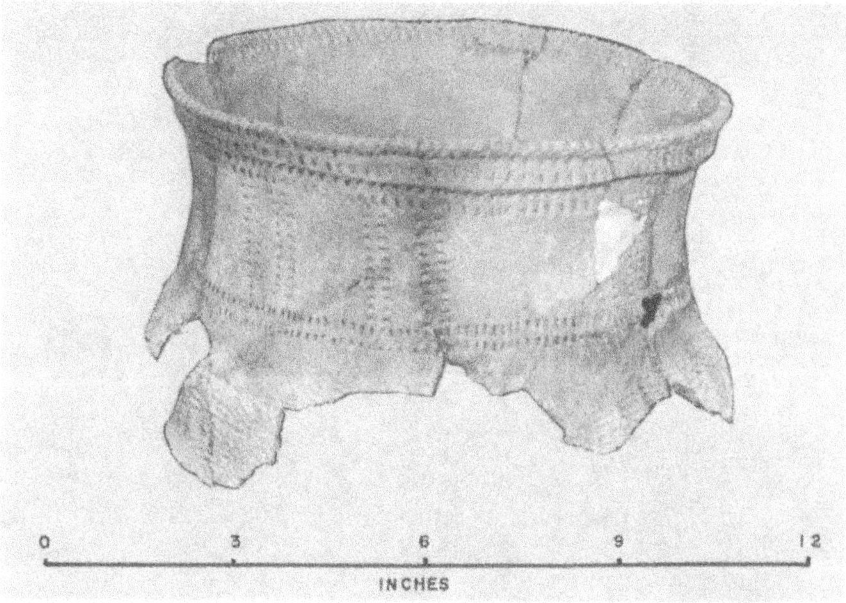

Vase Dentate vessel from the Riviere au Vase site (20 MB 3)

PLATE XIII

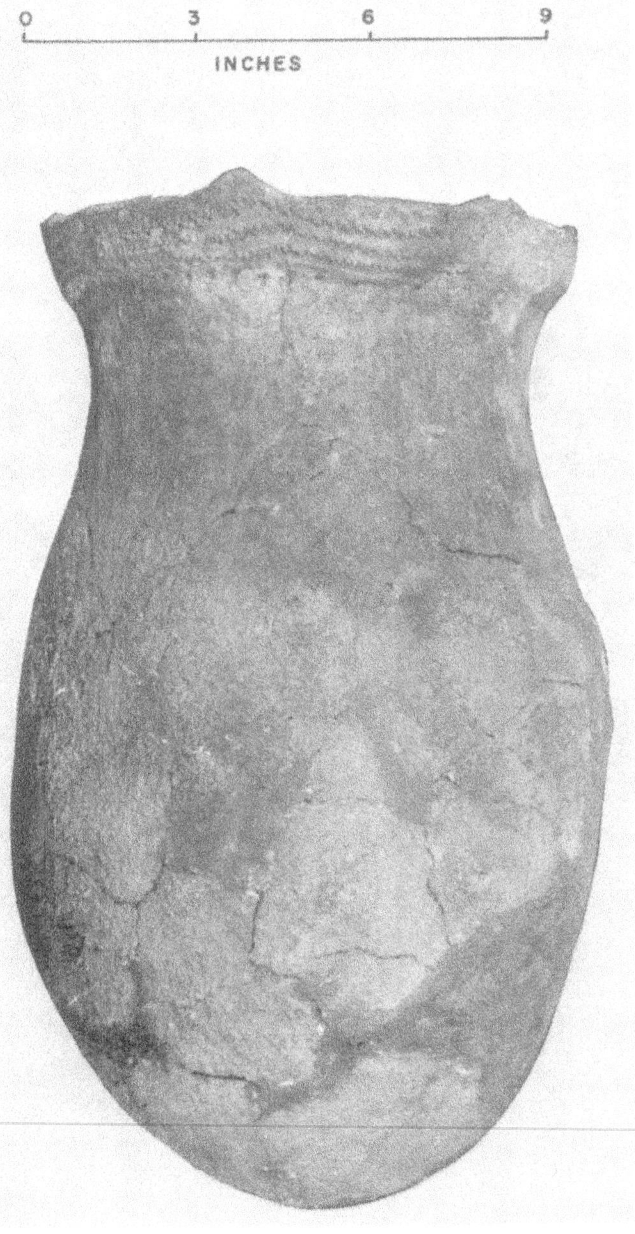

Macomb Linear-corded vessel from the Riviere au Vase site (20 MB 3)

PLATE XIV

Macomb Linear-corded vessel from the Riviere au Vase site (20 MB 3)

PLATE XV

Macomb Linear-corded sherds from the Riviere au Vase site (20 MB 3)

PLATE XVI

Macomb Interrupted-linear rim sherds from the Riviere au Vase site (20 MB 3)

PLATE XVII

Vase Tool-impressed rim sherds from the Riviere au Vase site (20 MB 3)

PLATE XVIII

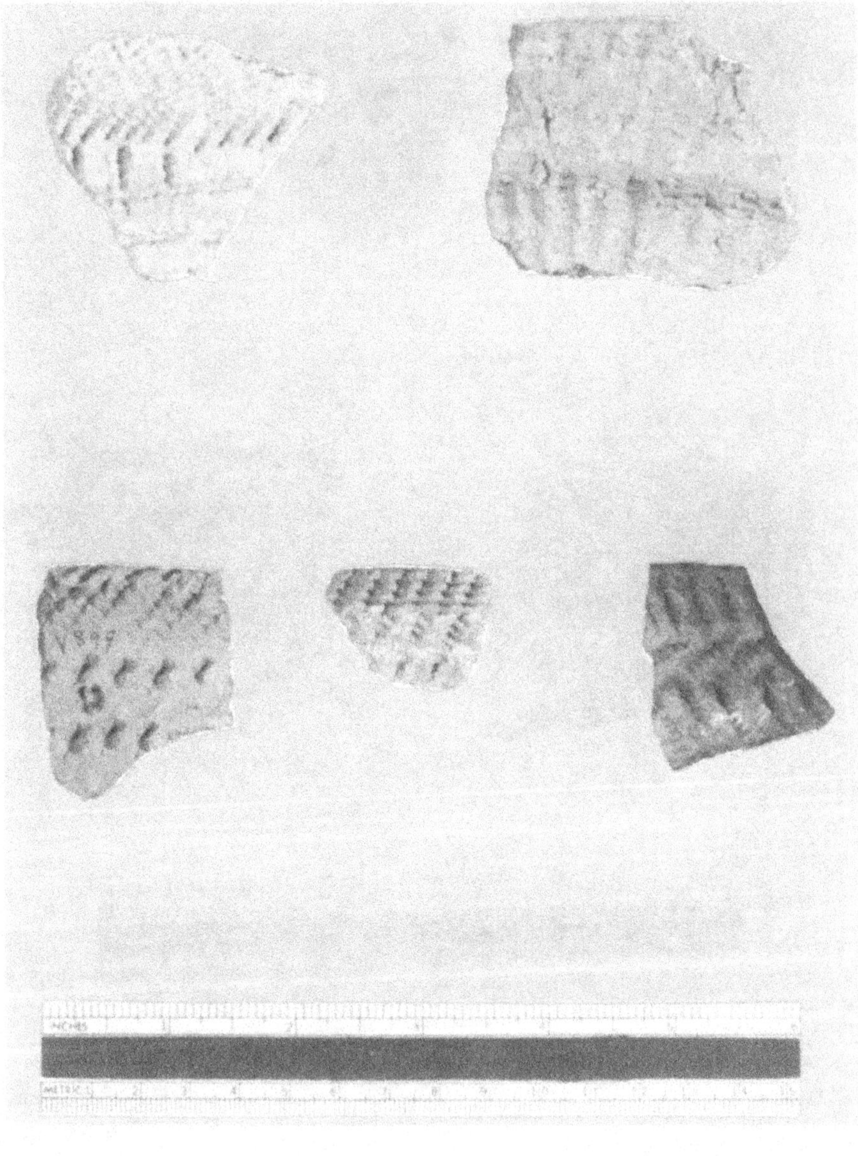

Vase Corded rim sherds from the Riviere au Vase site (20 MB 3)

PLATE XIX

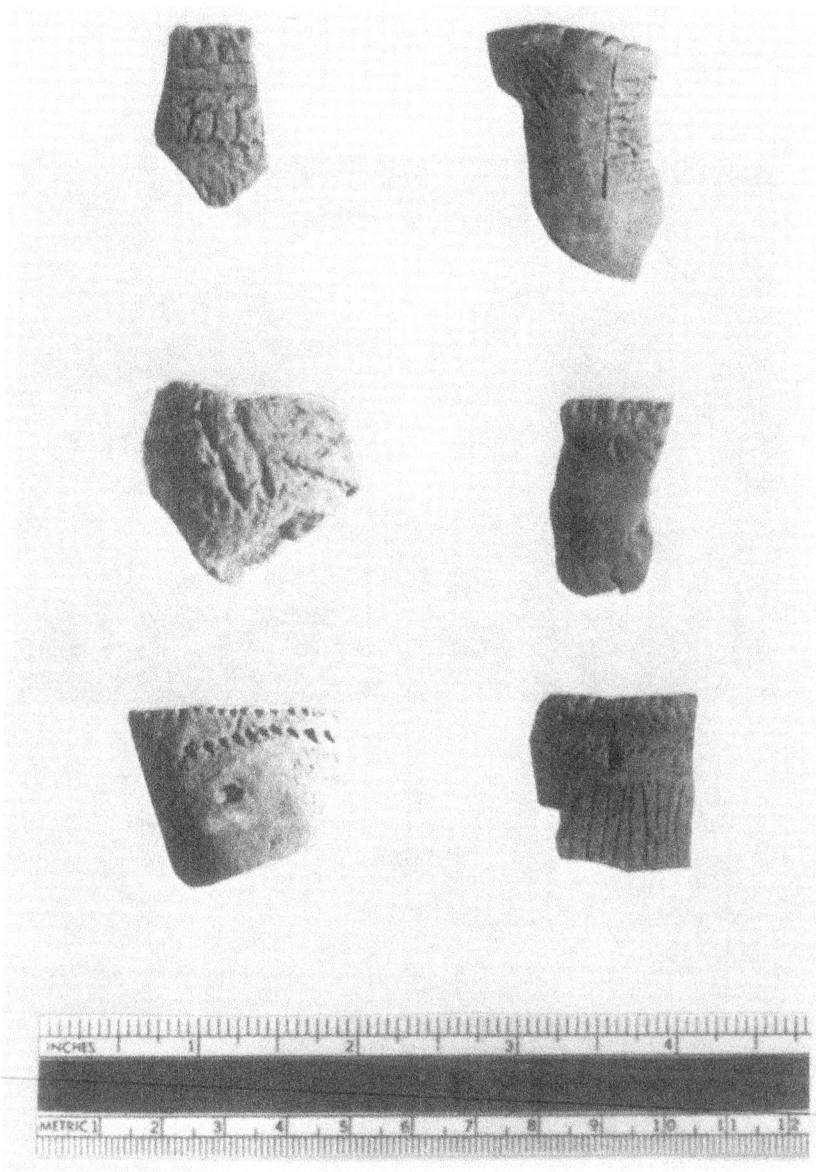

Miniature vessel decorated rim sherds from the Riviere au Vase site (20 MB 3)

PLATE XX

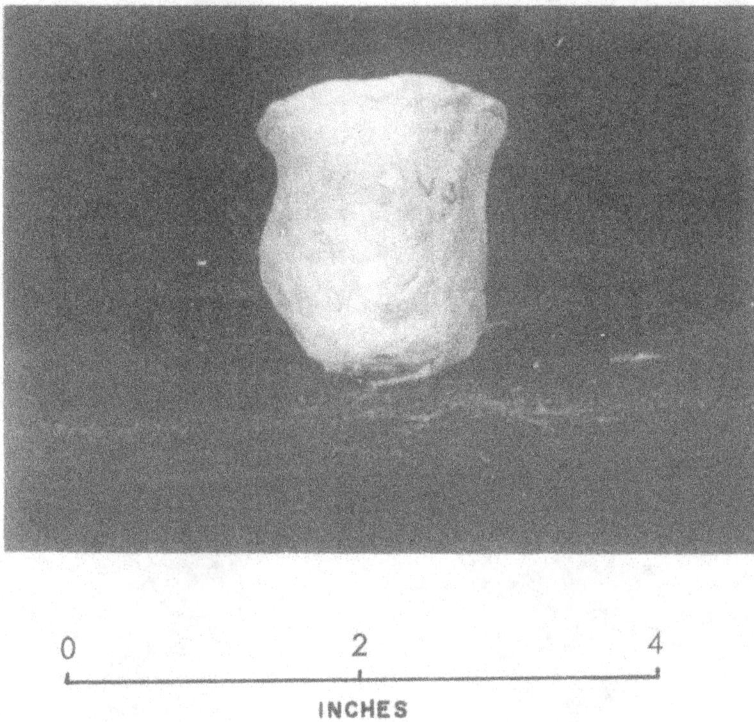

Plain miniature vessel from the Riviere au Vase site (20 MB 3)

PLATE XXI

Miniature vessel plain rim sherds from the Riviere au Vase site (20 MB 3)

PLATE XXII

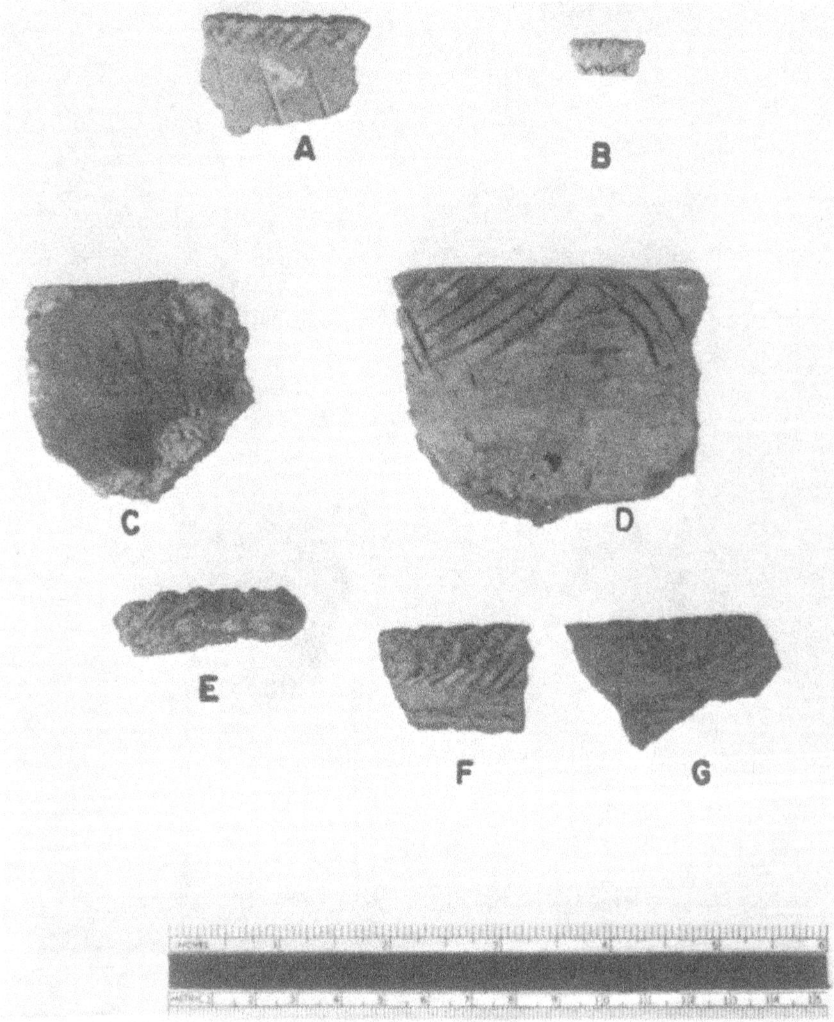

Aberrant rim sherds from the Riviere au Vase site (20 MB 3)

PLATE XXIII

Levanna points from the Riviere au Vase site (20 MB 3)

PLATE XXIV

Madison points from the Riviere au Vase site (20 MB 3)

PLATE XXV

Jack's Reef Corner-notched points from the Riviere au Vase site

PLATE XXVI

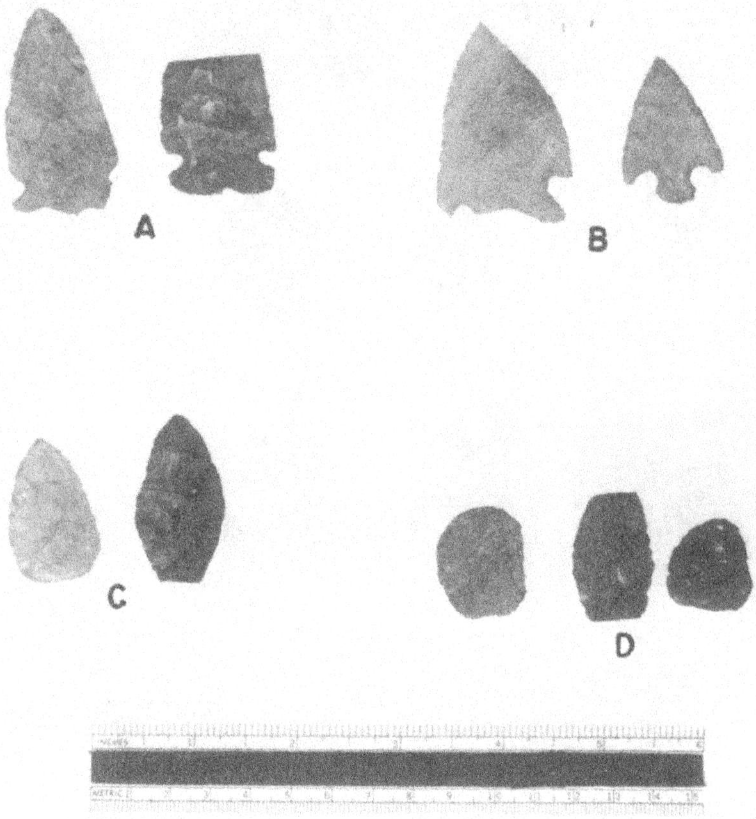

Projectile points from the Riviere au Vase site (20 MB 3)

PLATE XXVII

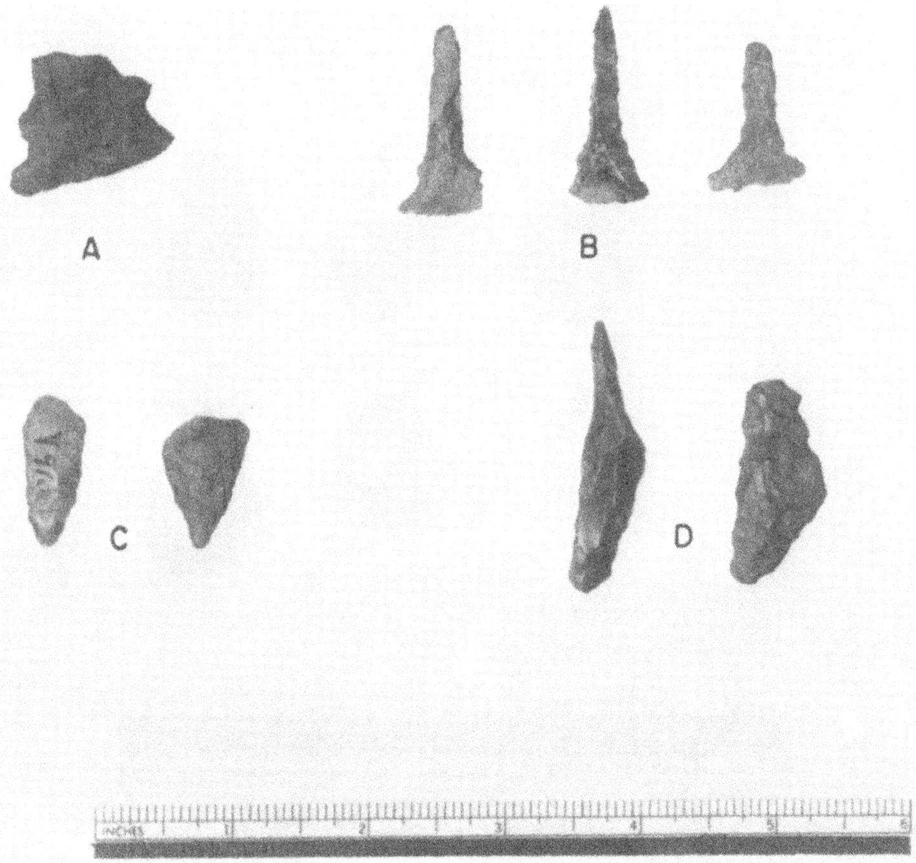

Drills, perforators, and crest blades from the Riviere au Vase site

PLATE XXVIII

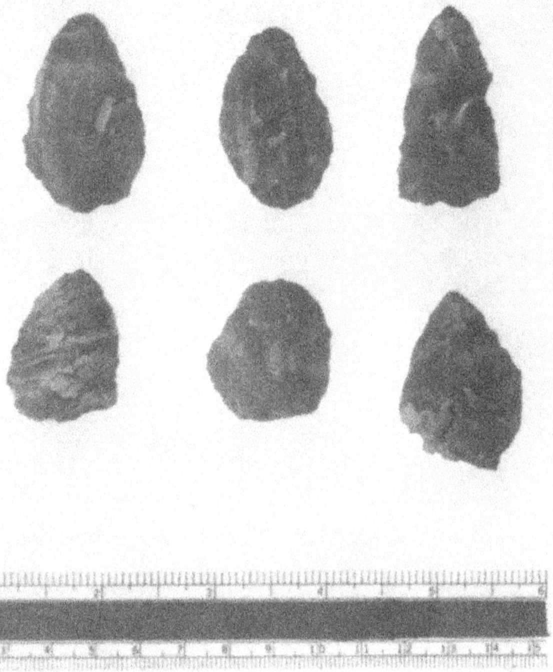

A cache of blanks from the Riviere au Vase site (20 MB 3)

PLATE XXIX

Ground-stone tools from the Riviere au Vase site (20 MB 3)

A) gorget fragment; B) gorget fragment; C) abrading stone; D) celt from Trench B; adze found with burial 5, II.

PLATE XXX

Copper from the Riviere au Vase site (20 MB 3)

PLATE XXXI

Aboriginal pipes from the Riviere au Vase site

PLATE XXXII

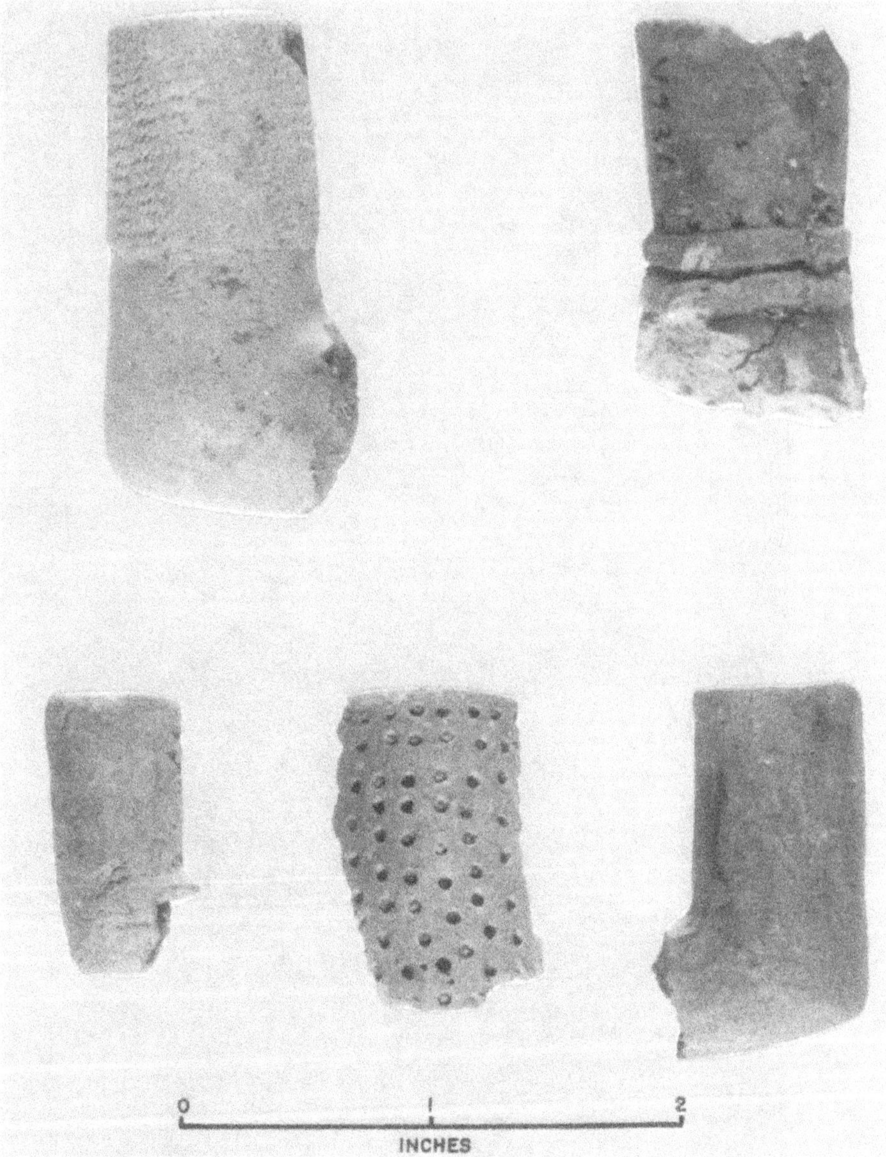

Aboriginal pipes and pipe fragments from the Riviere au Vase site (20 MB 3)

PLATE XXXIII

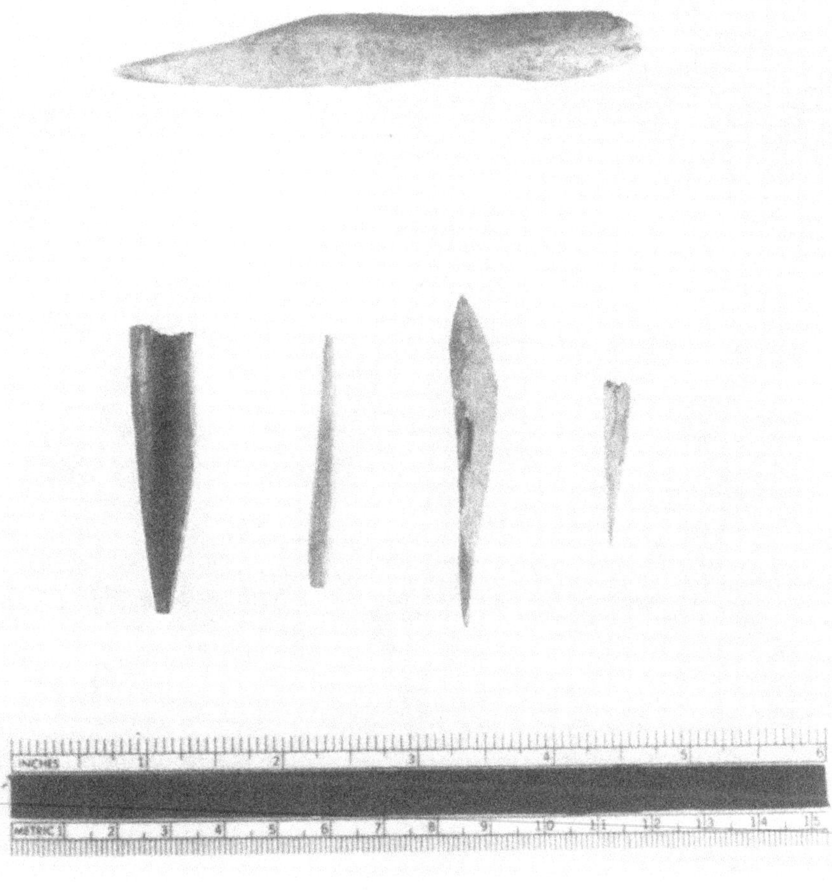

Bone awls from the Riviere au Vase site (20 MB 3)

PLATE XXXIV

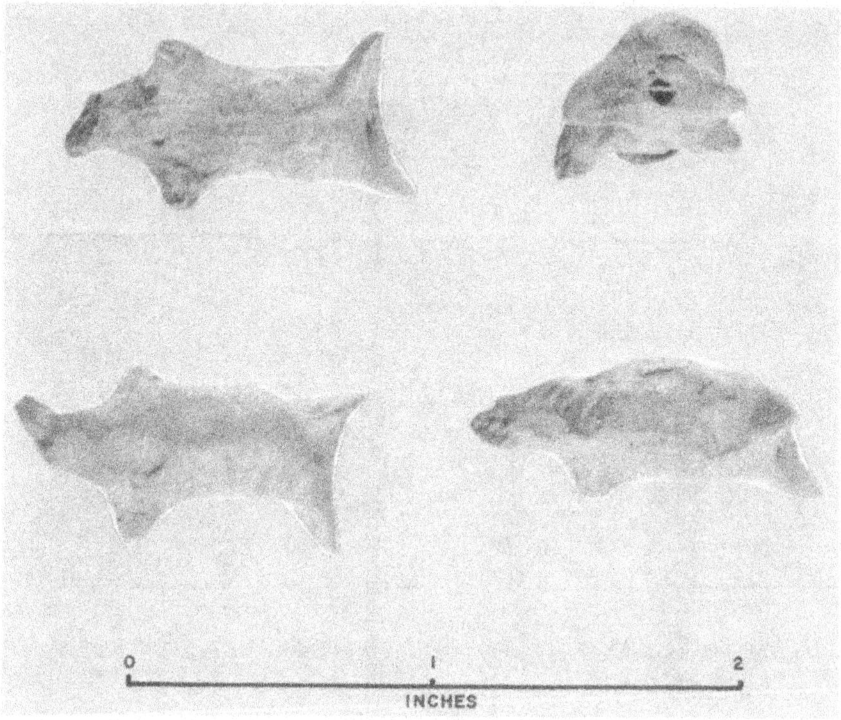

Clay effigy from the Riviere au Vase site (20 MB 3)

PLATE XXXV

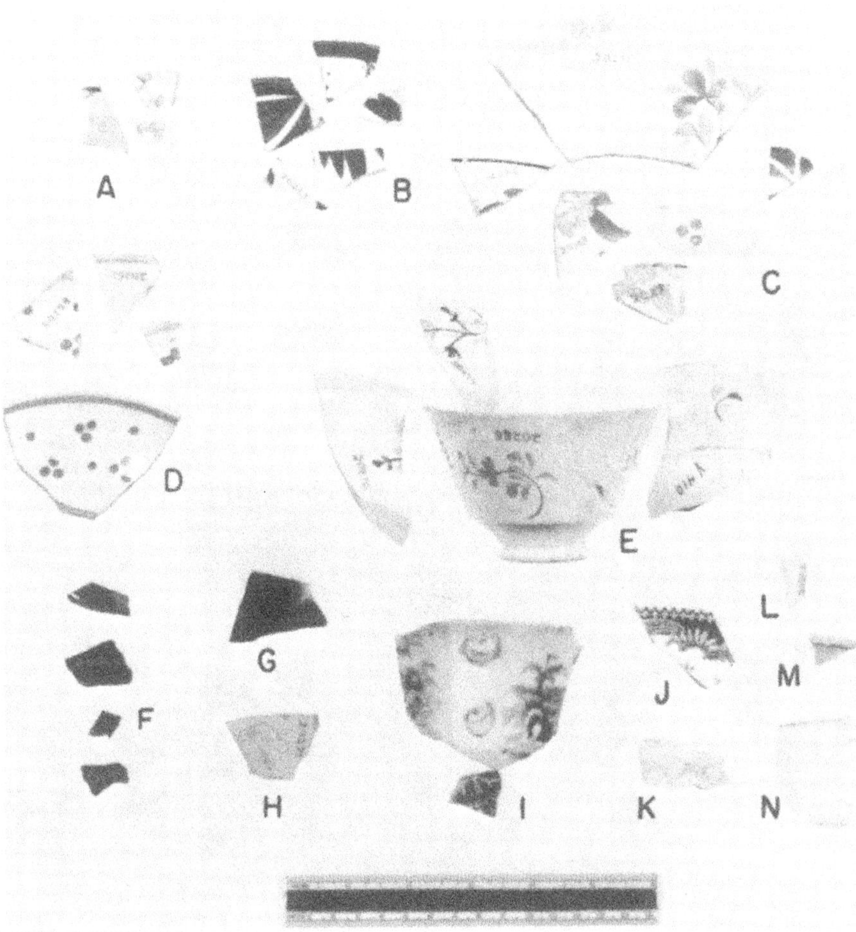

Historic ceramics from the Riviere au Vase site (20 MB 3)

A) Early Gaudy Dutch; B) Painted Blue; C) Middle Gaudy Dutch; D) Gaudy Dutch Polka Dot; E) Spring ware; F) Glazed Red Bisque earthenware; G) Brown Glaze; H) Common Yellow; I) Printed Glaze; J) Brown Print; K) Molded ware; L) Porcelaine; M) Majolica; N) Gilt Edge.

PLATE XXXVI

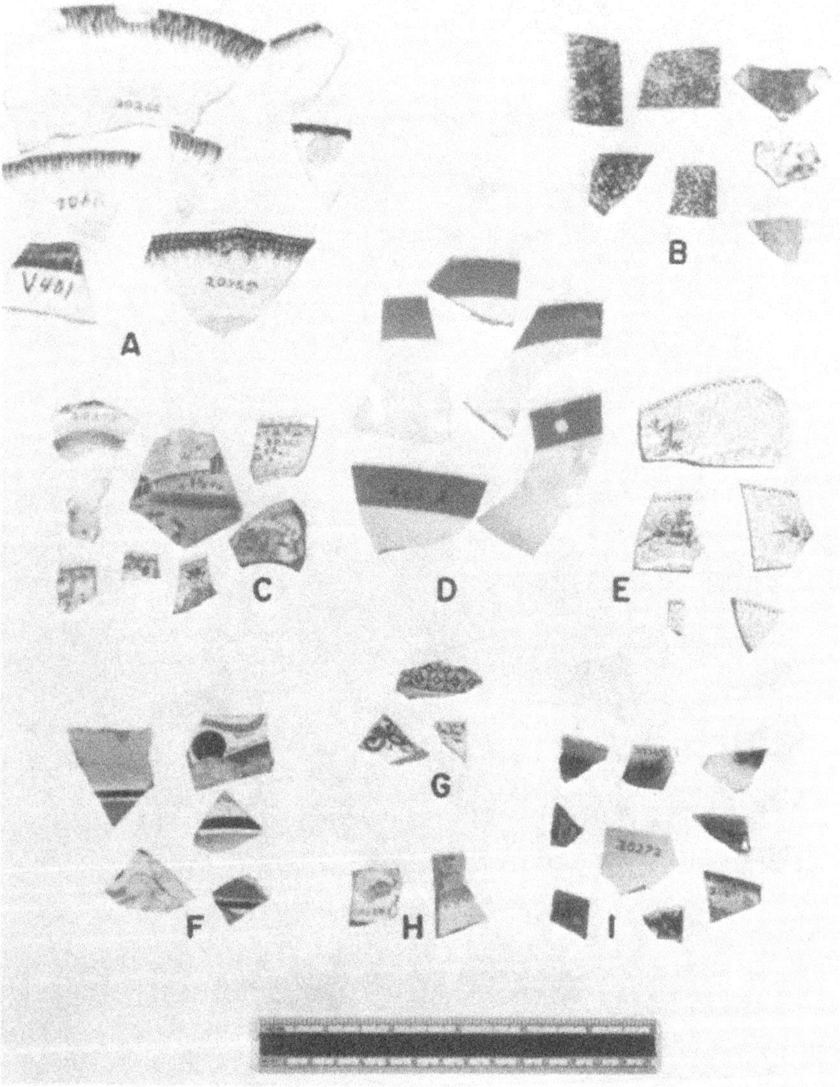

Historic ceramics from the Riviere au Vase site (20 MB 3)

A) Blue Edge; B) spatterware or spongeware; C) North Staffordshire Red Print; D) Light Blue Banded; E) Red Print Meander; F) Raised Glaze; G) Blue Printed Willow; H) Old Blue; I) Flowing Blue.

PLATE XXXVII

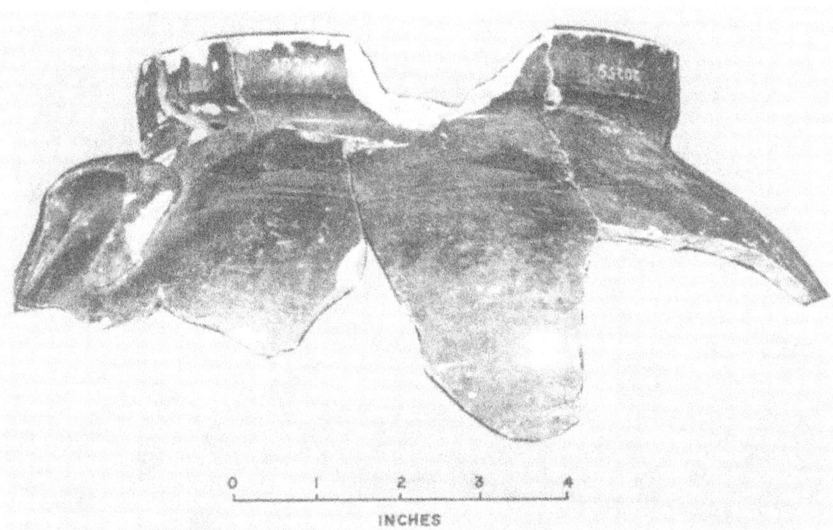

Red bisque earthenware vessel from the Riviere au Vase site (20 MB 3)

PLATE XXXVIII

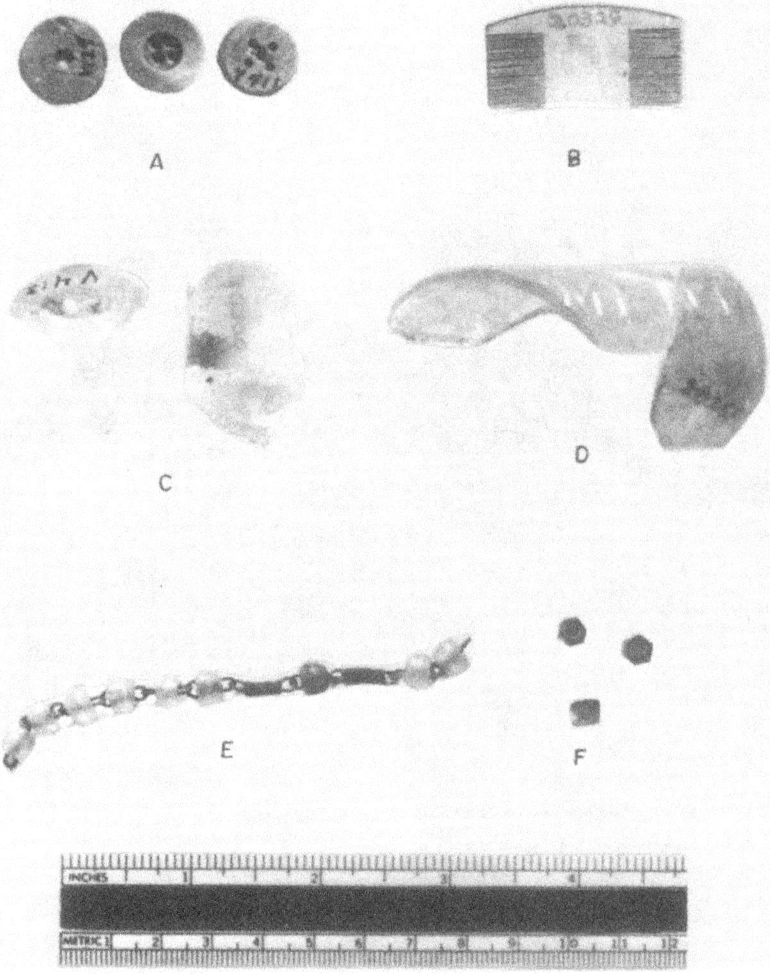

Historic artifacts from the Riviere au Vase site (20 MB 3)

A) bone buttons; B) bone comb; C) glass stoppers; D) raised glass bottle; E) rosary beads; F) hexagonal blue beads.

PLATE XXXIX

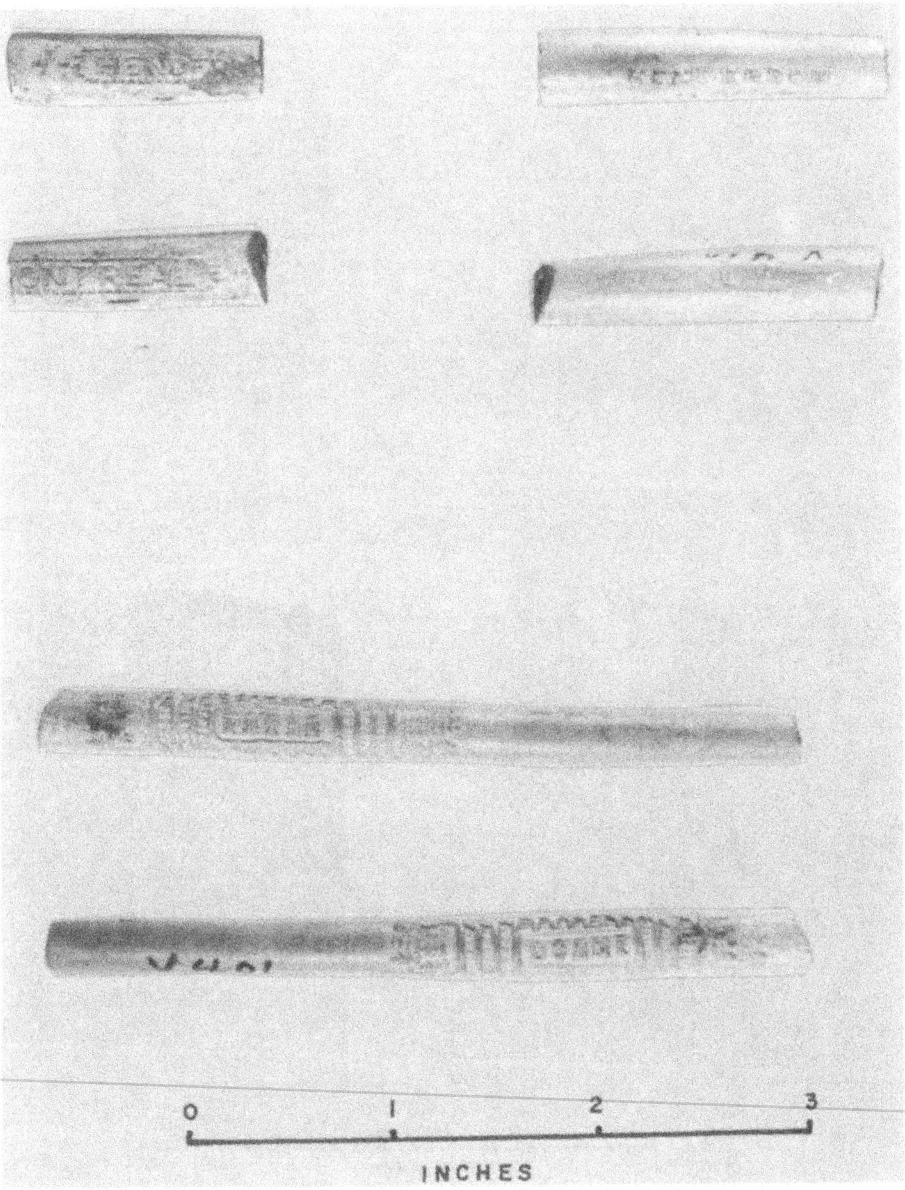

Historic pipestems from the Riviere au Vase site (20 MB 3)

PLATE XL

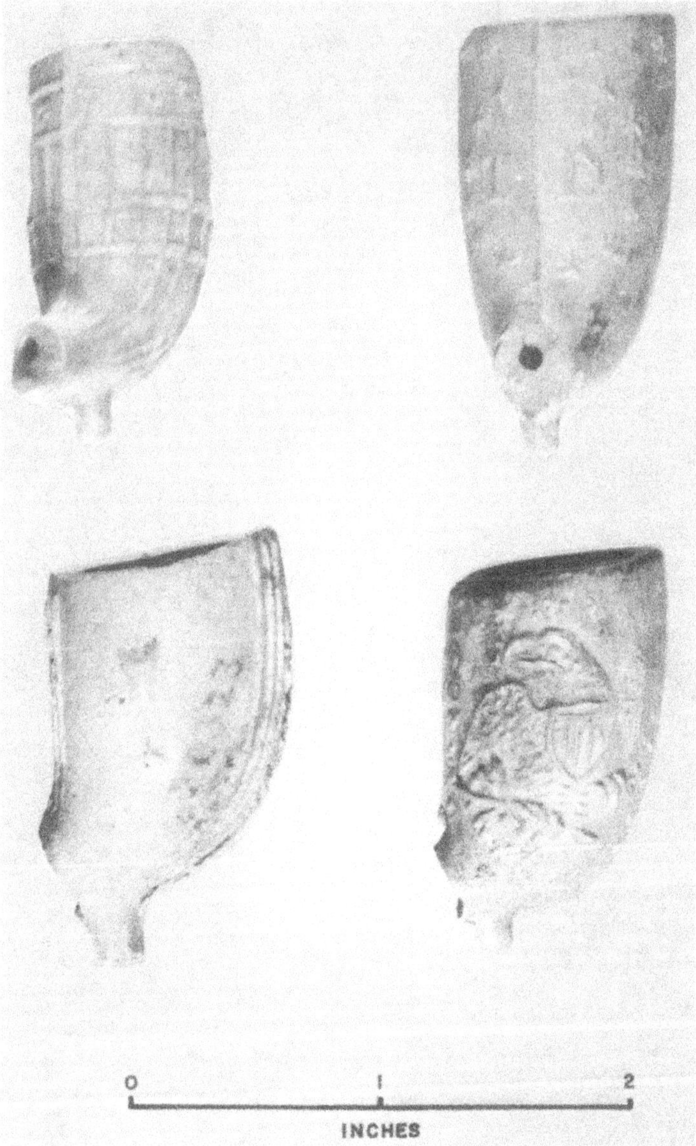

Historic pipe bowls from the Riviere au Vase site (20 MB 3)

PLATE XLI

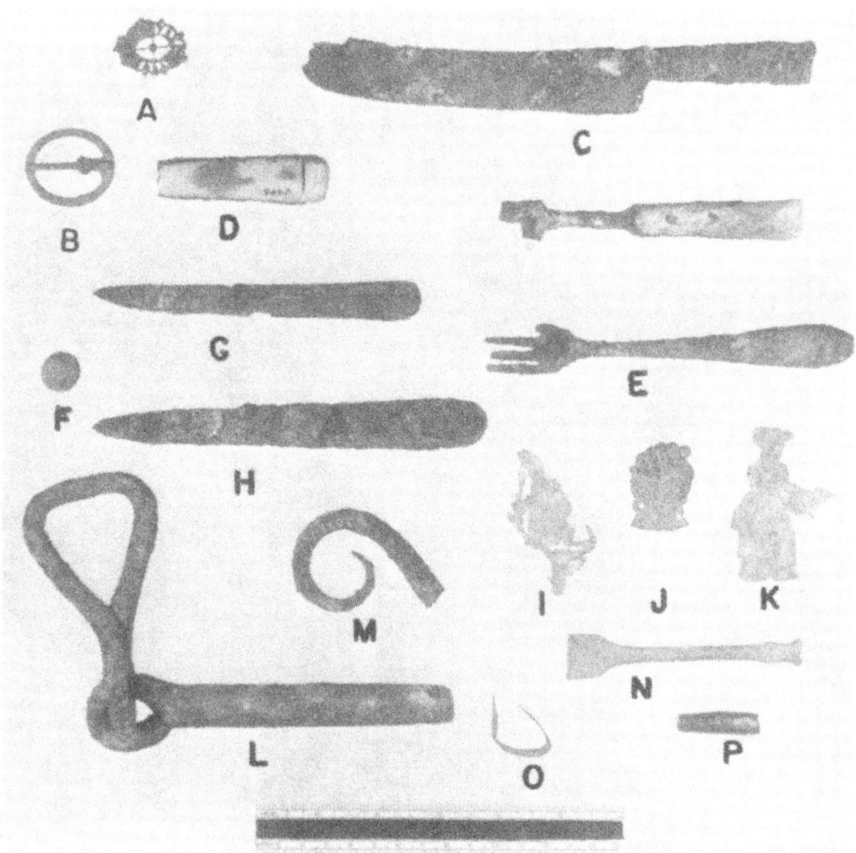

Historic artifacts from the Riviere au Vase site (20 MB 3)

A) broach; B) buckle; C) hoop iron table knife; D) bone knife handle; E) forks; F) thimble; G) penknife; H) utility knife; I-K) metal ornaments; L) pin and eye; O-P) copper objects.

PLATE XLII

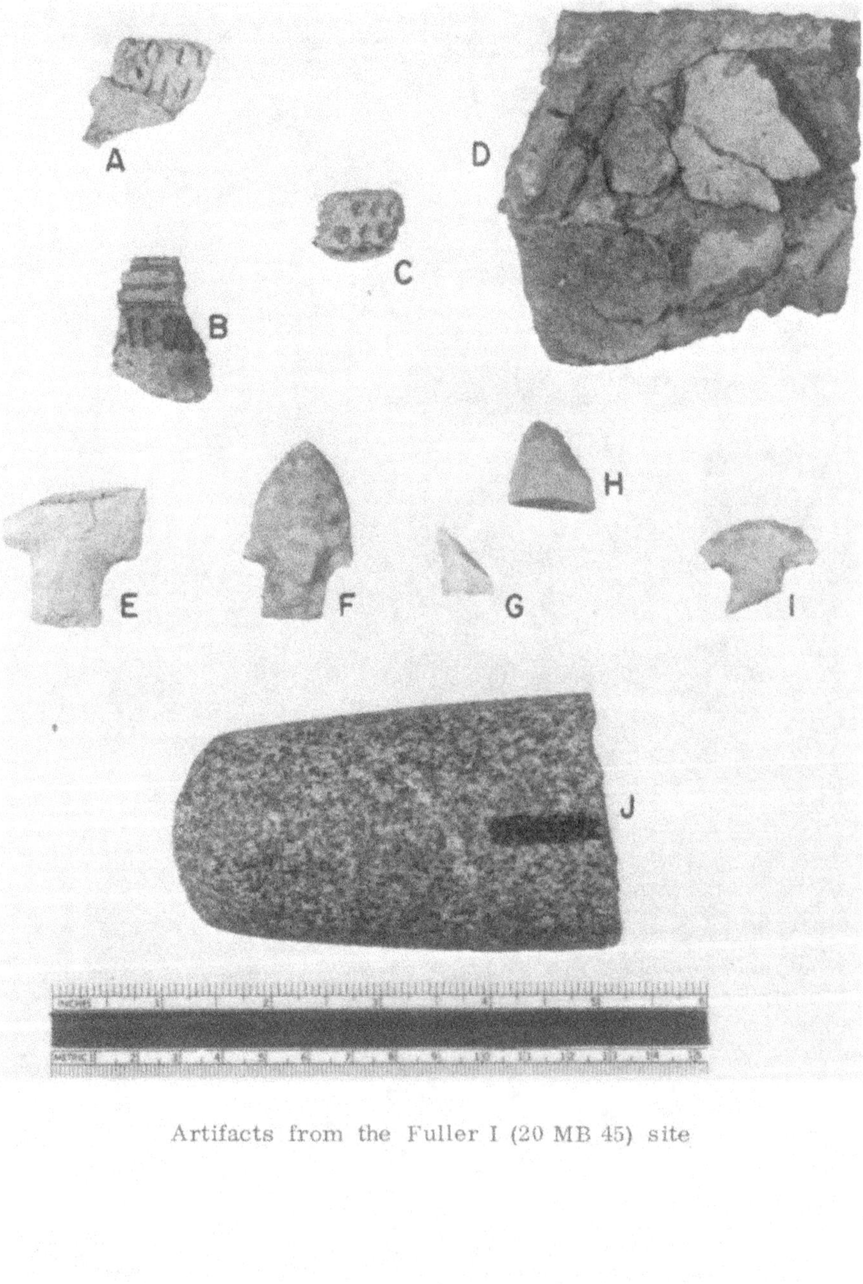

Artifacts from the Fuller I (20 MB 45) site

PLATE XLIII

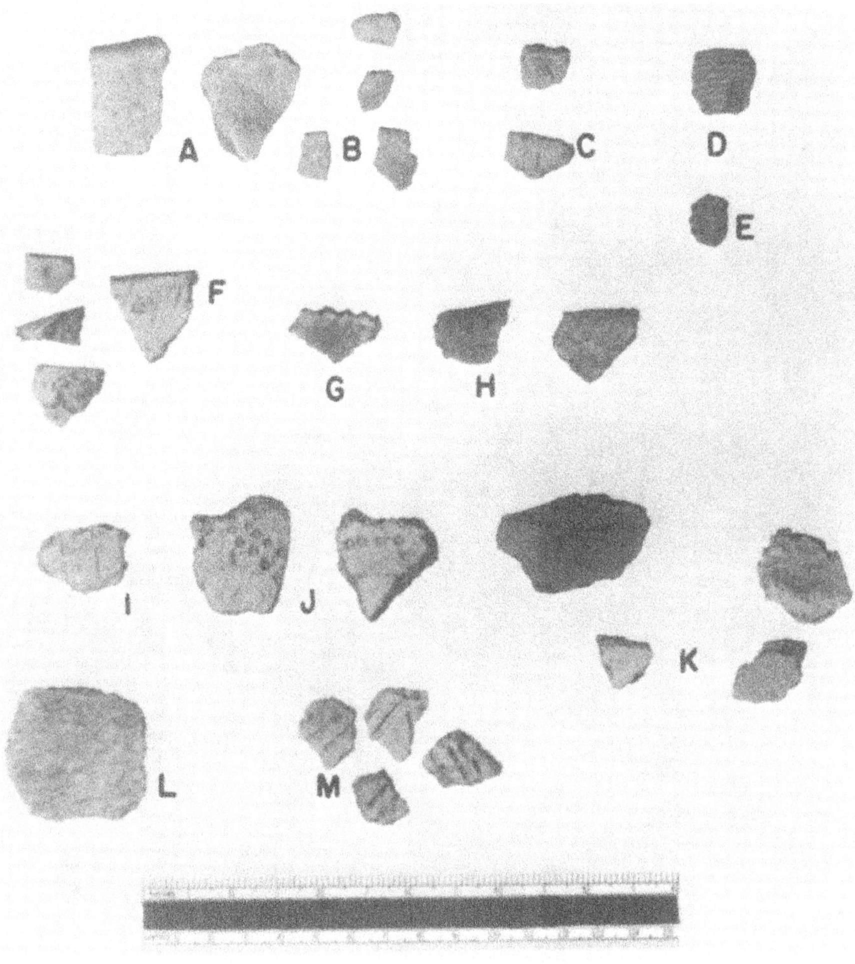

Artifacts from the Verchave I site (20 MB 178)

PLATE XLIV

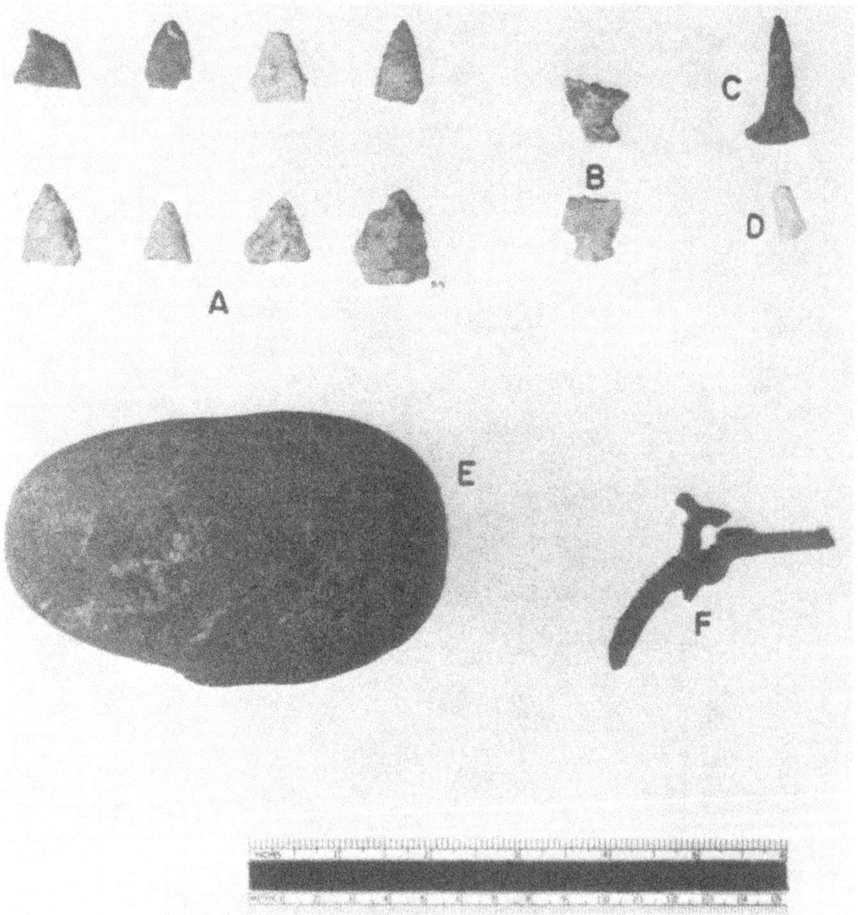

Artifacts from the Verchave I site (20 MB 178)

PLATE XLV

Base of vessel from Feature Number 2 at the Verchave II site (20 MB 181)

PLATE XLVI

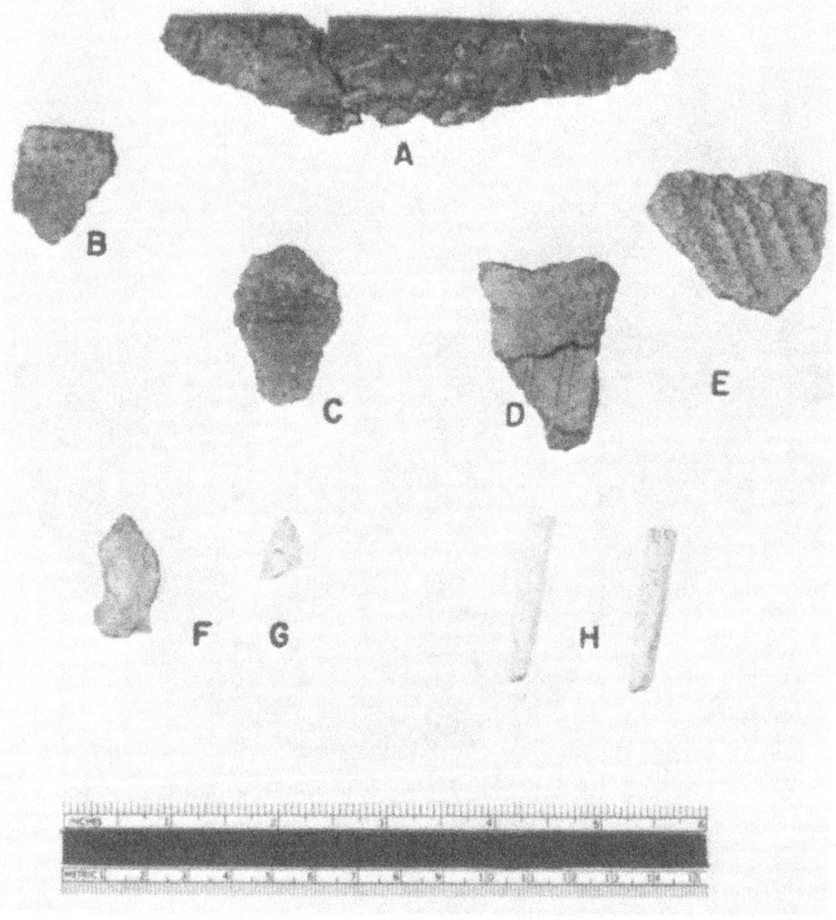

Artifacts from the Verchave II site (20 MB 181)

PLATE XLVII

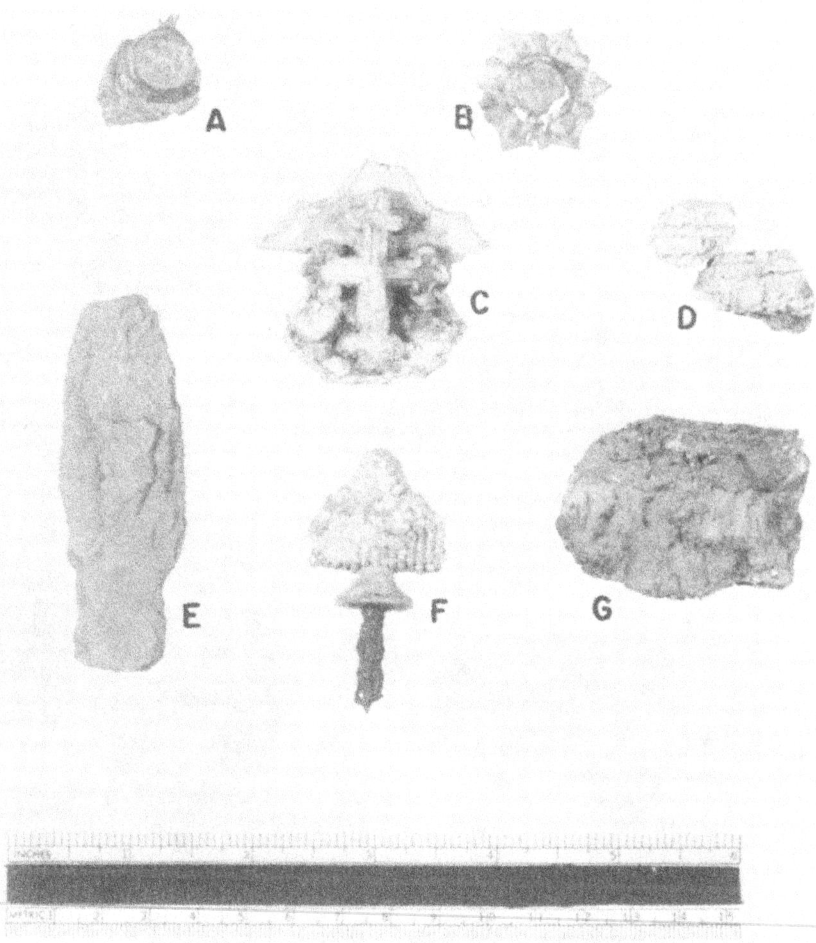

Artifacts from the Verchase III site (20 MB 182)

PLATE XLVIII

Springwells Net-impressed rim sherds from the Fort Wayne Mound

www.ingramcontent.com/pod-product-compliance
Lightning Source LLC
LaVergne TN
LVHW050021250826
846302LV00008B/42